Dictionary of Quotations in Communications

DICTIONARY OF QUOTATIONS IN COMMUNICATIONS

Compiled by
**Lilless McPherson Shilling
and Linda K. Fuller**

GREENWOOD PRESS
Westport, Connecticut • London

Library of Congress Cataloging-in-Publication Data

Dictionary of quotations in communications / compiled by Lilless
 McPherson Shilling and Linda K. Fuller.
      p.   cm.
   Includes bibliographical references (p.   ) and index.
   ISBN 0–313–30430–0 (alk. paper)
      1. Communication—Quotations, maxims, etc.   I. Shilling, Lilless
McPherson, 1942–   . II. Fuller, Linda K.
P90.D488   1997
302.2—DC21   97–5599

British Library Cataloguing in Publication Data is available.

Library of Congress Catalog Card Number: 97–5599
ISBN: 0–313–30430–0

First published in 1997

Greenwood Press, 88 Post Road West, Westport, CT 06881
An imprint of Greenwood Publishing Group, Inc.

Printed in the United States of America

The paper used in this book complies with the
Permanent Paper Standard issued by the National
Information Standards Organization (Z39.48–1984).

10 9 8 7 6 5 4 3 2 1

To my parents, Loue Pendleton McPherson and J. James McPherson, who delighted in my "quotations" when I was growing up, and to my daughter, Paz, who has delighted me with hers.

Lilless McPherson Shilling

George Gerbner, Dean Emeritus of the Annenberg School for Communication at the University of Pennsylvania and founder of the Cultural Environment Movement, has the distinction of being the most quoted communications scholar. He is also a leader, an educator, an editor, a family person, a gentleman, a visionary, an inspiration, and a mentor.

Linda K. Fuller

Our cultural environment is the system of stories and images that cultivates much of who we are, what we think, what we do, and how we conduct our affairs.

George Gerbner

Contents

List of Subject Headings

Preface

Even reviewers read a preface.
--Philip Guedalla, *The Missing Muse*

Whether you are a reader or a writer, a speaker or a listener, a poet or a photojournalist, an amateur or an impresario, a student or a scholar, this *Dictionary of Quotations in Communications* will stimulate and benefit you. You may use it as a reference source, to verify a half-remembered line, to find supporting statements for something you are creating on your own, to learn what others have said about a particular topic, or to enjoy as leisure reading. In the words of a Japanese proverb, "You can know ten things by learning one."

This dictionary, which contains more than three thousand quotations by over two thousand sources, grew out of our first collaboration, *Communicating Comfortably: Your Guide to Overcoming Speaking and Writing Anxieties.*[1] Reader response to the quotations in that book was so positive that we decided to collect more. After starting, we realized we had another book on our hands and, happily, we found a publisher who agreed.

Linda K. Fuller specializes in mass communications, Lilless Shilling in health communications. We both recognized how valuable it would be to have a volume of quotations covering the wide world of communications. While some quotation books are topic-specific, such as historical, religious, or business-oriented, no such compendium existed in the communications field.

We defined communications broadly when we were gathering and culling the quotations. In addition to quotations on reading, writing, speaking, and listening, the book covers related topics such as advertising, computers, education, film, international communication, journalism, language, photography, public relations, television, and many others. We hope to compile a future volume that will deal with the expanding world of technology.

Keeping in mind Gilbert K. Chesterton's comment, "You could compile the worst book in the world entirely out of selected passages from the best writers in the world," we were determined to be selective. We wanted to include a variety of sources and perspectives that would be helpful to readers, writers, speakers, and educators. This dictionary contains quotations from ancient and modern people and places. Some are serious, some humorous. Some are lengthy, some short. (As Sophocles said, "A short saying oft contains much wisdom.") Some quotations come from the famous, some from the infamous, and some from the lesser-known. We have used quotations from our students, teachers, colleagues around the world, and ourselves.

Multicultural diversity was one criterion for inclusion. The authors in this dictionary represent women and men from different ethnic groups, religions, and nationalities. You will see proverbs, maxims, and sayings from many countries.

Ranging from the classic to the contemporary, the quotations represent some of the best statements in the field of communication at this time. Legally, we have been careful to respect copyright laws by not using more than 300 words from any one source. Most of our choices were already part of the public domain; others we solicited directly from their authors.

Many other quotations merited inclusion. Almost everyone has said something quotable about communications. Children are particularly observant. Several quotations by Lilless's daughter Paz reflect the wisdom of children. When she was six years old, Paz said, "It's nice to know words, because then you can read--and learn."

Space constraints kept us from using thousands more quotations. Our next volume is begging to be compiled. As Robert Byrne, another quotation compiler said, "As fast as I skim the cream, more cream appears."[2]

In this dictionary, the quotations are arranged alphabetically by topic and within topics by author's last name. The author index will guide you to quotations by particular authors. You will find it useful to skim through the subject and author indexes to give you an idea of the broad variety of topics and authors. For those interested, one section contains quotations on quotations, such as Chamfort's, "Most anthologists . . . of quotations are like those who eat cherries . . . first picking the best ones and winding up by eating everything." Other sections have quotations on beginnings, endings, and indexes.

In many cases, we identified the source of the quotation in addition to the author; however, in some cases the sources were difficult to verify. Our work was made more difficult because reference sources sometimes disagree on dates and other bibliographical information. Rather than omit important quotations, we decided to include them even though we did not have complete information. If, despite our efforts to ensure accuracy, we have made errors, we apologize and take full responsibility for them.

This dictionary is a time capsule of communications quotations at the end of the twentieth century. We hope you will enjoy using it and we welcome your comments.

NOTES

1. Linda K. Fuller and Lilless McPherson Shilling, *Communicating Comfortably: Your Guide to Overcoming Speaking and Writing Anxieties*. (Amherst, MA: HRD Press, 1990).

2. Robert Byrne, *The Third--and Possibly the Best--637 Best Things Anybody Ever Said*. (New York: Atheneum, 1986).

QUOTATIONS

A

ACTING

Here's a rule I recommend: Never practice two roles at once.
    Tallulah Bankhead

One of my chief regrets during my years in the theatre is that I couldn't be in the audience and watch me.
    John Barrymore

An actor is a sculptor who carves in snow.
    Edwin Booth

An actor's a guy who, if you ain't talking about him, ain't listening.
    Marlon Brando

More than in the performing arts the lack of respect for acting seems to spring from the fact that every layman considers himself a valid critic.
    Uta Hagen

I am not sure acting is a thing for a grown man.
    Steve McQueen

Acting is a masochistic form of exhibitionism. It is not quite the occupation of an adult.
    Sir Laurence Olivier

Acting is not being emotional, but being able to express emotion.
    Kate Reid

Actors are the jockeys of literature. Others supply the horses, the plays, and we simply make them run.
    Ralph Richardson, recalled on his death

The art of acting consists in keeping people from coughing.
    Ralph Richardson

We're *actors*--we're the opposite of people! . . . Think, in your head, *now*, think of the most . . . *private* . . . *secret* . . . *intimate* thing you have ever done secure in the knowledge of its privacy . . . . Are you thinking of it? . . . well, *I saw you do it*!
    Tom Stoppard, *Rosencrantz and Guildenstern Are Dead*

An actor is never so great as when he reminds you of an animal--falling like a cat, lying like a dog, moving like a fox.
    François Truffaut, *The New Yorker*

ACTION

It doesn't matter if a cat is black or white, so long as it catches mice.
    Deng Xiaoping

Words are also actions, and actions are a kind of words.
    Ralph Waldo Emerson

Give me the ready hand rather than the ready tongue.
    Giuseppe Garibaldi

Whatever you can do, or dream you can, begin it.
Boldness has genius, power, and magic in it.
    Goethe

Things do not just happen. They are brought about.
    John Hay

Words without actions are the assassins of idealism.
    Herbert Hoover

Don't be afraid to take a big step. You can't cross a chasm in two small jumps.
    David Lloyd George

Inertia breeds despair. I find that action, even if not too well conceived, at least stimulates hope.
    Louis Nizer, *My Life in Court*

ADVERTISING

Advertising is the principal reason why the business man has come to inherit the earth.
    James Randolph Adams

Good times, bad times, there will always be advertising. In good times, people want to advertise; in bad times they have to.
  Bruce Barton

The advertiser who thinks he has to choose between the straight-forward and dull or the beautiful but dumb is mistaken. The trick is to be relevant as well as bright.
  William Bernbach

Doing business without advertising is like winking at a girl in the dark. You know what you are doing, but nobody else does.
  Stuart H. Britt

The business that considers itself immune to the necessity for advertising sooner or later finds itself immune to business.
  Derby Brown

Advertising promotes that divine discontent which makes people strive to improve their economic status.
  Ralph Starr Butler

I do not read advertisements--I would spend all my time wanting things.
  Archbishop of Canterbury

Advertising is what you do when you can't go see somebody.
  Fairfax Cone

You can tell the ideals of a nation by its advertisements.
  Norman Douglas

You know why Madison Avenue advertising has never done well in Harlem? We're not the only ones who know what it means to be Brand X.
  Dick Gregory

Advertising is found in societies which have passed the point of satisfying the basic animal needs.
  Marion Harper, Jr.

The trouble with us in America isn't that the poetry of life has turned to prose, but that it has turned to advertising copy.
  Louis Kronenberger

The product that will not sell without advertising, will not sell profitably with advertising.
  Albert Lasker

Kodak sells film, but they don't advertise film. They advertise memories.
Theodore Levitt, Harvard Business School

Who's kidding whom? What's the difference between Giant and Jumbo? Quart and *full*-quart? Two-ounce and *big* two-ounce? What does Extra Long mean? What's a *tall* 24-inch? And what busy shopper can tell?
Marya Mannes, *Life*

Advertising is the place where the selfish interests of the manufacturer coincide with the interests of society.
David Ogilvy

Advertising is the rattling of a stick inside a swill bucket.
George Orwell

Advertising is not spending; it's an investment to get a piece of the mind of millions of Americans.
Alph B. Peterson, Benrus

In the factory we make cosmetics; in the drugstore we sell hope.
Charles Revson

Advertising is the foot on the accelerator, the hand on the throttle, the spur on the flank that keeps our economy surging forward.
Robert W. Sarnoff

Advertising is the art of making whole lies out of half truths.
Edgar A. Shoaff

There is no such thing as modern art.
There is art--and there is advertising.
Albert Sternen

Many a small thing has been made large by the right kind of advertising.
Mark Twain

Advertising has annihilated the power of the most powerful adjectives.
Paul Valéry

Half the money I spend on advertising is wasted, and the trouble is I don't know which half.
John Wanamaker

In advertising, the beginning of greatness is to be conspicuous and different. The

beginning of failure is to be invisible and orthodox.
    Roy Whittier

ADVICE

It is easy when we are in prosperity to give advice to the afflicted.
    Aeschylus

We give advice by the bucket, but take it by the grain.
    William Rounseville Alger

Advice is like castor oil, easy enough to give but dreadful uneasy to take.
    Josh Billings

Advice is like kissing; it costs nothing and is a pleasant thing to do.
    Josh Billings

Advice is seldom welcome, and those who need it the most, like it the least.
    Lord Chesterfield

In those days he was wiser than he is now--he used frequently to take my advice.
    Winston Churchill

Nobody can give you wiser advice than yourself.
    Cicero

Advice is like snow; the softer it falls, the longer it dwells upon, and the deeper it sinks into the mind.
    Samuel Taylor Coleridge

It is always safe to learn even from our enemies, seldom safe to instruct even our friends.
    Charles Caleb Colton

No vice is so bad as advice.
    Marie Dressler

Don't give advice before you are called upon.
    Desiderius Erasmus

He that won't be counseled can't be helped.
    Benjamin Franklin

Advice is what we ask for when we already know the answer but wish we didn't.
    Erica Jong

No man is so foolish that he may sometimes give another good counsel, and no man so wise that he may not easily err if he takes no other counsel than his own. He that is taught only by himself has a fool for a master.
  Ben Jonson

He who can take advice is sometimes superior to he who can give it.
  Karl Ludwig von Knebel

Men give away nothing so liberally as their advice.
  François de La Rochefoucauld

Old people like to give good advice, as solace for no longer being able to provide bad examples.
  François de La Rochefoucauld

I give myself sometimes admirable advice, but I am incapable of taking it.
  Lady Mary Wortley Montagu

One can advise comfortably from a safe port.
  Friedrich von Schiller

The true secret of giving advice is, after you have honestly given it, to be perfectly indifferent whether it is taken or not and never persist in trying to set people right.
  Hannah Whitall Smith

Always do right. This will gratify some people, and astonish the rest.
  Mark Twain

If you have to swallow a frog, don't look at it too long. If you have to swallow two frogs, don't swallow the smaller one first.
  Mark Twain

The only thing to do with good advice is to pass it on. It is never of any use to oneself.
  Oscar Wilde

AGING

Anyone who stops learning is old, whether at 20 or 80.
  Henry Ford

The older I grow, the more I listen to people who don't say much.
  Germain G. Glidden

The man who is too old to learn was probably always too old to learn.
  Henry S. Haskins

At fifty, everyone has the face he deserves.
George Orwell

There is nothing more beautiful than cheerfulness in an old face.
Jean Paul Richter

How does an inexpressive face age? More slowly, one would suppose.
Susan Sontag

I haven't closed the book; I'm just opening a new chapter.
Lorraine Szala, on turning forty

One of the chief reasons for the generation gap is that as we grow older, most of us
begin to suffer from hardening of the attitudes.
Dorrine Anderson Turecamo, *The Toastmaster*

We laugh and laugh. Then cry and cry.
Then feebler laugh. Then die.
Mark Twain

In the waning light of day you see more clearly the things that are important.
Bishop Herbert Welch

AGREEMENT

Too much agreement kills a chat.
Eldridge Cleaver

I am always of the opinion with the learned, if they speak first.
William Congreve

Since when do you have to agree with people to defend them from injustice?
Lillian Hellman

Strange to see how a good dinner and feasting reconciles everybody.
Samuel Pepys

ANGER

I was angry with my friend:
I told my wrath, my wrath did end.
I was angry with my foe:
I told it not, my wrath did grow.
William Blake, "A Poison Tree"

Anger repressed can poison a relationship as surely as the cruelest words.
  Dr. Joyce Brothers

If you are patient in one moment of anger, you will escape a hundred days of sorrow.
  Chinese proverb

So long as a man is angry, he cannot be in the right.
  Chinese proverb

Truly to moderate your mind and speech when you are angry, or else to hold your peace, betokens no ordinary nature.
  Cicero

When anger arises, think of the consequences.
  Confucius

Beware the fury of a patient man.
  John Dryden

He who pursues revenge should dig two graves.
  Fortune cookie advice

Anger is never without a reason, but seldom with a good one.
  Benjamin Franklin

A fit of anger is as fatal to dignity as a dose of arsenic is to life.
  Josiah Holland

Anger is short-lived madness.
  Horace, *Epistles*

Ye shall know the truth, and the truth shall make you mad.
  Aldous Huxley

I never work better than when I am inspired by anger. When I am angry I can write, pray, and preach well. For then my whole temperament is quickened, my understanding sharpened, and all mundane vexations and temptations depart.
  Martin Luther

I found that one of my problems was getting angry at angry people.
  David McPherson

A soft answer turneth away wrath; but grievous words stir up anger.
  Proverbs 15:1

The moment you grab someone by the lapels, you're lost.
    Burt Reynolds

If anger is not restrained it is frequently more hurtful to us than the injury that provokes it.
    Seneca

If anger proceeds from a great cause, it turns to fury; if from a small cause, it is peevishness; and so is always either terrible or ridiculous.
    Jeremy Taylor

Darkness invades the life of somebody who's angry.
    John Trent

When angry, count to ten. When very angry, swear.
    Mark Twain

ANSWERS

There are four sides to every answer: Right and wrong, yours and mine.
    Bo Hamilton

I was gratified to be able to answer promptly. I said I don't know.
    Mark Twain

No answer is also an answer.
    Marcus Weissmann-Chajes

ARGUMENT

When a coward sees a man he can beat, he becomes hungry for a fight.
    Chinua Achebe

Don't make up your mind until you have heard both sides.
    Aristophanes, *The Wasps*

It is not necessary to understand things in order to argue about them.
    Pierre-Augustin de Beaumarchais

Repartee: What a person thinks of after he becomes a departee.
    Dan Bennett

Behind every argument is someone's ignorance.
    Louis D. Brandeis

The best argument is that which seems merely an explanation.
  Dale Carnegie

A book is like a quarrel: one word leads to another, and may erupt in blood or print, irrevocably.
  Will and Ariel Durant, *A Dual Autobiography*

Fear not those who argue but those who dodge.
  Marie Ebner von Eschenbach

Those whose cause is just will never lack good arguments.
  Euripides, *Hecuba*

Argument seldom convinces anyone contrary to his inclinations.
  Thomas Fuller, *Gnomologia*

There is no arguing with him, for if his pistol misses fire, he knocks you down with the butt end of it.
  Oliver Goldsmith

The best way I know of to win an argument is to start by being in the right.
  Lord Hailsham (Quintin Hogg)

The best thing for an argument is not words and ideas, but to stop arguing.
  Henry S. Haskins

Nothing was ever learned by either side in a dispute.
  William Hazlitt

No matter what side of an argument you're on, you always find some people on your side that you wish were on the other side.
  Jascha Heifetz

You can make up a quarrel, but it will always show where it was patched.
  Edgar Watson Howe, *Country Town Sayings*

It takes in reality only one to make a quarrel. It is useless for the sheep to pass resolutions in favor of vegetarianism, while the wolf remains of a different opinion.
  William R. Inge, *Outspoken Essays*

The aim of argument, or of discussion, should not be victory, but progress.
  Joseph Joubert, *Pensées*

If in argument we can make a man angry with us, we have drawn him from his vantage ground and overcome him.
  Walter Savage Landor, *Imaginary Conversations*

Quarrels would not last so long if the fault were only on one side.
　　François de La Rochefoucauld, *Maxims*

If a man will stand up and assert, and repeat, and re-assert that two and two do not make four, I know of nothing in the power of argument that can stop him.
　　Abraham Lincoln

Debate is the death of conversation.
　　Emil Ludwig

In arguing of the shadow, we forgo the substance.
　　John Lyly, *Euphues: The Anatomy of Wit*

The difficult part in an argument is not to defend one's opinion, but rather to know it.
　　André Maurois

He was one whom in an argument woe ever betides,
Because he always thought that there was much
to be said on both sides.
　　Ogden Nash, *The Strange Case of Mr. Pauncefoot's Broad Mind*

Quarreling binds men as closely as other things.
　　Charles Peguy

True disputants are like true sportsmen; their whole delight is in the pursuit.
　　Alexander Pope, "Thoughts on Various Subjects"

What renders the least flicker of an argument so profitless, so sterilizing, is that the minds of both the disputants are turned towards something quite different from either's authentic inner truth.
　　John Cowper Powys, *The Meaning of Culture*

Calmness in argument is a great advantage, for he who lets another chafe, warms him at his fire.
　　Ancient proverb

Wise men argue causes, fools often decide them.
　　Ancient proverb

In quarreling, the truth is always lost.
　　Publilius Syrus

Discussion is an exchange of knowledge; argument an exchange of ignorance.
　　Robert Quillen

There is no sense having an argument with a man so stupid he doesn't know you have the better of him.
John W. Raper, *What This World Needs*

The same arguments which we deem forcible as applied to others, seem feeble to us when turned against ourselves.
Joseph Roux, *Meditations of a Parish Priest*

Arguments only confirm people in their own opinions.
Booth Tarkington, *Looking Forward to the Great Adventure*

More than once I have heard good men come out second best to demagogues in argument because they have depended on their righteous indignation and neglected their homework.
Norman Thomas

Oh, the utter unpredictability of a quarrel! How inflammable words were to ignite each other until a blaze of them scorched and seared.
Agnes Sligh Turnbull

If the world should blow itself up, the last audible voice would be that of an expert saying it can't be done.
Sir Peter Ustinov

ART

All art is a kind of confession, more or less oblique. All artists, if they are to survive, are forced, at last, to tell the whole story, to vomit the anguish up.
James Baldwin, *Nobody Knows My Name*

Pop art is the inedible raised to the unspeakable.
Leonard Baskin

Art is the triumph over chaos.
John Cheever, *The Stories of John Cheever*

The true work of art is the one which the seventh wave of genius throws up on the beach where the under-tow of time cannot drag it back.
Cyril Connolly, *The Unquiet Grave*

Drawing is not what you see, but what you must make others see.
Edgar Degas

Art does not reproduce the visible; rather, it makes visible.
Paul Klee, *The Inward Vision*

The more minimal the art, the more maximum the explanation.
  Hilton Kramer

L'art est un anti-destin. (Art is a revolt against fate.)
  André Malraux, *Les voix du silence*

Impressionism is the newspaper of the soul.
  Henri Matisse

The true function of art is to criticize, embellish, and edit nature--particularly to edit it, and so make it coherent and lovely. The artist is a sort of impassioned proof-reader, blue-pencilling the bad spelling of God.
  H.L. Mencken

Art is much less important than life, but what a poor life without it!
  Robert Motherwell

Art is a reaching out into the ugliness of the world for vagrant beauty and the imprisoning of it in a tangible form.
  George Jean Nathan, *The Critic and the Drama*

Art is the difference between seeing and just identifying.
  Jean Mary Norman, *Art, of Wonder and a World*

Art comes to you proposing frankly to give nothing but the highest quality to your moments as they pass.
  Walter Pater, *The Renaissance*

It seems to me that all truly great art is propaganda.
  Ann Petry

All my life I've painted pictures so that certain people would drop dead when they looked at them, but I haven't succeeded yet. The worst painting can't hurt you, but a bad driver can kill you, a bad judge can send you to the chair, and a bad politician can ruin an entire country. That is why even a bad painting is sacred.
  Man Ray

Most events are inexpressible, taking place in a realm which no word has ever entered, and more inexpressible than all else are works of art, mysterious existences, the life of which, while ours passes away, endures.
  Rainer Maria Rilke, *Letters to a Young Poet*

The arts must study their occasions; they must stand modestly aside until they can slip in fitly into the interstices of life.
  George Santayana, *The Sense of Beauty*

And it came to pass that after a time the artist was forgotten, but the work lived.
    Olive Schreiner

Art is the signature of civilizations.
    Beverly Sills

There is no great art without reverence.
    Gerald Vann, *The Heart of Man*

Art happens--no hovel is safe from it, no prince may depend upon it, the vastest intelligence cannot bring it about.
    James McNeill Whistler, "Ten O'Clock"

Art is communication spoken by man for humanity in a language raised above the everyday happening.
    Mary Wigman

ARTISTS

An artist conscientiously moves in a direction which for some good reason he takes, putting one work in front of the other with the hope he'll arrive before death overtakes him.
    John Cage, "Erik Satie," *Silence*

The artistic temperament is a disease that afflicts amateurs.
    G.K. Chesterton, *Heretics*

An artist carries on throughout his life a mysterious, uninterrupted conversation with his public.
    Maurice Chevalier

An artist cannot speak about his art anymore than a plant can discuss horticulture.
    Jean Cocteau

Whatever happens, my audience mustn't know whether I'm spoofing or being serious; and likewise I mustn't know either. I'm in a constant interrogation: when does the deep and philosophically valid Dalí begin, and where does the loony and preposterous Dalí end?
    Salvador Dalí

The attitude that nature is chaotic and that the artist puts order into it is a very absurd point of view, I think. All that we can hope for is to put some order into ourselves.
    Willem de Kooning, *trans/formation*

The moment you cheat for the sake of beauty, you know you're an artist.
    Max Jacob, *Art poétique*

The artist, like the God of the creation, remains within or behind or beyond or above his handiwork, invisible, refined out of existence, indifferent, paring his fingernails.
James Joyce, *A Portrait of the Artist as a Young Man*

The first prerogative of an artist in any medium is to make a fool of himself.
Pauline Kael, *I Lost It at the Movies*

It is a mistake for a sculptor or a painter to speak or write very often about his job. It releases tension needed for his work.
Henry Moore

Then he asked me how it feels to be famous and what I think of those millions of Christmas cards made from my pictures. "Oh, I don't think about fame much. I keep my mind on what I am going to paint next. I have got a lot of catching up to do!"
Grandma Moses, *My Life's History*

An artist is his own fault.
John O'Hara, recalled on his death

Being an artist means ceasing to take seriously that very serious person we are when we are not an artist.
José Ortega y Gasset, *The Dehumanization of Art*

Artists--by definition innocent--don't steal. But they do borrow without giving back.
Ned Rorem, *Music from Inside Out*

Every time I paint a portrait I lose a friend.
John Singer Sargent

The true artist will let his wife starve, his children go barefoot, his mother drudge for his living at seventy, sooner than work at anything but his art.
George Bernard Shaw, *Man and Superman*

The world needs the artist who records, with dispassionate compassion, more than the missionary who proclaims with virulence unreal crusades against reality, especially those who want to put the clock back to an ideal past that never was.
Han Suyin

Immature artists imitate. Mature artists steal.
Lionel Trilling

To say to the painter that Nature is to be taken as she is, is to say to the player that he may sit on the piano.
James McNeill Whistler

This is the artist, then--life's hungry man, the glutton of eternity, beauty's miser, glory's slave.

Thomas Wolfe, *Of Time and the River*

If you ask me what I came to do in this world, I, an artist, will answer you: "I am here to live out loud."

Émile Zola, *Mes haines*

ATTITUDES

Argue for your limitations and they become yours. Argue for your heights and they are yours too.

Richard Bach

The optimist proclaims that we live in the best of all possible worlds; and the pessimist fears this is true.

James Branch Cabell

Amiability and good temper do not come easily when one is hungry.

A.J. Cronin

Nothing can bring you peace but yourself.

Ralph Waldo Emerson

Of cheerfulness, or a good temper--the more it is spent, the more of it remains.

Ralph Waldo Emerson, *Conduct of Life*

If you think you can or if you think you can't, you're absolutely right.

Henry Ford

No life is so hard that you can't make it easier by the way you take it.

Ellen Glasgow

Each one sees what he carries in his heart.

Goethe

If you treat people as they are, they will stay as they are; but if you treat them as if they were what they ought to be and could be, they will become what they ought to be and what they could be.

Goethe

The man whose habitual expression is supercilious, or distrustful, or apologetic, is making a statement of belief about himself in relation to other people though he may not hold the belief in verbal form.

D.W. Harding, *Experience into Words*

We awaken in others the same attitude of mind we hold toward them.
Elbert Hubbard

The greatest discovery of my generation is that human beings can alter their lives by altering their attitudes of mind.
William James

The more often I have a good attitude, the more often I have a good day.
Spencer and Constance Johnson, *The One-Minute Teacher*

I discovered I always have choices and sometimes it's only a choice of attitude.
Judith M. Knowlton

The mind is its own place, and in itself can make a heav'n of hell, a hell of heav'n.
John Milton

Change your thoughts and you change your world.
Norman Vincent Peale

Everytime you think you are not happy, say, "I am happy." Say it strongly to yourself, even if your feelings are contradictory. Remember, it is your self-image and not you. Just as fast as a fish can move in water, you can instantly change to a happy, balanced attitude.
Tarthang Tulku Rinpoche, *The Self-Image*

There is nothing either good or bad but thinking makes it so.
William Shakespeare, *Hamlet*

There is very little difference in people. But that little difference makes a big difference. The little difference is attitude. The big difference is whether it is positive or negative.
W. Clement Stone

I don't know what apathy means, and I don't care.
Julie Teitelbaum

AUDIENCE

For of the three elements in speech making--speaker, subject, and person addressed--it is the last one, the hearer, that determines the speech's end and object.
Aristotle

The best audience is one that is intelligent, well-educated--and a little drunk.
Alben W. Barkley

None speak false, when there is none to hear.
  James Beattie

What is this, an audience or an oil painting?
  Milton Berle

The audience gives you everything you need. They tell you. There is no director who can direct you like an audience.
  Fanny Brice

So long as you are mindful to say nothing unworthy of yourself, nothing untrue, nothing vulgar, you had better forget yourself altogether and think only of the audience, how to get them and how to hold them.
  James Bryce

If the speaker won't boil it down, the audience must sweat it out.
  Raymond Duncan

An author ought to write for the youth of his own generation, the critics of the next, and the schoolmasters of ever afterwards.
  F. Scott Fitzgerald

No tears in the writer, no tears in the reader.
  Robert Frost, *Collected Poems*

The conductor has the advantage of not seeing the audience.
  Andre Kostelanetz

I never saw dead people smoke before.
  Jackie Mason

They are only ten. [Said to have been posted in *The Times'* offices to remind the staff of their public's mental age.]
  Lord Northcliffe

I never failed to convince an audience that the best thing they could do was to go away.
  Thomas Love Peacock

You'd better do what you feel good about doing. If we [try] to figure out what it is the audience wants and then try to deliver it to them, we're lost souls on the ghost ship forever.
  Dan Rather

Applause is a receipt, not a note of demand.
  Artur Schnabel, *Saturday Review of Literature*

A good talker, even more than a good orator, implies a good audience.
　Leslie Stephen, *Samuel Johnson*

The pronoun *you* is more reader-centered than *I*. People are more interested in human beings than in things and more interested in themselves than in other human beings. Focusing your language on your reader helps you to focus your attention on him, to consider how he feels and how your words are affecting him.
　Henry Weihofen

A man really writes for an audience of about ten persons. Of course, if others like it, that is clear gain. But if those ten are satisfied, he is content.
　Alfred North Whitehead

AUTOBIOGRAPHY

Writing an autobiography and making a spiritual will are practically the same.
　Sholom Aleichem

Autobiography is now as common as adultery, and hardly less reprehensible.
　Lord Altrincham

You know writing one's life has a sobering effect on one--you get it together and you think: "Well! Look at the damn thing."
　S.N. Behrman, *Biography*

An autobiography is an obituary in serial form with the last installment missing.
　Quentin Crisp, *The Naked Civil Servant*

Every artist writes his own autobiography.
　Havelock Ellis, *The New Spirit*

Even if I set out to make a film about a fillet of sole, it would be about me.
　Federico Fellini, *Atlantic*

Autobiography is an unrivaled vehicle for telling the truth about other people.
　Philip Guedalla

Next to the writer of real estate advertisements, the autobiographer is the most suspect of prose artists.
　Donal Henahan

An autobiography usually reveals nothing bad about its writer except his memory.
　Franklin P. Jones

His memoir is a splendid artichoke of anecdotes, in which not merely the heart and leaves but the thistles as well are edible.
    John Leonard, on Brendan Gill's *Here at the New Yorker*

To write one's memoirs is to speak ill of everybody except oneself.
    Henri-Philippe Pétain

There ain't nothing that breaks up homes, country, and nations like somebody publishing their memoirs.
    Will Rogers, *Autobiography*

Autobiographies ought to begin with Chapter Two.
    Ellery Sedgwick, *The Happy Profession*

The best autobiographies are confessions; but if a man is a deep writer all his works are confessions.
    George Bernard Shaw, *Sixteen Self Sketches*

Only when one has lost all curiosity about the future has one reached the age to write an autobiography.
    Evelyn Waugh

B

BEGINNING (see also INTRODUCTION)

Nothing so difficult as a beginning.
    Lord Byron, *Don Juan*

The beginnings and endings of all human undertakings are untidy--the building of a
house, the writing of a novel, the demolition of a bridge, and eminently, the finish of
a voyage.
    John Galsworthy

Professional writers and editors find that the beginning of their first draft is no
beginning at all. It is a mess, a series of false beginnings in which the starter's pistol
goes off once, then twice, and the runners burst from their blocks only to stop and
come back again.
    Ken Macrorie

I always do the first line well, but I have trouble with the others.
    Molière, *The Ridiculous Précieuses*

I never lose an opportunity of urging a practical beginning, however small, for it is
wonderful how often the mustard-seed germinates and roots itself.
    Florence Nightingale

The last thing that we find in making a book is to know what we must put first.
    Blaise Pascal

As a queen sits down, knowing the chair will be there,
Or a general raises a hand and is given the field glasses,
Step off in the blank of your own mind.
Something will come to you.
    Richard Wilbur

BELIEFS

Does everyone just believe what he wants to?
As long as possible, sometimes longer.
    Isaac Asimov

Man is made by his belief. As he believes, so he is.
    Bhagavad-Gita

Man is what he believes.
    Anton Chekhov

A little credulity helps one on through life very smoothly.
    Elizabeth Cleghorn Gaskell

It is easier to believe than to doubt.
    Everett Dean Martin, *The Meaning of a Liberal Education*

A well-bred man keeps his beliefs out of his conversation.
    André Maurois

Doublethink means the power of holding two contradictory beliefs in one's mind simultaneously, and accepting both of them.
    George Orwell, *Nineteen Eighty-Four*

BIBLE

The Bible is a window in this prison-world, through which we may look into eternity.
    Timothy Dwight

The English Bible--a book which, if everything else in our language should perish, would alone suffice to show the whole extent of its beauty and power.
    Lord Thomas Babington Macaulay

You can learn more about human nature by reading the Bible than by living in New York.
    William Lyon Phelps

So long as tens of thousands of Bibles are printed every year, and circulated over the whole habitable globe, and the masses in all English-speaking nations revere it as the word of God, it is vain to belittle its influence.
    Elizabeth Cady Stanton

When a library expels a book of mine and leaves an unexpurgated Bible lying around

where unprotected youth can get ahold of it, the deep unconscious irony of it delights me.
  Mark Twain

BIOGRAPHY

To the biographer all lives bar none are dramatic constructions.
  Katharine Anthony

It is one of the ironies of biographical art that some details are more relevant than others, and many details have no relevance at all.
  Paul Bailey

None of the people I wrote about were as exciting in reality as I imagined them to be.
  Bettina Ballard

The best biographies leave their readers with a sense of having all but entered into a second life and of having come to know another human being in some ways better than he knew himself.
  Mary Cable

A well-written Life is almost as rare as a well-spent one.
  Thomas Carlyle

Any biographer must of necessity become a pilgrim . . . a peripatetic, obsessed literary pilgrim, a traveler with four eyes.
  Leon Edel

Once the implicit aim of biography was to *uplift* . . . now it is to *unveil*.
  Mark Feeney, *Boston Globe*

Biography, like big game hunting, is one of the recognized forms of sport, and it is [as] unfair as only sport can be.
  Philip Guedalla

Anybody who profits from the experience of others probably writes biographies.
  Franklin P. Jones

Then you take it all--the chronology, the letters, the interviews, your own knowledge, the newspaper cuttings, the history books, the diary, the thousand hours of contemplation, and you try to make a whole of it, not a chronicle but a drama, with a beginning and an end, the whole being given form and integrity because a man moves through it from birth to death, through all the beauty and terror of human life.
  Alan Paton, on writing biography

It is perhaps as difficult to write a good life as to live one.
  Lytton Strachey

Biographies are but the clothes and buttons of the man--the biography of the man himself cannot be written.
  Mark Twain

The lives of great men rarely remind us of anything sublime.
  Lord Vansittart

Just how difficult it is to write biography can be reckoned by anybody who sits down and considers just how many people know the truth about his or her love affairs.
  Dame Rebecca West

Biography lends to death a new terror.
  Oscar Wilde

Every great man nowadays has his disciples, and it is always Judas who writes the biography.
  Oscar Wilde

Biography is to give a man some kind of shape after his death.
  Virginia Woolf

BOOK REVIEWING

Several times I concluded that there was too much detail; always I returned to continue and enjoy the book.
  John Kenneth Galbraith

He who first praises a book becomingly is next in merit to the author.
  Walter Savage Landor, *Imaginary Conversations*

Prolonged, indiscriminate reviewing of books involves constantly *inventing* reactions towards books about which one has no spontaneous feelings whatever.
  George Orwell, "Confessions of a Book Reviewer"

The actual definition of reviewmanship is now, I think, stabilized. In its shortest form it is "How to be one-up on the author without actually tampering with the text." In other words, how, as a critic, to show that it is really you yourself who should have written the book, if you had had the time, and since you hadn't you are glad that someone else has, although obviously it might have been done better.
  Stephen Potter

I never read a book before reviewing it; it prejudices a man so.
  Sydney Smith, in Hesketh Pearson, *The Smith of Smiths*

Book critics are a weird journalistic subspecies: We may pull all-nighters, but they tend to take place at home, where page 648 leads inexorably to page 649.
Jean Strouse, *Newsweek*

I have long felt that any reviewer who expresses rage and loathing for a novel is preposterous. He or she is like a person who has put on full armor and attacked a hot fudge sundae or a banana split.
Kurt Vonnegut, Jr.

BOOKS

Books are the most mannerly of companions, accessible at all times, in all times, in all moods, frankly declaring the author's mind, without offense.
A. Bronson Alcott, *Concord Days*

What is even a wise book but a blast from the lungs made visible to the eyes?
Hervey Allen, *Anthony Adverse*

A book is like a garden carried in the pocket.
Arabic proverb

A real book is not one that's read, but one that reads us.
W.H. Auden, recalled on his death

Some books are to be tasted, others to be swallowed, and some few to be chewed and digested; that is, some books are to be read only in parts; others to be read, but not curiously; and some few to be read wholly, and with diligence and attention.
Sir Francis Bacon, "Of Studies," *Essays*

Books are the collective memory of mankind.
Herbert Smith Bailey, Jr.

Books say: she did this because. Life says: she did this. Books are where things are explained to you; life is where things aren't. I'm not surprised some people prefer books. Books make sense of life. The only problem is that the lives they make sense of are other people's lives, never your own.
Julian Barnes, *Flaubert's Parrot*

If we are told of some four-volume epic . . . we're apt to say, "How interesting," but we never will read it unless we have both legs in traction.
Martha Bayles

A book is a garden; a book is an orchard; a book is a storehouse; a book is a party. It

is company by the way; it is a counselor; it is a multitude of counselors.
  Henry Ward Beecher, *Proverbs from Plymouth Pulpit*

Where is human nature so weak as in the bookstore?
  Henry Ward Beecher

Books are the compasses and telescopes and sextants and charts which other men have prepared to help us navigate the dangerous seas of human life.
  Jesse Lee Bennett

These are my silent friends. My slaves. They sit in mute rows and they have nothing to say unless I ask them. By opening a book, I can make it speak eloquently for as long as I please. The words, the images, the stories, the knowledge, the history, the laughter, the edification, the tears of the world are in my hands.
  Jim Bishop

Books we must have though we lack bread.
  Alice Williams Brotherton, *Ballade of Poor Bookworms*

They do most by books, who could much without them.
  Sir Thomas Browne, *Christian Morals*

The possession of a book becomes a substitute for reading it.
  Anthony Burgess

I go to books and to nature as a bee goes to the flower, for a nectar that I can make into my own honey.
  John Burroughs, *The Summit of the Years*

Whosoever therefore acknowledges himself to be a zealous follower of truth, of happiness, of wisdom, of science, or even of faith, must of necessity make himself a lover of books.
  Richard de Bury, *Philobiblon*

The oldest books are still only just out to those who have not read them.
  Samuel Butler

A great book is like great evil.
  Callimachus

Books are the blessed chloroform of the mind.
  Robert W. Chambers, *What English Literature Gives Us*

A good book, a good friend.
  Selwyn Gurney Champion, *Racial Proverbs*

Books are the true levellers. They give to all, who will faithfully use them, the society, the spiritual presence, of the best and greatest of our race.
William Ellery Channing, *Self-Culture*

Every book must be chewed to get out its juice.
Chinese proverb

A book is like a piece of rope; it takes on meaning only in connection with the things it holds together.
Norman Cousins

Books cannot always please, however good;
Minds are not ever craving for their food.
George Crabbe, *The Borough*

There are books which I love to see on the shelf. I feel a virtue goes out of them, but I should think it undue familiarity to read them.
Samuel McChord Crothers

Books should to one of these four ends conduce,
For wisdom, piety, delight, or use.
John Denham, *Of Prudence*

There is more treasure in books than in all the pirates' loot on Treasure Island . . . and best of all, you can enjoy these riches every day of your life.
Walt Disney

Thank you very much for sending me the book. I shall lose no time in reading it.
Benjamin Disraeli

Cave ab homine unius Libri. (Beware of the man of one book.)
Isaac D'Israeli, *Curiosities of Literature*

Who, without books, essays to learn,
Draws water in a leaky urn.
Austin Dobson, *A Bookman's Budget*

If we encounter a man of rare intellect, we should ask him what books he reads.
Ralph Waldo Emerson

When I get a little money, I buy books; and if any is left, I buy food and clothes.
Desiderius Erasmus

How pure the joy when first my hands unfold
The small, rare volume, black with tarnished gold.
John Ferriar, *The Bibliomania*

Women are by nature fickle, and so are men . . . . Not so with books, for books cannot change. A thousand years hence they are what you find them today, speaking the same words, holding forth the same comfort.

    Eugene Field

I suspect that the only books that influence us are those for which we are ready, and which have gone a little further down our particular path than we have yet gone ourselves.

    E.M. Forster, *Two Cheers for Democracy*

Never lend books, for no one ever returns them; the only books I have in my library are books that other folks have lent me.

    Anatole France

The first time I read an excellent book, it is to me just as if I had gained a new friend. When I read over a book I have perused before, it resembles the meeting with an old one.

    Oliver Goldsmith, *The Citizen of the World*

Even bad books are books and therefore sacred.

    Günter Grass, *The Tin Drum*

Paperbacks blink in and out of print like fireflies. They also, as older collectors have ruefully discovered, fade and fall apart even more rapidly than their owners.

    Paul Gray

The book is here to stay. What we're doing is symbolic of the peaceful coexistence of the book and the computer.

    Vartan Gregorian

Some of the new books are so down to earth they should be plowed under.

    Anna Herbert

These are not books, lumps of lifeless paper, but minds alive on the shelves. From each of them goes out its own voice . . . and just as the touch of a button on our set will fill the room with music, so by taking down one of these volumes and opening it, one can call into range the voice of a man far distant in time and space, and hear him speaking to us, mind to mind, heart to heart.

    Gilbert Highet

The foolishest book is a kind of leaky boat on a sea of wisdom; some of the wisdom will get in anyhow.

    Oliver Wendell Holmes, Sr., *The Poet at the Breakfast Table*

The book which you read from a sense of duty, or because for any reason you must,

does not commonly make friends with you.
    William Dean Howells, *My Literary Passions*

This will never be a civilized country until we expend more money for books than we do for chewing gum.
    Elbert Hubbard, *The Philistine* (periodical)

Spend your money on good books, and you'll find its equivalence in gold of intelligence.
    Immanuel of Rome, *Mahberot*

There is no worse robber than a bad book.
    Italian proverb

What a sense of superiority it gives one to escape reading some book which everyone else is reading.
    Alice James, *Diary*

As long as mixed grills and combination salads are popular, anthologies will undoubtedly continue in favor.
    Elizabeth Janeway, *The Writer's Book* (periodical)

The book is man's best invention so far.
    Carolina Maria de Jesus

When a man travels and finds books which are not known in his hometown, it is his duty to buy them, rather than anything else, and bring the books back home with him.
    Judah of Regensburg

Literature is my Utopia. Here I am disenfranchised. No barrier of the senses shuts me out from the sweet, gracious discourse of my book friends. They talk to me without embarrassment or awkwardness.
    Helen Keller

A little known law of physics postulates that the number of books you have borrowed and failed to return equals the number of books you are owed. This law is called the Conservation of Literature.
    Martin F. Kohn

A book is a friend whose face is constantly changing. If you read it when you are recovering from an illness, and return to it years after, it is changed surely, with the change in yourself.
    Andrew Lang, *The Library*

The love of books is a love which requires neither justification, apology, nor defence.
    John Alfred Langford, *The Praise of Books*

For a good book has this quality, that it is not merely a petrification of its author, but that once it has been tossed behind, like Deucalion's little stone, it acquires a separate and vivid life of its own.
    Carolina LeJeune

Books, books, these are the only things that have come to my aid! In the end, it makes one terribly arrogant, always to do without one's equals!
    Marie Leneru

Book--what they make a movie out of for television.
    Leonard Louis Levinson

A book is a mirror; if an ass peers into it, you can't expect an apostle to peer out.
    Georg C. Lichtenberg

There can hardly be a stranger commodity in the world than books. Printed by people who don't understand them; sold by people who don't understand them; bound, criticized, and read by people who don't understand them; and now even written by people who don't understand them.
    Georg C. Lichtenberg, *Aphorisms*

Books serve to show a man that those original thoughts of his aren't very new after all.
    Abraham Lincoln

The things I want to know are in books; my best friend is the man who'll get me a book I ain't read.
    Abraham Lincoln

All books are either dreams or swords;
You can cut, or you can drug, with words.
    Amy Lowell, *Sword Blades and Poppy Seed*

We profit little by books we do not enjoy.
    John Lubbock, *The Pleasures of Life*

It was a book to kill time for those who liked it better dead.
    Rose Macaulay

The walls of books around him, dense with the past, formed a kind of insulation against the present world and its disasters.
    Ross Macdonald

Never disregard a book because the author of it is a foolish fellow.
    Lord Melbourne

As good almost kill a man as kill a good Book; who kills a Man kills a reasonable creature, Gods Image; but hee who destroyes a good Booke, kills reason itselfe, kills the Image of God, as it were in the eye.
John Milton, *Areopagitica*

Show me the books he loves and I shall know
The man far better than through mortal friends.
S. Weir Mitchell

A man loses contact with reality if he is not surrounded by his books.
François Mitterrand

If good books did good, the world would have been converted long ago.
George Moore

A book is the only place in which you can examine a fragile thought without breaking it, or explore an explosive idea without fear it will go off in your face . . . . It is one of the few havens remaining where a man's mind can get both provocation and privacy.
Edward P. Morgan, *Clearing the Air*

The real purpose of books is to trap the mind into doing its own thinking.
Christopher Morley

When you sell a man a book you don't sell him just twelve ounces of paper and ink and glue--you sell him a whole new life.
Christopher Morley

The desire to have many books, and never use them, is like the child that will have a candle burning by him all the while he is sleeping.
Henry Peacham

Wear the old coat and buy the new book.
Austin Phelps, *The Theory of Preaching*

The best of mural decorations is books; they are more varied in color and appearance than any wall-paper. They are attractive in design.
William Lyon Phelps

Collecting books is like collecting other people's minds, like having people on the shelves--only, you can just put them away when you want to.
John Prizeman, *Esquire*

The greatest book is not the one whose message engraves itself on the brain . . . but the one whose vital impact opens up other viewpoints, and from writer to reader spreads the fire that is fed by the various essences, until it becomes a vast

conflagration from forest to forest.
Romain Rolland, *Journey Within*

Teachers of wisdom, who could once beguile
My tedious hours, lighten every toil,
I now resign to you.
William Roscoe, "To My Books on Parting with Them"

After love, book collecting is the most exhilarating sport of all.
A.S.W. Rosenbach, *A Book Hunter's Holiday*

A good book makes my nostrils quiver. In all other respects, I like to think, I am a clean, wholesome American boy.
Leo Rosten, *The Many Worlds of L*E*O R*O*S*T*E*N*

Books are often wiser than their readers.
Russian proverb

If a drop of ink fell at the same time on your books and on your coat, clean first the book and then the garment.
Sefer Hasidim (Book of the Righteous)

While you converse with lords and dukes,
I have their betters here--my books.
Thomas Sheridan, *My Books*

A good book should leave you . . . slightly exhausted at the end. You live several lives while reading it.
William Styron, in *Writers at Work*

Books are the treasured wealth of the world and the fit inheritance of generations and generations.
Henry David Thoreau, *Walden*

Books must be read as deliberately and reservedly as they were written.
Henry David Thoreau

Books are the carriers of civilization. Without books, history is silent, literature dumb, science crippled, thought and speculation at a standstill.
Barbara Tuchman, *Authors' League Bulletin*

A good book is the best of friends, the same today and forever.
Martin Farquhar Tupper, *Proverbial Philosophy*

It is with books as with men: a very small number play a great part.
Voltaire

Why is it that reality, when set down untransposed in a book, sounds false?
    Simone Weil

The books we think we ought to read are poky, dull, and dry;
The books that we would like to read we are ashamed to buy;
The books that people talk about we never can recall;
And the books that people give us, oh, they're the worst of all.
    Carolyn Wells

Good books are the most precious blessings to a people; bad books are among the worst of curses.
    Edwin Percy Whipple, *Essays and Reviews*

Camerado, this is no book. Who touches this, touches a man.
It is I you hold and who holds you,
I spring from the pages into your arms.
    Walt Whitman, *Leaves of Grass*

I would never read a book if it were possible for me to talk half an hour with the man who wrote it.
    Woodrow Wilson

BOOK WRITING

I can't understand why a person will take a year to write a novel when he can easily buy one for a few dollars.
    Fred Allen

Fiction is not a dream. Nor is it guess work. It is imagining based on facts, and the facts must be accurate or the work of imagining will not stand up.
    Margaret Culkin Banning

For several days after my first book was published I carried it about in my pocket, and took surreptitious peeps at it to make sure that the ink had not faded.
    Sir James M. Barrie

I don't keep any copy of my books around . . . . They would embarrass me. When I finish writing my books, I kick them in the belly, and have done with them.
    Ludwig Bemelmans

I take the view, and always have done, that if you cannot say what you have to say in twenty minutes, you should go away and write a book about it.
    Lord Brabazon

I sympathize with my youthful neighbor, who is struggling to inject a little order, a

little taste and style--a little readability, in short--into a mass of manuscript that is supposed to be a book.
    Van Wyck Brooks

Who knows whether in retirement I shall be tempted to the last infirmity of mundane minds, which is to write a book.
    Archbishop of Canterbury

There are men that will make you books, and turn them loose into the world, with as much dispatch as they would do a dish of fritters.
    Miguel de Cervantes, *Don Quixote*

Writing a book is an adventure. To begin with, it is a toy and an amusement. Then it becomes a mistress, then it becomes a master, then it becomes a tyrant. The last phase is that just as you are about to be reconciled to your servitude, you kill the monster, and fling him to the public.
    Winston Churchill

Someday I hope to write a book where the royalties will pay for the copies I give away.
    Clarence Darrow

Writing every book is like a purge; at the end of it one is empty . . . like a dry shell on the beach, waiting for the tide to come in again.
    Daphne du Maurier

People who want to write sociology should not write a novel.
    Ralph Ellison

Everything goes by the board: honor, pride, decency . . . to get the book written.
    William Faulkner, in *Writers at Work*

I wish I could write a beautiful book to break those hearts that are soon to cease to exist: a book of faith and small neat words and of people who live by the philosophies of popular songs.
    Zelda Fitzgerald

Unprovided with original learning, unformed in the habits of thinking, unskilled in the arts of composition, I resolved to write a book.
    Edward Gibbon

For a dyed-in-the-wool author, nothing is as dead as a book once it is written . . . . She is rather like a cat whose kittens have grown up.
    Rumer Godden

Whatever an author puts between the two covers of his book is public property;

whatever of himself he does not put there is private property, as much as if he had never written a word.

Gail Hamilton

A book, like a child, needs time to be born. Books written quickly--within a few weeks--make me suspicious of the author. A respectable woman does not bring a child into the world before the ninth month.

Heinrich Heine, *Thoughts and Fancies*

I look with pleasure on my book, however defective, and deliver it to the world with the spirit of a man who has endeavored well.

Samuel Johnson

It helps if you have someone to talk to, it really helps. I have my husband to talk to. It helps very much if I say to him, "I think I've painted myself into a corner. Now I have three or four different solutions." . . . we discuss the solutions, and I pick the one I like best. I don't think you can write a book completely alone.

Judith Krantz

Royalties are nice and all that, but shaking the beads brings in money quicker.

Gypsy Rose Lee

With each book I write, I become more and more convinced that [the books] have a life of their own, quite apart from me.

Madeleine L'Engle, *Anglican Digest*

I put things down on sheets of paper and stuff them in my pockets. When I have enough, I have a book.

John Lennon

I try to leave out the parts that people skip.

Elmore Leonard

During the final stages of publishing a paper or a book, I always feel strongly repelled by my own writing . . . . It appears increasingly hackneyed and banal and less worth publishing.

Konrad Lorenz

If you have one strong idea, you can't help repeating it and embroidering it. Sometimes I think that authors should write one book and then be put in a gas chamber.

John Marquand

A sequel is an admission that you've been reduced to imitating yourself.

Don Marquis

There are three rules for writing a novel. Unfortunately, no one knows what they are.
> W. Somerset Maugham

Give me a condor's quill! Give me Vesuvius's crater for an inkstand! . . .
To produce a mighty book you must choose a mighty theme.
> Herman Melville, *Moby Dick*

Writing is hard. If writing was easy, everyone would do it. You must sit in a chair six or seven hours a day for two years to write a book.
> James Michener

Writing a book is not as tough as it is to haul thirty-five people around the country and sweat like a horse five nights a week.
> Bette Midler

A person who publishes a book willfully appears before the populace with his pants down . . . . If it is a good book nothing can hurt him. If it is a bad book nothing can help him.
> Edna St. Vincent Millay

First you're an unknown, then you write one book and you move up to obscurity.
> Martin Myers

Whoever is able to write a book and does not, it is as if he has lost a child.
> Nachman of Bratslav

I write because, exacting as it may be to do so, it is still more difficult to refrain, and because--however conscious of one's limitations one may be--there is always at the back of one's mind an irrational hope that this next book will be different: it will be the rounded achievement, the complete fulfillment. It never has been: yet I am still writing.
> Iris Origo

Make 'em laugh; make 'em cry; make 'em wait.
> Charles Reade, "Recipe for a Successful Novel"

A great novelist must open the reader's heart, allow the reader to remember the vastness and glory--and the shame and shabbiness--of what it is to be human.
> Carolyn See

I've always been a compulsive talker. I can talk for two hours about nothing. I just talked a book.
> Beverly Sills

The profession of book writing makes horse racing seem like a solid, stable business.
> John Steinbeck, Nobel Prize address

I've given my memoirs far more thought than any of my marriages. You can't divorce a book.
  Gloria Swanson

When I write, I aim in my mind not toward New York but toward a vague spot a little east of Kansas. I think of the books on library shelves, without their jackets, years old, and a countryish teen-aged boy finding them, and having them speak to him. The reviews, the stacks in Brentano's, are just hurdles to get over, to place the books on that shelf.
  John Updike

Each book, before the contract, is beautiful to contemplate. By the middle of the writing, the book has become, for the author, a hate object. For the editor, in the middle of editing, it has become a two-ton concrete necklace. However, both author and editor will recover the gleam in their eyes when the work is complete, and see the book as the masterwork it really is.
  Sam Vaughan

I quit writing if I feel inspired, because I know I'm going to have to throw it away. Writing a novel is like building a wall brick by brick; only amateurs believe in inspiration.
  Frank Yerby

BREVITY

The Ten Commandments contain 297 words. The Bill of Rights is stated in 463 words. Lincoln's Gettysburg Address contains 266 words. A recent Federal directive to regulate the price of cabbage contains 26,911 words.
  Atlanta Journal, letter to the editor

No man pleases by silence; many please by speaking briefly.
  Ausonius, *Epistulae*

As man grows wiser he talks less and says more.
  Roger Babson

Praised be he who can state a cause in a clear, simple, and succinct manner, and then stop.
  Judge Harry H. Belt

I don't care how much a man talks, if he only says it in a few words.
  Josh Billings

Deliver your words not by number but by weight.
  Sir Henry George Bohn, *A Handbook of Proverbs*

No speech can be entirely bad, if it is short enough.
　　Irvin S. Cobb

One never repents of having spoken too little, but often of having spoken too much.
　　Philippe de Commynes, *Mémoires*

Spartans, stoics, heroes, saints, and gods use a short and positive speech.
　　Ralph Waldo Emerson

The more you say, the less people remember. The fewer the words, the greater the profit.
　　François Fénelon

The fewer thy words the fewer thine errors.
　　Solomon Ibn Gabirol, *Choice of Pearls*

Talk as if you were making your will: the fewer words the less litigation.
　　Baltasar Gracian, *The Art of Worldly Wisdom*

Well said is soon said.
　　Baltasar Gracian, *The Art of Worldly Wisdom*

It is nothing short of genius that uses one word when twenty will say the same thing.
　　David Grayson, *The Friendly Road*

When you've got a thing to say,
Say it! Don't take half a day.
When your tale's got little in it,
Crowd the whole thing in a minute!
　　Joel Chandler Harris, *Advice to Writers for the Daily Press*

Polyverbosity . . . is a common disease of seniors and young instructors, and of some professors also. It should be repressed and sternly. Once a student can be persuaded that the best writing is usually the briefest . . . [he learns] that his "yes" must be "yes" and not "semantic affirmation."
　　G.G. Harrison

The most valuable of all talents is that of never using two words when one will do.
　　Thomas Jefferson

A mediocre speech can never be too short.
　　Madame Constant de Lambert

As it is the mark of a great mind to say much in a few words, so it is the mark of a little one to talk much and say little.
　　François de La Rochefoucauld, *Maxims*

To a reporter assigned a thousand words for an article but insisting on fifteen hundred came the wire: "1000, MOSES COVERED THE CREATION IN 864."
    Lawrence E. Nelson, *Our Roving Bible*

Thinketh big.
Sayeth small.
    Ron Nickel

It is either better to be silent or say things of more value than silence. Sooner throw a pearl at hazard than an idle or useless word; and do not say a little in many words, but a great deal in a few.
    Pythagoras

He replies nothing but monosyllables. I believe he would make three bites of a cherry.
    François Rabelais, *Pantagruel*

Always be shorter than anybody dared to hope.
    Lord Reading

There are things which don't deserve to be said briefly.
    Jean Rostand

Therefore, since brevity is the soul of wit,
And tediousness the limbs and outward flourishes,
I will be brief.
    William Shakespeare, *Hamlet*

If Moses had been paid newspaper rates for the Ten Commandments, he might have written the Two Thousand Commandments.
    Isaac Bashevis Singer, *New York Times*

It is with words as with sunbeams--the more they are condensed the deeper they burn.
    Robert Southey

Vigorous writing is concise. A sentence should contain no unnecessary words, a paragraph no unnecessary sentences for the same reason that a drawing should have no unnecessary lines and a machine no unnecessary parts. This requires not that the writer make all his sentences short, or that he avoid all detail and treat his subjects only in outline, but that every word tell.
    William Strunk, *Elements of Style*

Don't quote Latin; say what you have to say, and then sit down.
    Duke of Wellington (Arthur Wellesley), advice to a new member of Parliament

Little said is soonest mended.
    George Wither, *The Shepheard's Hunting*

BUSINESS COMMUNICATION

If Asia has been targeted for opening and offering the potentially most lucrative market for advertising industries, consider women there as the ultimate niche.
    Linda K. Fuller, Association for Business Communication

We've long believed there's nothing to be gained by telling our competitors how we do things.
    Edward G. Harness

A company is judged by the president it keeps.
    James Hulbert

Business today consists in persuading crowds.
    Gerald Stanley Lee, *Crowds*

"My door is always open--bring me your problems." This is guaranteed to turn on every whiner, lackey, and neurotic on the property.
    Robert F. Six, Continental Airlines

C

CENSORSHIP

In some respects the life of a censor is more exhilarating than that of an emperor. The best the emperor can do is to snip off the heads of men and women, who are mere mortals. The censor can decapitate ideas which but for him might have lived forever.
Heywood Broun, *Pieces of Hate*

Censor--A self-appointed snoophound who sticks his noes into other people's business.
Bennett Cerf, *The Laugh's on Me*

You have a right to burn books or destroy books if you can prove that they can do harm.
Thomas Devine

Every burned book enlightens the world.
Ralph Waldo Emerson, "Compensation," *Essays*

Blessed are the censors for they shall inhibit the earth.
Official Bulletin, Guild of Film Critics (England)

The burning of an author's books, imprisonment for opinion's sake, has always been the tribute that an ignorant age pays to the genius of its time.
Joseph Lewis

I'm going to introduce a resolution to have the Postmaster General stop reading dirty books and deliver the mail.
Senator Gale McGee

I am a man of a thousand faces, all of them blacklisted.
Zero Mostel

We all know that books burn--yet we have the greater knowledge that books cannot be killed by fire. People die, but books never die . . . . No man and no force can put thought in a concentration camp forever.
     Franklin D. Roosevelt

The ultimate censorship is the flick of the dial.
     Tom Smothers

Censorship reflects a society's lack of confidence in itself.
     Potter Stewart

What is hard today is to censor one's own thoughts--
To sit by and see the blind man
On the sightless horse, riding into the bottomless abyss.
     Arthur Waley, *Censorship*

CHILDREN

You know how it is in the kid's book world: It's just bunny eat bunny.
     Anonymous

Child! do not throw this book about;
Refrain from the unholy pleasure
Of cutting all the pictures out!
Preserve it as your chiefest pleasure.
     Hilaire Belloc, *The Bad Child's Book of Beasts*

Before a child of our time finds his way clear to opening a book, his eyes have been exposed to such a blizzard of changing, colorful, conflicting letters that his chances of penetrating the archaic stillness of the book are slight.
     Walter Benjamin, *One-Way Street*

Young children's concern with words is more like that of the poet, since they too are more than usually aware of their physical qualities, and show this by the way they play with sounds, making jingles and rhymes and puns and mixing in nonsense sounds.
     James Britton, *Language and Learning*

It may be that we have to lose that knowledge and understanding which children have and then perhaps it comes back to us through living experience and wisdom.
     Louis Bromfield

The Chinese believe that there's an age in which to learn everything. If you try to teach a child too young, he can't learn it; and you just wear yourself out and ruin his temper and your own too.
     Pearl Buck

Every adult needs a child to teach; it's the way adults learn.
    Frank A. Clark

The prime function, therefore, of the children's book writer is to write a book that is so absorbing, exciting, funny, fast, and beautiful that the child will fall in love with it. And that first love affair between the young child and the young book will hopefully lead to other loves for other books and when that happens the battle is probably won. The child will have found a crock of gold. He will also have gained something that will help to carry him most marvelously through the tangles of his later years.
    Roald Dahl, in Jim Trelease, *The Read-Aloud Handbook*

A misbehaving child is a discouraged child.
    Rudolf Dreikurs

Teach your child to hold his tongue. He'll learn fast enough to speak.
    Benjamin Franklin, *Poor Richard's Almanack*

A kid is a guy I never wrote down to. He's interested in what I say if I make it interesting. He is also the last container of a sense of humor, which disappears as he gets older, and he laughs only according to the way the boss, society, politics, or race want him to. Then he becomes an adult. And an adult is an obsolete child.
    Theodore Geisel (Dr. Seuss)

When a child writes, "My sister was hit by a terck yesterday" and the teacher's response is a red-circled "terck" with no further comment, educational standards may have been upheld, but the child will think twice before entering the writing process again. Inane and apathetic writing is often the writer's only means of self-protection.
    Donald H. Graves

Perhaps it is only in childhood that books have any deep influence on our lives . . . in childhood all books are books of divination, telling us about the future, and like the fortune-teller who sees a long journey in the cards or death by water, they influence the future. I suppose that is why books excited us so much. What do we ever get nowadays from reading to equal the excitement and revelation of those first fourteen years?
    Graham Greene

Children who are not spoken to by live and responsive adults will not learn to speak properly. Children who are not answered will stop asking questions. They will become incurious. And children who are not told stories and who are not read to will have few reasons for wanting to learn to read.
    Gail E. Haley

One laugh of a child will make the holiest day more sacred still.
    Robert G. Ingersoll, *The Liberty of Man, Woman, and Child*

Children are likely to live up to what you believe of them.
> Lady Bird Johnson

There are many little ways to enlarge [your child's] world. Love of books is the best of all.
> Jacqueline Kennedy

The real menace in dealing with a five-year-old is that in no time at all you begin to sound like a five-year-old.
> Jean Kerr, *Please Don't Eat the Daisies*

There is frequently more to learn from the unexpected questions of a child than the discourses of men, who talk in a road, according to the notions they have borrowed and the prejudices of their education.
> John Locke, *Some Thoughts concerning Education*

The important thing is not so much that every child should be taught as that every child should be given the wish to learn.
> John Lubbock, *The Pleasures of Life*

Children and fools speak true.
> John Lyly, *Endymion*

Of all people children are the most imaginative. They abandon themselves without reserve to every illusion. No man, whatever his sensibility may be, is ever affected by Hamlet or Lear as a little girl is affected by the story of poor Red Riding-hood.
> Lord Thomas Babington Macaulay, *Edinburgh Review*

People with bad consciences always fear the judgment of children.
> Mary McCarthy

Children will watch anything, and when a broadcaster uses crime and violence and other shoddy devices to monopolize a child's attention it's worse than taking candy from a baby. It is taking precious time from the process of growing up.
> Newton Minow

Children are inclined to learn from television [because] it is never too busy to talk to them, and it never has to brush them aside while it does household chores.
> National Commission on Causes and Prevention of Violence

Every child is an artist. The problem is how to remain an artist once he grows up.
> Pablo Picasso

A child's words preserve innocence and truth.
> Elizabeth Ricciardone

Grown-ups never understand anything for themselves, and it is tiresome for children to be always and forever explaining things to them.
    Antoine de Saint-Exupéry, *The Little Prince*

Children read books, not reviews. They don't give a hoot about the critics.
    Isaac Bashevis Singer

The impact of even one good book on a child's mind is surely an end in itself, a valid experience which helps him form standards of judgment and taste at the time when his mind is most sensitive to impressions of every kind.
    Lillian H. Smith, *The Unreluctant Years*

A child tells in the street what its father and mother say at home.
    Talmud

CLARITY

With pen and pencil we're learning to say
Nothing, more clearly every day.
    William Allingham, *Blackberries*

What is conceived well is expressed clearly.
And the words to say it with arrive with ease.
    Nicolas Boileau, *L'art poétique*

Those who write clearly have readers; those who write obscurely have commentators.
    Albert Camus

Except you utter by the tongue words easy to be understood, how shall it be known what is spoken? For ye shall speak into the air.
    I Corinthians 14:9

The chief virtue that language can have is clearness, and nothing detracts from it so much as the use of unfamiliar words.
    Galen, *On the Natural Faculties*

Some experience of popular lecturing had convinced me that the necessity of making things plain to uninstructed people was one of the best means of clearing up the obscure corners in one's own mind.
    Thomas H. Huxley, *Man's Place in Nature*

A thinker who cannot set forth weighty thoughts in simple and clear language should be suspected, primarily, of lacking talent for thought.
    Jacob Klatzkin, *In Praise of Wisdom*

You must always explain things frankly and explicitly to your lawyer . . . . It is for him to embroil them afterwards.
    Alessandro Manzoni

Good prose is like a window pane.
    George Orwell, *Collected Essays*

The great enemy of clear language is insincerity. When there is a gap between one's real and one's declared aims, one turns as it were instinctively to long words and exhausted idioms, like a cuttlefish squirting out ink.
    George Orwell, *Shooting an Elephant*

A man who has the knowledge but lacks the power clearly to express it is no better off than if he never had any ideas at all.
    Pericles

Making something perfectly clear only confuses everybody.
    George Rockwell, *Down East*

If a man has something to say, it should drop from him directly, like a stone to the ground.
    Henry David Thoreau

A sentence should be read as if its author, had he held a plough instead of a pen, could have drawn a furrow deep and straight to the end.
    Henry David Thoreau

The difference between the right word and the almost right word is the difference between lightning and the lightning bug.
    Mark Twain

It's hard to be funny when you have to be clear.
    Mae West

CLASSICS

Books that have become classics--books that have had their day and now get more praise than perusal--always remind me of retired colonels and majors and captains who, having reached the age limit, find themselves retired on half pay.
    Thomas Bailey Aldrich, *Ponkapog Papers*

When you reread a classic you do not see more in the book than you did before; you see more in *you* than there was before.
    Clifton Fadiman, *Any Number Can Play*

We find little in a book but what we put there. But in great books, the mind finds room to put many things.
Joseph Joubert, *Pensées*

Every man with a belly full of classics is an enemy of the human race.
Henry Miller

Masterpieces are no more than the shipwrecked flotsam of great minds.
Marcel Proust

A classic is something that everyone wants to have read and nobody wants to read.
Mark Twain, "The Disappearance of Literature"

CLICHÉS

Funny how people despise platitudes, when they are usually the truest thing going. A thing has to be pretty true before it gets to be a platitude.
Katherine F. Gerould

Our writers are full of clichés just as old barns are full of bats. There is obviously no rule about this, except that anything that you suspect of being a cliché undoubtedly is one and had better be removed.
Wolcott Gibbs, "Theory and Practice of Editing *New Yorker* Articles"

Critics are probably more prone to clichés than fiction writers who pluck things out of the air.
Penelope Gilliatt

At the beginning there was the Word--at the end just the Cliché.
Stanislaw Lec, *Unkempt Thoughts*

Journalistic clichés migrate from broadcast to broadcast.
Dmitri Lyubosvetov, *Pravda* columnist

The truths of the past are the clichés of the present.
Ned Rorem, *Music from Inside Out*

I think to be oversensitive about clichés is like being oversensitive about table manners.
Evelyn Waugh

CLOTHING

No one has ever had an idea in a dress suit.
Sir Frederick G. Banting

When in doubt wear red.
   Bill Blass

A man becomes the creature of his uniform.
   Napoléon Bonaparte

Dress is a very foolish thing, and yet it is a very foolish thing for a man not to be well dressed.
   Lord Chesterfield, *Letters to His Son*

Dressing a pool player in a tuxedo is like putting whipped cream on a hot dog.
   Minnesota Fats

The subjective actress thinks of clothes only as they apply to her; the objective actress thinks of them only as they affect others, as a tool for the job.
   Edith Head

Nothing makes men more alike than putting dress suits on them.
   Will Rogers

The desire to please by outward charms, which we know naturally invite lust, does not spring from a sound conscience. Why should you rouse an evil passion?
   Tertullian, *Women's Dress,* third century

Beware of all enterprises that require new clothes, and not rather a new wearer of clothes.
   Henry David Thoreau

Modesty died when clothes were born.
   Mark Twain

COMMITTEE

A committee is a group of people who, individually, can do nothing, but collectively can meet and decide that nothing can be done.
   Anonymous

A committee is a group that keeps minutes and loses hours.
   Milton Berle

A committee is a cul-de-sac down which ideas are lured and then quietly strangled.
   Sir Barnett Cocks

We always carry out by committee anything in which any one of us alone would be too reasonable to persist.
   Frank Moore Colby

No grand idea was ever born in a conference, but a lot of foolish ideas have died there.
F. Scott Fitzgerald

Could Hamlet have been written by a committee, or the Mona Lisa painted by a club? Could the New Testament have been composed as a conference report? Creative ideas do not spring from groups, they spring from individuals. The divine spark leaps from the finger of God to the finger of Adam.
Alfred Whitney Griswold

If you want to kill any idea in the world today, get a committee working on it.
Charles Kettering

If people in a group want to interrupt serious discussion with some diversion or personal expression--let them. Then bring them back to the agenda. Committees work best when the talk swings between the personal and the purposeful.
Irving Lee, *How to Talk with People*

Committees are to get everybody together and homogenize their thinking.
Art Linkletter, *A Child's Garden of Misinformation*

COMMUNICATION

If my possessions were taken from me, with one exception, I would choose to keep the power of communication; for by it I would soon regain all the rest.
Stephen Vincent Benét, *The Devil and Daniel Webster*

Social intercourse--a very limited thing in a half civilized country, becomes in our centers of civilization a great power.
Elizabeth Blackwell, *Medicine as a Profession for Women*

In communication training, my approach is digital--my ten fingers and hands on!
George Boston, *BBC Open University*

Communication doesn't flow. Sometimes it leaks, spurts, and dribbles.
Edgar Dale

Communication is a process of sharing experience till it becomes a common possession. It modifies the disposition of both parties who partake in it.
John Dewey

You can't not communicate.
Sigmund Freud

Talking is a hydrant in the yard, and writing is the faucet upstairs in the house; opening

the first takes the pressure off the second.
   Robert Frost

Communication is power.
   Senator J. William Fulbright

The unexpressed, then, is always of greater value than the expressed.
   Zona Gale

Speaking or writing without thinking is like shooting without aiming.
   Arnold Glasgow

We are all of us calling and calling across the incalculable gulfs which separate us.
   David Grayson

People strike sparks off each other; that is what I try to note down. But mark well, they only do this when they are talking together. After all, we don't write letters now, we telephone.
   Henry Green, in *Writers at Work*

People change and forget to tell each other.
   Lillian Hellman

All is never said.
   Ibo proverb

From listening comes wisdom, and from speaking repentance.
   Italian proverb

The most immutable barrier in nature is between one man's thoughts and another's.
   William James

A word cannot pick up an idea and carry it over to another mind. Ideas become effective in a group only in so far as all the members of the group have learned forms of thought which are common.
   Charles H. Judd, *The Psychology of Social Institutions*

You can send a message around the world in less than a second but it takes years to get it through the human skull.
   Charles Kettering

One of the reasons our society has become such a mess is that we're isolated from each other.
   Maggie Kuhn

If you can't communicate, the least you can do is to shut up.
    Tom Lehrer

Good communication is as stimulating as black coffee, and just as hard to sleep after.
    Anne Morrow Lindbergh, *Gift from the Sea*

To understand is not only to pardon but in the end to love.
    Walter Lippmann

The chief end of language in communication being to be understood, words serve not well for that end when any word does not excite in the hearer the same idea which it stands for in the mind of the speaker.
    John Locke

Communication is something so simple and difficult that we can never put it in simple words.
    T.S. Matthews

We seek pitifully to convey to others the treasures of our heart, but they have not the power to accept them, and so we go lonely, side by side but not together, unable to know our fellows and unknown by them.
    W. Somerset Maugham, *The Moon and Sixpence*

You'll never really know what I mean and I'll never know exactly what you mean.
    Mike Nichols

If only everyone talked the way we do in my household. I mean . . . if only everyone . . . like . . . talked . . . you know . . . the way we do . . . right? It would be so much . . . like . . . easier . . . you know . . . understand . . . right?
    Robert Nordell

If you don't talk straight, and you don't write straight, there is a good possibility that you don't think straight.
    Charles Osgood

Not only to say the right thing in the right place, but far more difficult, to leave unsaid the wrong thing at the tempting moment.
    George Sala

He who receives a benefit with gratitude repays the first installment on his debt.
    Seneca, *Moral Essays*

Sometimes it's nice to have a large vocabulary. Other times it's nice to be understood.
    Frank Thompson

The big print giveth and the small print taketh away.
Tom Waitts

It is difficult to be emphatic when no one is emphatic on the other side.
Charles Dudley Warner, *My Summer in a Garden*

It only takes a minute to be considerate.
Valerie T. West

Think like a man but communicate in the language of the people.
William Butler Yeats

COMPETITION

Show me a good loser, and I'll show you a loser.
Red Auerbach, former general manager of the Boston Celtics

Win as if you were used to it, lose as if you enjoyed it for a change.
Eric Mark Golnik

If you can react the same way to winning and losing, that . . . quality is important because it stays with you the rest of your life.
Chris Evert Lloyd

The joy of winning doesn't motivate me any more. It's the fear of losing.
Randy Matson, world champion shot-putter

This [defeat] has taught me a lesson, but I'm not sure what it is.
John McEnroe

I just try to concentrate on concentrating.
Martina Navratilova

A horse never runs so fast as when he has other horses to catch up and outpace.
Ovid, *The Art of Love*

I admit disappointment but not defeat.
John Patrick

COMPUTERS

At an Italian restaurant in Reading [United Kingdom], known for its computer industries, someone was overheard ordering a chilled bottle of "Ascii spumante."
Martin Allard

The computer is down. I hope it's something serious.
Stanton Delaplane

The computer is a moron.
Peter Drucker

Computers can figure out all kinds of problems, except the things in the world that just don't add up.
James Magary

In a few minutes a computer can make a mistake so great that it would take many men many months to equal it.
Merle L. Meacham

To err is human; to really foul things up requires a computer.
Bill Vaughan

CONCLUSION (see also ENDING)

Only on the edge of the grave can man conclude anything.
Henry Brooks Adams, *The Education of Henry Adams*

I knew a wise man that had it for a byword, when he saw men hasten to a conclusion. "Stay a little, that we may make an end."
Sir Francis Bacon, *Essays of Dispatch*

Life is the art of drawing sufficient conclusions from insufficient premises.
Samuel Butler, II, "Lord, What is Man?" *Note-Books*

I am no athlete--but at one sport I used to be an expert. It was a dangerous game, called "jumping to conclusions."
Eddie Cantor, *The Way I See It*

A conclusion is the place where you get tired thinking.
Martin H. Fischer

I have come to the conclusion, after many years of sometimes sad experiences, that you cannot come to any conclusion at all.
Victoria Sackville-West

CONFLICT

The injury we do and the one we suffer are not weighed in the same scales.
Aesop

For every man there is something in the vocabulary that would stick to him like a

second skin. His enemies have only to find it.
Ambrose Bierce, *The Devil's Dictionary*

He that wrestles with us strengthens our nerves, and sharpens our skill. Our antagonist is our helper.
Edmund Burke, *Reflections on the Revolution in France*

Man is a social animal who dislikes his fellow men.
Eugène Delacroix, *Journal*

The first human being who hurled an insult instead of a stone was the founder of civilization.
Attributed to Sigmund Freud

You cannot shake hands with a clenched fist.
Indira Gandhi

If men would think how often their own words are thrown at their heads, they would less often let them go out of their mouths.
Lord Halifax

Opposition brings discord. Out of discord comes the fairest harmony.
Heraclitus

In a fight between you and the world, bet on the world.
Franz Kafka

Pick battles big enough to matter, small enough to win.
Jonathan Kozol

What is important here is not that men disagree, but that they become disagreeable about it.
Irving Lee, *How to Talk with People*

In the Chinese family system, there is superficial quiet and calmness and quarreling is frowned upon, but in reality all is in conflict.
Ting Ling

If you wish to make someone your enemy, say simply, "You are wrong." This method works every time.
Henry C. Link

Whoever fights monsters should see to it that in the process he does not become a monster. And when you look long into an abyss, the abyss also looks into you.
Friedrich Nietzsche

We have met the enemy, and he is us.
    Pogo

Opposition inflames the enthusiast, never converts him.
    Friedrich von Schiller

And do as adversaries do in law--
Strive mightily, but eat and drink as friends.
    William Shakespeare, *Taming of the Shrew*

A man never tells you anything until you contradict him.
    George Bernard Shaw

One of the most time-consuming things is to have an enemy.
    E.B. White

Have you not learned great lessons from those who reject you and brace themselves against you? Or treat you with contempt, or dispute the passage with you?
    Walt Whitman

Many promising reconciliations have broken down because, while both parties came prepared to forgive, neither party came prepared to be forgiven.
    Charles Williams

If you want to make enemies, try to change something.
    Woodrow Wilson

Make sure to be in with your equals if you're going to fall out with your superiors.
    Yiddish proverb

CONSUMERS

Consumers with dollars in their pockets are not, by any stretch of the imagination, weak. To the contrary, they are the most merciless, meanest, toughest market disciplinarians I know.
    Edwin S. Bingham

The responsiveness of a firm to the consumer is directly proportionate to the distance on the organization chart from the consumer to the chairman of the board.
    Virginia H. Knauer, U.S. Office of Consumer Affairs

The consumer today is the victim of the manufacturer who launches on him a regiment of products for which he must make room in his soul.
    Mary McCarthy, *On the Contrary*

CONVERSATION

For parlor use, the vague generality is a life-saver.
George Ade, *Forty Modern Fables*

It is all right to hold a conversation but you should let go of it now and then.
Richard Armour

In dinner talk it is allowable to fling any faggot rather than let the fire go out.
Sir James M. Barrie, *Tommy and Grizel*

Men prominent in life are mostly hard to converse with. They lack small-talk, and at the same time one doesn't like to confront them with their own great themes.
Max Beerbohm, *Mainly on the Air*

He never spares himself in conversation. He gives himself so generously that hardly anybody else is permitted to give anything in his presence.
Aneurin Bevan, on Winston Churchill

A good conversationalist is not one who remembers what was said, but says what someone wants to remember.
John Mason Brown

When you talk to the half-wise, twaddle; when you talk to the ignorant, brag; when you talk to the sagacious, look very humble, and ask their opinion.
Edward George Bulwer-Lytton, *Paul Clifford*

Conversations are like those trips we take on the water; we set sail almost without noticing it, and we do not realize that we have left the land until we are already far from it.
Sébastien-Roch Nicolas de Chamfort, *Maximes et pensées*

Never hold anyone by the button or the hand in order to be heard out; for if people are unwilling to hear you, you had better hold your tongue than them.
Lord Chesterfield

Well, many times I say only yes or no to people. Even that's too much. It winds them up for twenty minutes more.
Calvin Coolidge

It has been estimated that from the first "good morning" to the last "good night" the average man engages in approximately thirty conversations a day.
Roy S. Dunton

The art of conversation, or the qualification for a good companion, is a certain self-

control, which now holds the subject, now lets it go, with a respect for the emergencies of the moment.
  Ralph Waldo Emerson

Conversation is a game of circles.
  Ralph Waldo Emerson, "Circles," *Essays*

Conversation is an exchange of thought that leaves all parties to it a grain wiser.
  Alfred Whitney Griswold

The boneless quality of English conversation . . . so far as I have heard it, is all form and no content. Listening to Britons dining out is like watching people play first-class tennis with imaginary balls.
  Margaret Halsey, *With Malice toward Some*

A perpetual succession of good things puts an end to common conversation.
  William Hazlitt

A person who talks with equal vivacity on every subject, excites no interest in any. Repose is as necessary in conversation as in a picture.
  William Hazlitt, *Characteristics*

Inject a few raisins of conversation into the tasteless dough of existence.
  O. Henry (William Sydney Porter), *Complete Life of John Hopkins*

Conversation is the slowest form of human communication.
  Don Herold

The misfortune of Goldsmith in conversation is this: he goes on without knowing how he is to get off.
  Samuel Johnson

A gossip is one who talks to you about others; a bore is one who talks to you about himself; and a brilliant conversationalist is one who talks to you about yourself.
  Lisa Kirk

The success of conversation consists less in being witty than in bringing out wit in others; the man who leaves after talking with you, pleased with himself and his own wit, is perfectly pleased with you.
  Jean de La Bruyère, *Characters*

The conversation was dull, as is always the case when we are speaking only favorably of our fellow men.
  Pierre de Laclos

Conversation should be pleasant without scurrility, witty without affectation, free without indecency, learned without conceitedness, novel without falsehood.
François de La Rochefoucauld

If the art of conversation stood a little higher, we would have a lower birthrate.
Stanislaw Lec

A single conversation across the table with a wise man is better than ten years' study of books.
Henry Wadsworth Longfellow

The art of conversation is not knowing what you ought to say, but what one ought not to say.
F.L. Lucas

Conversation means being able to disagree and still continue the conversation.
Dwight MacDonald

A young man once went to Socrates in order to learn conversation. In the opening commonplaces he talked so incessantly that Socrates said he could not accept him as a pupil without a double fee. "Why charge me double?" asked the loquacious student. "Because," Socrates answered, "I must teach you two things. The one how to hold your tongue, and the other how to speak!"
Patrick Mahony, *You Can Find a Way*

He knew that his conversation had the power to fascinate, and he used it like a prodigal man who knew he had an everlasting fortune.
Princess Mathilde

Conversation would be vastly improved by the constant use of four simple words: I do not know.
André Maurois

We do not talk--we bludgeon one another with facts and theories gleaned from cursory readings of newspapers, magazines, and digests.
Henry Miller, *The Air-conditioned Nightmare*

It is good to rub and polish our brain against that of others.
Michel de Montaigne, *Essays*

The real art of conversation is not only to say the right thing in the right place but to leave unsaid the wrong thing at the tempting moment.
Dorothy Nevill

Ideal conversation must be an exchange of thought, and not, as many of those who

worry most about their shortcomings believe, an eloquent exhibition of wit or oratory.
    Emily Post

It is not what we learn in conversation that enriches us. It is the elation that comes of swift contact with tingling currents of thought.
    Agnes Repplier, *Compromises*

I am annoyed by individuals who are embarrassed by pauses in a conversation. To me, every conversational pause refreshes.
    George Sanders

Conversation, like a salad, should have various ingredients and should be well stirred with salt, oil, and vinegar.
    Joaquín Setanti, *Centellas*

The trouble with her is that she lacks the power of conversation but not the power of speech.
    George Bernard Shaw

One way to prevent conversation from being boring is to say the wrong thing.
    Frank Sheed

That amenity which the French have developed into a great art . . . conversation.
    Cornelia Otis Skinner

It is an impertinent and unreasonable fault in conversation for one man to take up all the discourse.
    Sir Richard Steele, *The Spectator*

One of the best rules of conversation is, never to say a thing which any of the company can reasonably wish had been left unsaid.
    Jonathan Swift

There are some people whose good manners will not suffer them to interrupt you, but what is almost as bad, will discover an abundance of impatience, and lie upon the watch until you have done, because they have started something in their own thoughts, which they long to be delivered of.
    Jonathan Swift, "Hints toward an Essay on Conversation"

Conversation, the commerce of minds.
    Cyril Tourneur

I happen to disagree with the well-entrenched theory that the art of conversation is merely the art of being a good listener. Such advice invites people to be cynical with one another and full of fake; when a conversation becomes a monologue, poked along

with tiny cattle-prod questions, it isn't a conversation any more.
    Barbara Walters

There is no such thing as conversation. It is an illusion. There are intersecting monologues, that is all.
    Dame Rebecca West

When people talk to us about others they are usually dull. When they talk to us about themselves they are nearly always interesting.
    Oscar Wilde, "The Critic as Artist"

COURTESY

Curtsy while you're thinking what to say. It saves time.
    Lewis Carroll, *Through the Looking-Glass*

Who fears to offend takes the first step to please.
    Colley Cibber

We Occidentals have a congenial, it may even be said fatal, need for good manners, or you might say ceremony, in our approach to meaning, I suppose to make up for our crudeness in living.
    Eleanor Clark

Courtesy is not dead--it has merely taken refuge in Great Britain.
    Georges Duhamel

How sweet and gracious, even in common speech,
Is that fine sense which men call Courtesy!
    James T. Fields

A civil guest will no more talk all, than eat all the feast.
    George Herbert, *The Church-Porch*

Everyone has to think to be polite; the first impulse is to be impolite.
    Edgar Watson Howe, *Country Town Sayings*

If we are polite in manner and friendly in tone, we can without immediate risk be really rude to many a man.
    Arthur Schopenhauer, *Parerga and Paralipomena*

Anyone can be a barbarian; it requires a terrible effort to be or remain a civilized man.
    Leonard Woolf

CREATIVITY (see also ORIGINALITY)

I would call the personality of man the gland of creativity.
Sholem Asch, *What I Believe*

Originality is the essence of true scholarship. Creativity is the soul of the true scholar.
Nnamdi Azikiwe

Creative people can stand more chaos than ordinary people.
Frank Barron

Don't keep forever on the public road, going only where others have gone. Leave the beaten track occasionally and drive into the woods. You will be certain to find something you have never seen before. Of course it will be a little thing, but do not ignore it. Follow it up, explore all around it; one discovery will lead to another, and before you know it you will have something worth thinking about to occupy your mind. All really big discoveries are the results of thought.
Alexander Graham Bell

With a little creativity, you can turn a sow's ear into a silk purse. But you've got to have the sow's ear to start with.
Frederick Buggie

A hunch is creativity trying to tell you something.
Frank Capra

Creativity is something new and different for you.
Marie Collart

The artistic impulse seems not to wish to produce finished work. It certainly deserts us half-way, after the idea is born; and if we go on, art is labor.
Clarence Day, *This Simian World*

Creation is a drug I can't do without.
Cecil B. De Mille

I have not failed 10,000 times. I have successfully found 10,000 ways that will not work.
Thomas Edison

The answer comes . . . while you are eating an apple.
Albert Einstein

How do I work? I grope.
Albert Einstein

Creative minds have always been known to survive any kind of bad training.
Anna Freud

Everything has been thought of before, but the problem is to think of it again.
Goethe

First . . . a new theory is attacked as absurd; then it is admitted to be true, but obvious and insignificant; finally it is seen to be so important that its adversaries claim that they themselves discovered it.
William James, *Pragmatism*

The creative mind plays with the objects it loves.
Carl Jung, *Psychological Types*

Creative activity could be described as a type of learning process where the teacher and pupil are located in the same individual.
Arthur Koestler

An essential aspect of creativity is not being afraid to fail.
Edwin Land

Those who dream by night . . . wake in the day to find that it was vanity: but the dreamers of the day are dangerous men, for they may act their dreams with open eyes, to make it possible.
T.E. Lawrence

It terrified me to have an idea that was solely mine to be no longer a part of my mind, but totally public.
Maya Lin, on her design for the Vietnam Veterans Memorial

A good analogy is the violin string. If it is too taut, it will be out of tune; but if *no* tension is applied to it, it won't produce a note.
Tom Mach, on creative tension

A first-rate soup is more creative than a second-rate painting.
Abraham Maslow

Honor your divergent thinking phase.
Jane Mayo

"*L'improvisation de la vie humaine*," he said. "There's nothing that makes you so aware of the improvisation of human existence as a song unfinished. Or an old address book."
Carson McCullers, "The Sojourner"

One of the advantages of being disorderly is that one is constantly making exciting discoveries.
A.A. Milne

Theoretical insights flourish best when the thinker is apparently wasting time.
J. Robert Oppenheimer

All great discoveries are made by men whose feelings run ahead of their thinking.
Charles H. Parkhurst

Every act of creation is first of all an act of destruction.
Pablo Picasso

I invent nothing. I rediscover.
Auguste Rodin

Every creation is born out of the dark. Every birth is bloody.
May Sarton

It hinders the creative work of the mind if the intellect examines too closely the ideas as they pour in.
Friedrich von Schiller

I like to build the bridge but I don't want to be the one who stands there collecting a quarter from everyone who crosses it.
John Snyder

Our current obsession with creativity is the result of our continued striving for immortality in an era when most people no longer believe in an after-life.
Arianna Stassinopoulos

The very people who have done the breaking through are themselves often the first to try to put a scab on their achievement.
Igor Stravinsky, in Robert Craft, *Conversations with Igor Stravinsky*

Discovery consists of seeing what everybody has seen, and thinking what nobody has thought.
Albert Szent-Györgyi

A mind truly cultivated never feels that the intellectual process is complete until it can reproduce in some media the thing which it has absorbed.
Ida Tarbell, *The Ways of Woman*

Periods of tranquility are seldom prolific of creative achievement. Mankind has to be stirred up.
Alfred North Whitehead

The race in writing is not won by the swift, but by the original.
William K. Zinsser

CRITICISM

Ridicule is the deadliest of weapons against a lofty cause.
Samuel Hopkins Adams, *Tenderloin*

Personally I have no enthusiasm for organized jeering sections but I hold that the spontaneous right of raspberry should be denied to no one in America.
Heywood Broun

I do not resent criticism, even when, for the sake of emphasis, it parts for the time with reality.
Winston Churchill

We make more enemies by what we say than friends by what we do.
John Churton Collins

I love criticism just so long as it's unqualified praise.
Noël Coward

Criticism is easy, art is difficult.
Philippe Destouches, *Le glorieux*

The blow of a whip raises a welt, but a blow of the tongue crushes bones.
Ecclesiasticus, *Apocrypha*

Criticism is not just a question of taste, but of whose taste.
James Grand

If you must speak ill of another, do not speak it . . . write it in the sand near the water's edge.
Napoleon Hill

A just criticism is a commendation, rather than a detraction.
Henry Jacob

Criticism--a big bite out of someone's back.
Elia Kazan

Criticism of our contemporaries is not criticism; it is conversation.
François Lemaître

A torn jacket is soon mended; but hard words bruise the heart of a child.
Henry Wadsworth Longfellow, "Driftwood"

The only graceful way to accept an insult is to ignore it; if you can't ignore it, laugh at it; if you can't laugh at it, it's probably deserved.
  Russell Lynes

Criticism is asserted superiority.
  Cardinal Henry Edward Manning, *Pastime Papers*

People ask you for criticism, but they only want praise.
  W. Somerset Maugham, *Of Human Bondage*

I criticize not by finding fault but with a new creation.
  Michelangelo

Criticism is the art wherewith a critic tries to guess himself into a share of the artist's fame.
  George Jean Nathan, *The House of Satan*

Impersonal criticism is like an impersonal fist fight or an impersonal marriage, and as successful.
  George Jean Nathan

They have a right to censure that have a heart to help.
  William Penn, *Some Fruits of Solitude*

It is folly to censure him whom all the world adores.
  Publilius Syrus, *Moral Sayings*

Indifference is probably the severest criticism that can be applied to anything.
  Ann Schade

Someone has said that even criticism is better than silence. I don't agree to this. Criticism can be very harmful unless it comes from a master; and in spite of the fact that we have hundreds of critics these days, it is one of the most difficult of professions.
  Janet Scudder

Pay no attention to what the critics say; no statue has ever been put up to a critic.
  Jean Sibelius

As far as criticism is concerned, we don't resent that unless it is absolutely biased, as it is in most cases.
  John Voster

The modern world is not given to uncritical admiration. It expects its idols to have feet

of clay, and can be reasonably sure that press and camera will report their exact dimensions.
    Barbara Ward, *Saturday Review*

Our criticism is always devoting itself to . . . watching the sticks and straws on the surface of the current, without interest, apparently, in the natural force of the stream, the style and turn of the whole composition, its communicative social imagination.
    Edith Franklin Wyatt

Criticism comes easier than craftsmanship.
    Zeuxis

CRITICS

Never answer a critic, unless he's right.
    Bernard Baruch

Critics are like eunuchs in a harem. They're there every night, they see it done every night, they see how it should be done every night, but they can't do it themselves.
    Brendan Behan

A good writer is not, per se, a good book critic. No more so than a good drunk is automatically a good bartender.
    Jim Bishop

Praise not the critic, lest he think
You crave the shelter of his ink.
    Alice Brown

Next to the author of a good book is the man who makes a good commentary on it.
    Chang Chao, *Yumengying*

Take heed of criticks: they bite, like fish, at anything, especially at bookes.
    Thomas Dekker, *News from Hell*

Critics are like brushers of other men's clothes.
    English proverb

The first man who objected to the general nakedness, and advised his fellows to put on clothes, was the first critic.
    E.L. Godkin, *Problems of Modern Democracy*

Confronted by an absolutely infuriating review it is sometimes helpful for the victim to do a little personal research on the critic. Is there any truth to the rumor that he had no formal education beyond the age of eleven? In any event, is he able to construct a

simple English sentence? Do his participles dangle? When moved to lyricism does he write "I had a fun time"? Was he ever arrested for burglary? I don't know that you will prove anything this way, but it is perfectly harmless and quite soothing.
 Jean Kerr

A critic is a man created to praise greater men than himself, but he is never able to find them.
 Richard Le Gallienne

Nature fits all her children with something to do,
He who would write and can't write, can surely review.
 James Russell Lowell, *A Fable for Critics*

A critic knows more than the author he criticizes, or just as much, or at least somewhat less.
 Cardinal Henry Edward Manning, *Pastime Papers*

If the critics were always right we should be in deep trouble.
 Robert Morley

Asking a working writer what he thinks about critics is like asking a lamppost what it feels about dogs.
 John Osborne

A critic is a legless man who teaches running.
 Channing Pollock, *The Green Book*

Can't a critic give his opinion of an omelette without being asked to lay an egg?
 Clayton Rawson, *No Coffin for the Corpse*

Don't be afraid of criticism. Anyone who can fill out a laundry slip thinks of himself as a writer. Those who can't fill out a laundry slip think of themselves as critics.
 George Seaton

There is a certain justice in criticism. The critic is like a midwife--a tyrannical midwife.
 Stephen Spender, *New York Times*

I had another dream the other day about music critics. They were small and rodent-like with padlocked ears, as if they had stepped out of a painting by Goya.
 Igor Stravinsky

Reviewing music or reviewing anything is a writing job. It's nice if you are experienced in the field you are writing about, but writing is what you are doing.
 Virgil Thomson

A critic is a man who knows the way but can't drive the car.
    Kenneth Tynan

It is probably not necessary for a critic to be insane to survive all those opening nights, but I assure you that it helps.
    Alexander Woollcott

CROSS-CULTURAL COMMUNICATION

You cannot speak of ocean to a wellfrog,
--the creature of a narrower sphere.
You cannot speak of ice to a summer insect,
--the creature of a season.
    Chuang Tzu, "Autumn Floods"

The real test of whether whites can communicate with blacks as human beings is not what they reply to Ralph Bunche but how they respond to Rap Brown.
    James Cone

The predominating power of the African race is lyric. In that I should expect the writers of my race to excel. Their poetry will not be exotic or differ much from that of whites.
    Paul Laurence Dunbar

As academe and the wider society move to advance and celebrate multiculturalism, there are a anumber of barriers--both real and fabricated, due to preconceived and constructed media images--that need to be overcome.
    Linda K. Fuller, *U.S. Media and the Middle East*

While the world is changing, the obsolete and damanging image--bound media system is becoming increasingly rigid, commercialized, concentrated, and globalized.
    George Gerbner, Introduction to *U.S. Media and the Middle East*

The Berlin Wall is down, but between East Harlem and West Hampton, Chinatown and Tarrytown, suburbia and the ghettos, the walls go up and up. Has the cold war ended abroad to usher in the hot war at home?
    Bette Bao Lord, address at Skidmore College, 1992

D

DEADLINES

When facing a deadline just hours away, I can work with children crawling on my back and across my desk.
  Hal Kanter

A journalist is stimulated by a deadline; he writes worse when he has time.
  Karl Kraus

DIARY

It's the good girls who keep diaries; the bad girls never have the time.
  Tallulah Bankhead

The life of every man is a diary in which he means to write one story, and writes another; and his humblest hour is when he compares the volume as it is with what he vowed to make it.
  Sir James M. Barrie, *The Little Minister*

It's not a bad idea to get in the habit of writing down one's thoughts. It saves one having to bother anyone else with them.
  Isabel Colegate

So the point of my keeping a notebook has never been, nor is it now, to have an accurate factual record of what I have been doing or thinking . . . . Perhaps it never did snow that August in Vermont; perhaps there never were flurries in the night wind, and maybe no one else felt the ground hardening and summer already dead even as we pretended to bask in it, but that was how it felt to me, and it might as well have snowed, could have snowed, did snow.
  Joan Didion

I soothe my conscience now with the thought that it is better for hard words to be on paper than that Mummy should carry them in her heart.
  Anne Frank

If you want to be a writer, you keep an honest, unpublishable journal for all your junk.
  Madeleine L'Engle

Why do women keep diaries? . . . The form has been an important outlet for women partly because it is an analogue to their lives: emotional, fragmentary, interrupted, modest, not to be taken seriously, private, restricted, daily, trivial, formless, concerned with self, as endless as their tasks.
  Mary Jane Moffat

What is a diary as a rule? A document useful to the person who keeps it, dull to the contemporary who reads it, invaluable to the student, centuries afterwards, who treasures it!
  Ellen Terry

I always say, keep a diary and some day it'll keep you.
  Mae West, "Every Day's a Holiday," film

I never travel without my diary; one should always have something sensational to read in the train.
  Oscar Wilde

DICTIONARY

Words fascinate me. They always have. For me, browsing in a dictionary is like being turned loose in a bank.
  Eddie Cantor, *The Way I See It*

Le premier livre d'une nation est le dictionnaire de sa langue. (The most important book of a nation is the dictionary of its language.)
  Constantin, Comte de Volney, *Sayings*

Neither is a dictionary a bad book to read . . . . It is full of suggestions--the raw material of possible poems and history.
  Ralph Waldo Emerson

The responsibility of a dictionary is to record a language, not set its style.
  Philip Gove, editor-in-chief of *Webster's Third New International Dictionary*

The *English Dictionary* was written with little assistance of the learned, and without any patronage of the great; not in the soft obscurities of retirement, or under the shelter of academick bowers, but amidst inconvenience and distraction, in sickness and in

sorrow.... If our language is not here fully displayed, I have only failed in an attempt which no human powers have hitherto completed.
    Samuel Johnson

From the actual use I have made of my dictionary I have got little but sorrow. Many excellent words are ruined by too definite a knowledge of their meaning.
    Aline Kilmer

A dictionary is but an index to the literature of a given speech; or rather it bears to language the relation which a digest bears to a series of legal reports. Neither is an authority; and he is but a sorry lawyer who cites the one, an indifferent scholar who quotes the other as such.
    George Perkins Marsh, *Lectures on the English Language*

As sheer casual reading-matter, I still find the English dictionary the most interesting book in our language.
    Albert Jay Nock, *Memoirs of a Superfluous Man*

It is a little hard to believe but the *Oxford Dictionary* carries 14,070 different definitions for the 500 most used words in English. This is an average of 28 separate definitions per word.
    John O'Hayre

DIPLOMACY

Diplomacy is the art of saying "Nice doggie" until you can find a rock.
    Will Rogers

Diplomat: a man who thinks twice before saying nothing.
    Frederick Sawyer

Once the Xerox copier was invented, diplomacy died.
    Andrew Young

DRAFTS

My first drafts are very rough. I wouldn't want anybody to read one. If, when I die, there should be a first draft lying on my desk, ... I want it to be burned.
    Lois Duncan

Try simply to steer your mind in the direction or general vicinity of the thing you are trying to write about and start writing and keep writing.
    Peter Elbow, *Writing without Teachers*

This practice of drafting illustrates the truth that the best form of education is to put one's own words on paper.
Arthur L. Goodhart

Remember you are hitting practice shots.
Ken Macrorie

Only ambitious nonentities and hearty mediocrities exhibit their rough drafts. It is like passing around samples of one's sputum.
Vladimir Nabokov

The greatest pleasure when I started making money was not buying cars or yachts but finding myself able to have as many freshly typed drafts as possible.
Gore Vidal

DREAMS

Hollywood as the "Dream Factory " is in actuality an outdated, oxymoronic notion.
Linda K. Fuller, *Beyond the Stars: Studies in American Popular Film*

Dreams have as much influence as actions.
Stéphane Mallarmé

The future belongs to those who have been supported in their dream.
Eleanor Roosevelt

I dream for a living.
Steven Spielberg, *Time*

Saddle your dreams before you ride 'em.
Mary Webb

E

EDITING

In an art form like film-making, we know that editing and revising cannot be dismissed as superfluous, for they are an integral part of the whole process. In fact, what we eventually see on the screen is not what was filmed, but what was edited.
    William Irmscher

Editing while you write is like pruning seeds.
    Kenneth Koch

A wise editor will always make a point of inquiry for information, from one who knows, who is not necessarily a literary, scientific, or learned person. Good editing consists in knowing not only who's who, but who knows what.
    Sir Edward Parry

Editing is like searching your beard for fleas.
    Kenneth Rexroth

Editing is the same as quarreling with writers--same thing exactly.
    Harold Ross, *Time*

Don't pass judgment on a manuscript as it is, but as it can be made to be.
    M. Lincoln Schuster, "An Open Letter to a Would-Be Editor"

Against the misuse of words every editorial prejudice should be fixed in concrete.
    Ellery Sedgwick, *The Happy Profession*

Editing can be such a relief! Now's your chance to unburden every sentence.
    Fran Shaw, *30 Ways to Help You Write*

One thing [the editors] taught me was the value of cutting out the last paragraph of

stories, something I pass down as a tip to all writers. The last paragraph in which you tell what the story is about is almost always best left out.
    Irwin Shaw

This is what I find encouraging about the writing trades: they allow mediocre people who are patient and industrious to revise their stupidity, to edit themselves into something like intelligence. They also allow lunatics to seem saner than sane.
    Kurt Vonnegut, Jr.

Poets lose half the praise they should have got,
Could it be known what they discreetly blot.
    Edmund Waller

Every man is bound to leave a story better than he found it.
    Mary Augusta Ward

Editing is the most companionable form of education.
    Edward Weeks, *In Friendly Candor*

No passion in the world, no love or hate, is equal to the passion to alter someone else's draft.
    H.G. Wells

EDITORS

If an editor can only make people angry enough, they will write half his newspaper for him for nothing.
    G.K. Chesterton, *Heretics*

An editor is a man who knows what he wants, but doesn't know what it is.
    Walter Davenport

An editor should tell the author his writing is better than it is. Not a lot better, a little better.
    T.S. Eliot

Some editors are failed writers, but so are most writers.
    T.S. Eliot

I never said anything good about an editor until he or she had published something of mine.
    Robert Fontaine, *That's a Good Question*

Authors are vain because they cherish every article as they would a sweetheart. Editors are entitled to trample on vanity.
    Reginald Heber Smith

An editor is one who separates the wheat from the chaff and prints the chaff.
   Adlai Stevenson, in Bill Adler, *The Stevenson Wit*

A great editor is a man of outstanding talent who owns 51 per cent of his newspaper's stock.
   Henry Watterson

I became the editor of a weekly newspaper because I wanted to be my own particular kind of a damn fool.
   William Allen White

EDUCATION

Let your concern for learning
Be greater than for teaching.
By the latter you benefit others;
By the former, yourself.
   Pierre Abélard, *Astrolabius*

There are obviously two educations. One should teach us how to make a living. The other should teach us how to live.
   James Truslow Adams

Education is an ornament in prosperity and a refuge in adversity.
   Aristotle

We'd be limited to very narrow and provincial lives if we depended upon direct experience to familiarize ourselves with the world in which we live.
   Franklin Bobbitt, *The Curriculum of Modern Education*

We begin with the hypothesis that any subject can be taught effectively in some intellectually honest form to any child at any stage of development.
   Jerome S. Bruner, *The Process of Education*

Experience is a comb which nature gives us when we are bald.
   Chinese proverb

Train up a fig tree in the way it should go, and when you are old sit under the shade of it.
   Charles Dickens, *Dombey and Son*

Education fills in blank spots with knowledge.
   Lucinda S. Duncan

Human beings ultimately decide for themselves. And, in the end, education must be education toward the ability to decide.
    Viktor Frankl

If a man empties his purse into his head, no one can take it from him.
    Benjamin Franklin

Education is the ability to listen to almost anything without losing your temper or your self-confidence.
    Robert Frost

You cannot teach a man anything. You can only help him to find it within himself.
    Galileo

All too often we are giving students cut flowers when we should be teaching them to plant their own.
    John Gardner

To teach rigor while preserving imagination is an unsolved challenge to education.
    R.W. Gerard, "The Biological Basis of Imagination"

We need a combination of practice and reflection. Reflection only without practice leads to theories that gather a lot of learned papers and a lot of dust. Practice without reflection leads to calling last year's mistakes experience and then making them again this year.
    Mary Graham

In nature there are neither rewards nor punishment--there are consequences.
    Robert G. Ingersoll

Education by means of pre-fabricated ideas is propaganda.
    Mordecai M. Kaplan, *Reconstructionist*

The purpose of all higher education is to make men aware of what was and what is; to incite them to probe into what may be. It seeks to teach them to understand, to evaluate, to communicate.
    Otto Kleppner

Learn from the masses, and then teach them.
    Mao Zedong

I read in the newspapers they are going to have 30 minutes of intellectual stuff on television every Monday from 7:30 to 8 . . . to educate America. They couldn't educate America if they started at 6:30.
    Groucho Marx, *Boston Globe*

It is, indeed, one of the capital tragedies of youth--and youth is the time of real tragedy --that the young are thrown mainly with adults they do not quite respect.
    H.L. Mencken

School days, I believe, are the unhappiest in the whole span of human existence. They are full of dull, unintelligible tasks, new and unpleasant ordinances, brutal violations of common sense and common decency.
    H.L. Mencken

A faithful study of the liberal arts humanizes character and permits it not to be cruel.
    Ovid, *Epistulae ex Ponto*

Education consists of example and love--nothing else.
    Johann Heinrich Pestalozzi

'Tis education forms the common mind;
Just as the twig is bent the tree's inclined.
    Alexander Pope, *Moral Essays*

A well-informed mind . . . is the best security against the contagion of folly and of vice.
    Ann Radcliffe

You can trust the student. You can trust him to desire to learn in every way which will maintain or enhance self; you can trust him to make use of resources which will serve this end; you can trust him to evaluate himself, which will make for self-progress; you can trust him to grow, provided the atmosphere for growth is available to him.
    Carl Rogers

Everything educates, and some things educate more than others.
    Harold Taylor

His studies were pursued but never effectually overtaken.
    H.G. Wells

Experience is the name everyone gives to their mistakes.
    Oscar Wilde, *Lady Windermere's Fan*

ELOQUENCE

Borrowed eloquence, if it contains as good stuff, is as good as our own eloquence.
    John Adams, letter to Benjamin Rush

To be truly eloquent is to speak to the purpose.
    Hugh Blair

Eloquence is thought on fire.
William Jennings Bryan

No man can be eloquent on a subject that he does not understand.
Cicero

The finest eloquence is that which gets things done.
David Lloyd George

Eloquence is a painting of thought.
Blaise Pascal, *Pensées*

A mighty thing is eloquence . . . nothing so much rules the world.
Pope Pius II

Use a sweet tongue, courtesy, and gentleness, and thou mayest manage to guide an
elephant with a hair.
Sa'di, *Gulistan*

Take eloquence and wring its neck.
Paul Verlaine, "L'art poétique"

The prime purpose of eloquence is to keep other people from speaking.
Louis Vermeil

EMOTIONS

Pity makes the world soft to the weak and noble for the strong.
Edwin Arnold

The hardest sentiment to tolerate is pity, especially when it's deserved. Hatred is a
tonic, it vitalizes us, it inspires vengeance; but pity deadens, it makes our weakness
weaker.
Honoré de Balzac, *La peau de chagrin*

There's just so much worry and responsibility in the air. If we take it all on ourselves,
there's none left for the people around us. It overworks us and underworks them.
Melody Beattie

There is no state of mind, however simple, which does not change every moment.
Henri Bergson, *Introduction to Metaphysics*

The child's sob in the silence curses deeper
Than the strong man in his wrath.
Elizabeth Barrett Browning

If you want to make people weep, you must weep yourself. If you want to make people laugh, your face must remain serious.
Giovanni Jacopo Casanova

The price of hating other human beings is loving oneself less.
Eldridge Cleaver, *Soul on Ice*

At the heart of the matter is the matter of the heart.
Tom Cooper, Emerson College

Worry is misuse of the imagination.
Mary Crowley

I think that in order to write really well and convincingly, one must be somewhat poisoned by emotion. Dislike, displeasure, resentment, fault-finding, imagination, passionate remonstrance, a sense of injustice--they all make fine fuel.
Edna Ferber

Sentimentality--that's what we call the sentiment we don't share.
Graham Greene

Writing is a form of therapy; sometimes I wonder how all those who do not write, compose, or paint can manage to escape the madness, the melancholia, the panic fear which is inherent in a human situation.
Graham Greene

Silence is no certain token
That no secret grief is there;
Sorrow which is never spoken
Is the heaviest load to bear.
Frances Ridley Havergal

My life is in the hands of any rascal who chooses to annoy or tease me.
John Hunter

There is a sacredness in tears. They are not the mark of weakness, but of power. They speak more eloquently than ten thousand tongues. They are the messengers of overwhelming grief, or deep contrition, and of unspeakable love.
Washington Irving

Pity may represent little more than the impersonal concern which prompts the mailing of a check, but true sympathy is the personal concern which demands the giving of one's soul.
Martin Luther King, Jr., *Strength to Love*

How can you write if you can't cry?
    Ring Lardner

People don't ask for facts in making up their minds. They would rather have one good, soul-satisfying emotion than a dozen facts.
    Robert Keith Leavitt, *Voyages and Discoveries*

We are stimulated to emotional response not by works that confirm our sense of the world, but by works that challenge it.
    Joyce Carol Oates

Sympathy is two hearts tugging at *one* load.
    Charles H. Parkhurst

I'm never so happy as when I'm filled with righteous indignation.
    Carolyn Thiedke

Let's not forget that the little emotions are the great captains of our lives and we obey them without realizing it.
    Vincent Van Gogh

I'm very much in favor of the creative use of guilt. Guilt is an underused national resource.
    David Waters

EMPATHY

Empathy is akin to sympathy, but whereas sympathy says, "I feel as you do," empathy says, "I know how you feel." In other words, empathy enables us to use our heads more than our hearts, and allows us to appreciate another person's feelings without becoming emotionally involved with him.
    R.W. Armstrong

Universal responsibility is feeling for other people's suffering just as we feel for our own. It is the realization that even our enemy is entirely motivated by the quest for happiness. We must recognize that all human beings want the same thing we want.
    The XIV Dalai Lama

The comforter's head never aches.
    Italian proverb

It is not granted to the fortunate to understand the sorrow of others.
    A.V. Platen

No one really understands the grief or joy of another.
    Franz Schubert

A warm man never knows how a cold man feels.
    Alexander Solzhenitsyn

ENDING (see also CONCLUSION)

That's all there is, there isn't any more.
    Ethel Barrymore

If I were to stop now and summarize what I've said, I'd find it very difficult. It's easier to stop than to summarize.
    Clive Brock

The important thing is not what the author, or any artist, had in mind to begin with but at what point he decided to stop.
    D.W. Harding, *Experience into Words*

Which, of all defects, has been the one most fatal to a good style? The not knowing when to come to an end.
    Sir Arthur Helps, *Companions of My Solitude*

Great is the art of beginning, but greater the art of ending.
    Henry Wadsworth Longfellow

A speech is like a love affair. Any fool can start it, but to end it requires considerable skill.
    Lord Mancroft

If I didn't know the ending of a story, I wouldn't begin. I always write my last line, my last paragraph, my last page first.
    Katherine Anne Porter

ENTHUSIASM

Enthusiasm is the greatest asset in the world. It beats money and power and influence.
    Henry Chester

The real secret of success is enthusiasm.
    Walter Chrysler

The world belongs to the Enthusiast who keeps cool.
    William McFee

EPITAPH

Alcuin was my name: learning I loved.
> Alcuin, his own epitaph

I have but one request to ask at my departure from this world--it is the charity of silence. Let there be no inscription on my tomb. Let no man write my epitaph.
> Robert Emmet

The final condensation.
> DeWitt Wallace, founder of *Reader's Digest*, self-epitaph, recalled on his death

EXAMPLE

We have too many high sounding words, and too few actions that correspond with them.
> Abigail Adams

He that gives good advice, builds with one hand; he that gives good counsel and example, builds with both; but he that gives good admonition and bad example, builds with one hand and pulls down with the other.
> Sir Francis Bacon

Though language forms the preacher, 'tis "good works" make the man.
> Eliza Cook

Use what language you will, you can never say anything but what you are.
> Ralph Waldo Emerson, "Worship"

What you do speaks so loud that I cannot hear what you say.
> Ralph Waldo Emerson

A man of words and not of deeds,
Is like a garden full of weeds.
> English proverb

The shortest answer is doing.
> English proverb

Actions speak louder than words--but not so often.
> *Farmer's Almanac*

One has to grow up with good talk in order to form the habit of it.
> Helen Hayes

A thousand words will not leave so deep an impression as one deed.
    Henrik Ibsen

A good name, like good will, is got by many actions and lost by one.
    Lord Francis Jeffrey

Children need models rather than critics.
    Joseph Joubert, *Pensées*

It is not so much what you believe in that matters, as the way in which you believe it,
and proceed to translate that belief into action.
    Lin Yutang

The actions of men are the best interpreters of their thoughts.
    John Locke

Plebeia ingenia magis exemplis quam ratione capiuntur. (Vulgar minds are more
impressed by examples than by reasons.)
    Ambrosius Theodosius Macrobius

Train up a child in the way he should go; and when he is old he will not depart from
it.
    Proverbs 22:6

Example is not the main thing influencing others. It is the only thing.
    Albert Schweitzer

Shape or be shaped--the choice is ours.
    B.F. Skinner

Factis ut credam facis. (Words gain credibility by deeds.)
    Terence, *Hecyra*

At the Day of Judgment we shall not be asked what we read but what we have done.
    Thomas à Kempis

There are few things harder to put up with than the annoyance of a good example.
    Mark Twain, *Pudd'nhead Wilson's Calendar*

Actions lie louder than words.
    Carolyn Wells

EXPLANATION

If you can describe clearly without a diagram the proper way to make this or that knot,

then you are a master of the English tongue.
Hilaire Belloc

I am master of everything I can explain.
Theodor Haecker, *Journal in the Night*

Never explain. Your friends do not need it and your enemies will not believe you anyway.
Elbert Hubbard, *The Note Book of Elbert Hubbard*

Remember that your prime purpose is to *explain* something, not prove you're smarter than your readers.
Edward T. Thompson

F

FACTS

A fact in itself is nothing. It is valuable only for the idea attached to it, or for the proof which it furnishes.
Claude Bernard, *Introduction to the Study of Experimental Medicine*

Facts are never neutral; they are impregnated with value judgments.
Peter Gay, *Style in History*

In reporting with some accuracy, at times we have to go much further than the strictly factual. Facts are part of the perceived whole.
Alastair Reid

She always says, my lord, that facts are like cows. If you look them in the face hard enough they generally run away.
Dorothy L. Sayers, *Clouds of Witness*

FAME

No public character has ever stood the revelation of private utterance and correspondence.
Lord Acton

It's the place where my prediction from the sixties finally came true: "In the future everyone will be famous for fifteen minutes." I'm bored with that line. I never use it anymore. My new line is, "In fifteen minutes everybody will be famous."
Andy Warhol, *Andy Warhol's Exposures*

FAMILY

Family jokes, though rightly cursed by strangers, are the bond that keeps more families alive.
   Stella Benson

It takes about three neurons for you to interact normally with your family. "Good morning." "How'd you sleep?" "Pass the sugar, please."
   Hiram Curry

A mother is not a person to lean on but a person to make leaning unnecessary.
   Dorothy Canfield Fisher, *Her Son's Wife*

The most important thing a father can do for his children is to love their mother.
   Theodore M. Hesburgh

I felt like you can write forever, but you have a short time to raise a family. And I think a family is a lot more important than writing.
   Ken Kesey

One of the oldest human needs is having someone to wonder where you are when you don't come home at night.
   Margaret Mead

Whatever else anybody invents to replace it, the family always creeps back.
   Margaret Mead

FEAR

Fear is stronger than arms.
   Aeschylus, *Seven against Thebes*

No man fears what he has seen grow.
   African proverb

Tell us your phobias, and we will tell you what you are afraid of.
   Robert Benchley

Behind everything we feel, there is always a sense of fear.
   Ugo Betti, *Struggle till Dawn*

No passion so effectually robs the mind of all its powers of acting and reasoning as fear.
   Edmund Burke, *A Philosophical Inquiry into the Origin of Our Ideas of the Sublime and Beautiful*

It is better to suffer the worst at once, than to live in perpetual fear of it.
    Julius Caesar

Fear is sharp-sighted, and can see things under ground, and much more in the skies.
    Miguel de Cervantes, *Don Quixote*

We are all dangerous till our fears grow thoughtful.
    John Ciardi, "Incident"

Nothing in life is to be feared. It is only to be understood.
    Marie Curie

Taking a new step, uttering a new word is what people fear most.
    Fyodor Dostoevsky

Do the thing you fear, and the death of fear is certain.
    Ralph Waldo Emerson

He has not learned the lesson of life who does not every day surmount a fear.
    Ralph Waldo Emerson

Many of our fears are tissue-paper-thin, and a single courageous step would carry us
clear through them.
    Brendan Francis

He that fears you present will hate you absent.
    Thomas Fuller, *Gnomologia*

Where there is fear there is no religion.
    Mohandas K. Gandhi

A good scare is worth more to a man than good advice.
    Edgar Watson Howe, *Country Town Sayings*

Bravery is being the only one who knows you're afraid.
    Franklin P. Jones

Let us never negotiate out of fear. But let us never fear to negotiate.
    John F. Kennedy, inaugural address, 1961

Of all the liars in the world, sometimes the worst are your own fears.
    Rudyard Kipling

I don't have big anxieties. I wish I did. I'd be much more interesting.
    Roy Lichtenstein

From this arises the question whether it is better to be loved rather than feared, or feared rather than loved. It might perhaps be answered that we should wish to be both; but since love and fear can hardly exist together, if we must choose between them, it is far safer to be feared than loved.
Niccolò Machiavelli, *The Prince*

He who fears he shall suffer, already suffers what he fears.
Michel de Montaigne, *Essays*

Fear has the largest eyes of all.
Boris Pasternak, "Hoarfrost"

What we fear comes to pass more speedily than what we hope.
Publilius Syrus, *Moral Sayings*

So first of all let me assert my firm belief that the only thing we have to fear is fear itself--nameless, unreasoning, unjustified terror which paralyzes needed efforts to convert retreat into advance.
Franklin D. Roosevelt, first inaugural address, 1933

Were the diver to think on the jaws of the shark he would never lay hands on the precious pearl.
Sa'di, *Gulistan*

The mind that is anxious about the future is miserable.
Seneca

Where fear is, happiness is not.
Seneca, *Letters to Lucilius*

Present fears
Are less than horrible imaginings.
William Shakespeare, *Macbeth*

In this world, there is always danger for those who are afraid of it.
George Bernard Shaw

To him who is in fear everything rustles.
Sophocles

Curiosity will conquer fear even more than bravery will.
James Stephens, *The Crock of Gold*

It takes up too much time, being afraid.
Pierre Trudeau

To fear a crowd, and yet fear solitude; to fear to go unguarded, to fear the very guards themselves; to be unwilling to dispense with an armed escort, and yet to feel displeasure at the sight of one's attendants carrying arms: what a hateful predicament.
Xenophon

FICTION

The best part of the fiction in many novels is the notice that the characters are all purely imaginary.
Franklin Pierce Adams

Good fiction reveals feeling, refines events, locates importance, and, though its methods are as mysterious as they are varied, intensifies the experience of living our own lives.
Vincent Canby

Fiction is like a spider's web, attached ever so slightly perhaps, but still attached to life at all four corners.
Virginia Woolf, *A Room of One's Own*

FIGURES OF SPEECH

A simile must be as precise as a slide rule and as natural as the smell of dill.
Isaac Babel

The coldest Word was once a glowing new metaphor.
Thomas Carlyle, *Past and Present*

Similes are like songs in love;
They much describe; they nothing prove.
Matthew Prior, *Alma*

Every writer writes in metaphor. I'm not talking about my grandchild. I'm talking about the universal grandchild.
Andy Rooney

The man who writes about himself and his own time is the only man who writes about all people and about all time.
George Bernard Shaw

A simile committing suicide is always a depressing spectacle.
Oscar Wilde, *A Critic in Pall Mall*

FILM

Good movies make you care, make you believe in possibilities again.
 Pauline Kael

Does art reflect life? In movies, yes. Because more than any other art form, films have been a mirror held up to society's porous face.
 Marjorie Rosen

Some films could only have been cast in one way: screen tests were given and the losers got the parts.
 Gene Shalit

I don't know any other business that tells you not to go in and buy their product.
 Jack Valenti, President, Motion Picture Association of America, on film rating

FLATTERY

While your head is in the lion's mouth, stroke his back.
 African proverb

A compliment is something like a kiss through a veil.
 Victor Hugo, *Les misérables*

Flattery is all right--if you don't inhale.
 Adlai Stevenson

FREE PRESS

Provided I do not write about the government, religion, politics, morals, people in power, official institutions, the Opera, the other theatres, or about anybody attached to anything, I am free to print anything, subject to the inspection of two or three censors.
 Pierre-Augustin de Beaumarchais

Congress shall make no law . . . abridging the freedom of speech, or of the press.
 Constitution of the United States, First Amendment

When men cannot freely convey their thoughts to one another, no other liberty is secure.
 William Ernest Hocking, *Freedom of the Press*

Freedom of the press is guaranteed only to those who own one.
 A.J. Liebling

We have a reasonably free press in this country, but there are far too many captive editors who cannot even be heard to rattle their chains.
Carl E. Lindstrom

FREE SPEECH

What this country needs is more free speech worth listening to.
Hansell B. Duckett

The right to be heard does not automatically include the right to be taken seriously. To be taken seriously depends entirely upon what is being said.
Hubert Humphrey

The only way to make sure people you agree with can speak is to support the rights of people you don't agree with.
Eleanor Holmes Norton

Happy the country where an honest man speaks as loud as a scoundrel.
Lord Palmerston (Henry John Temple)

Every man has a right to be heard, but no man has the right to strangle democracy with a single set of vocal chords.
Adlai Stevenson

I disapprove of what you say, but I will defend to the death your right to say it.
Voltaire

Free speech is like garlic. If you are perfectly sure of yourself, you enjoy it and your friends tolerate it.
Lynn White

FRIENDSHIP

Friendship is one mind in two bodies.
Aristotle

Wishing to be friends is quick work, but friendship is a slow-ripening fruit.
Aristotle, *Nicomachean Ethics*

There is little friendship in the world, and least of all between equals.
Sir Francis Bacon, *Essays*

This communicating of a man's self to his friend works two contrary effects, for it redoubleth joys, and cutteth griefs in half.
Sir Francis Bacon, *Essays*

Nothing strengthens a friendship as much as the conviction by each one that he is superior to the other.
    Honoré de Balzac

Friends are the thermometers by which we may judge the temperature of our fortune.
    Countess of Blessington

Friendships multiply joys and divide griefs.
    Sir Henry George Bohn

One of the curious superstitions of friendship is that we somehow choose our friends. To the connoisseur in friendship no idea could be more amazing and incredible. Our friends are chosen for us by some hidden law of sympathy, and not by our conscious wills.
    Randolph S. Bourne

Here's to Friendship--Love without his wings.
    Lord Byron

You can make more friends in two months by becoming interested in other people than you can in two years by trying to get other people interested in you.
    Dale Carnegie

That two men may be real friends, they must have opposite opinions, similar principles, and different loves and hatreds.
    François-René de Chateaubriand

True friendship is like sound health: the value of it is seldom known until it be lost.
    Charles Caleb Colton

Don't go to visit your friend in the hour of his disgrace.
    Rabbi Simeon Ben Eleazar, *Ethics of the Fathers*

Animals are such agreeable friends--they ask no questions, they pass no criticisms.
    George Eliot

A friend is one before whom I may think aloud.
    Ralph Waldo Emerson

It is not so much our friends' help that helps as the confidence of their help.
    Epicurus

Instead of making and maintaining friendships, people stay home to watch "Friends" on TV.
    Linda K. Fuller, *Media-Mediated Relationships*

Better lose a jest than a friend.
  Thomas Fuller, *Gnomologia*

A friend is a speaking acquaintance who also listens.
  Arnold Glasgow

Friendship is having the latchkey of another's mind.
  Edgar J. Goodspeed

In times of difficulty friendship is on trial.
  Greek proverb

We have fewer friends than we imagine, but more than we know.
  Hugo von Hofmannsthal, *The Book of Friends*

Without wearing any mask we are conscious of, we have a special face for each friend.
  Oliver Wendell Holmes, Sr., *Journals*

Probably no man ever had a friend that he did not dislike a little.
  Edgar Watson Howe

The friend is the man who knows all about you, and still likes you.
  Elbert Hubbard, *The Note Book of Elbert Hubbard*

The feeling of friendship is like that of being comfortably filled with roast beef; love, like being enlivened with champagne.
  Samuel Johnson

It is only the great-hearted who can be true friends; the mean and cowardly can never know what true friendship means.
  Charles Kingsley

Our friendships should be immortal, our enmities mortal.
  Titus Livius

Friendship is an arrangement by which we undertake to exchange small favors for big ones.
  Montesquieu

If everybody knew what one says of the other, there would not be four friends left in the world.
  Blaise Pascal, *Pensées*

Vulgare amici nomen, sed rara est fides. (The name of friend is common, but true friendship is rare.)
    Gaius Velleius Paterculus

You have made the steep places level.
    Plautus, *Miles Gloriosus*

That friendship will not continue to the end that is begun for an end.
    Francis Quarles

The friend who understands you, creates you.
    Romain Rolland

Friendship is almost always the union of a part of one mind with a part of another; people are friends in spots.
    George Santayana

She became for me an island of light, fun, wisdom where I could run with my discoveries and torments and hopes at any time of day and find welcome.
    May Sarton

The friends thou hast, and their adoption tried
Grapple them to thy soul with hooks of steel.
    William Shakespeare, *Hamlet*

There is no possession more valuable than a good and faithful friend.
    Socrates

Friendship based solely upon gratitude is like a photograph; with time it fades.
    Carmen Sylva

Friendship is to be valued for what there is in it, not for what can be gotten out of it.
    H. Clay Trumbell

To grow, you need the mirror of one trusted friend.
    Voltaire

Seek no friend to make him useful, for that is the negation of friendship; but seek him that you may be useful, for this is of friendship's essence.
    Henry A. Wallace

We cherish our friends not for their ability to amuse us, but for ours to amuse them.
    Evelyn Waugh

G

GENDER

Women like silent men. They think they're listening.
    Marcel Achard

Debate is masculine; conversation is feminine.
    A. Bronson Alcott, *Concord Days*

A man would never get the notion of writing a book on the peculiar situation of the human male.
    Simone de Beauvoir, *The Second Sex*

The basic discovery about any people is the discovery of the relationship between its men and women.
    Pearl Buck

A man is already halfway in love with a woman who listens to him.
    Brendan Francis

Fighting is essentially a masculine idea; a woman's weapon is her tongue.
    Hermione Gingold

As soon as a woman crosses the border into male territory, the nature of professional combat changes.
    Françoise Giroud

Everyone needs a wife; no one needs a husband.
    Germaine Greer

To be successful, a woman has to be much better at her job than a man.
    Golda Meir

It is the general rule that all superior men inherit the elements of superiority from their mothers.
    Jules Michelet

Whatever the "real" differences between the sexes may be, we are not likely to know them until the sexes are treated differently, that is, alike.
    Kate Millett

Remember, Ginger Rogers did everything Fred Astaire did, but she did it backwards and in high heels.
    Faith Whittlesey

Women have served all these centuries as looking glasses possessing the magic and delicious power of reflecting the figure of man at twice its natural size.
    Virginia Woolf

I realize that were I a man, I would be at the battlefront fighting amidst bullets and explosives, instead of sitting serenely at my desk.
    Kieko Yamamuro, *Essay*

GOLDEN RULE

Golden Rule of Writing: Write unto others as you would be written unto.
    Robert Gunning

Fail to honor people, they fail to honor you.
    Lao-Tse

All things whatsoever ye would that men should do to you, do ye even so to them: for this is the law and the prophets.
    Matthew 7:12

If you want a golden rule that will fit everybody, this is it: Have nothing in your houses that you do not know to be useful, or believe to be beautiful.
    William Morris, *The Beauty of Life*

Do not do unto others as you would that they should do unto you. Their tastes may not be the same.
    George Bernard Shaw, *Man and Superman*

GOSSIP

Half the gossip of society would perish if the books that are truly worth reading were but read.
    George Dawson

I have been taught that gossip, whether inspired by malice or not . . . begins in a lie and generally ends in truth.
José Echegaray

Gossip is a sort of smoke that comes from the dirty tobacco-pipes of those who diffuse it; it proves nothing but the bad taste of the smoker.
George Eliot, *Daniel Deronda*

Gossip is the henchman of rumor and scandal.
Octave Feuillet

Today's gossip is tomorrow's headline.
Walter Winchell

GOVERNMENT

Every nation has the government it deserves.
Joseph de Maistre, letter

It's all papers and forms, the entire Civil Service is like a fortress made of papers, forms, and red tape.
Aleksandr Ostrovsky

The government is the only known vessel that leaks from the top.
James Reston

I don't make jokes; I just watch the government and report the facts.
Will Rogers

There is no trick to being a humorist when you have the whole government working for you.
Will Rogers

GRAMMAR

This is the sort of nonsense up with which I refuse to put.
Winston Churchill, on being criticized for ending a sentence with a preposition

Grammar is to speech what salt is to food.
Moses Ibn Ezra, *Shirat Yisrael*

The adjective is the banana peel of the parts of speech.
Clifton Fadiman

You can be a little ungrammatical if you come from the right part of the country.
Robert Frost, *Atlantic*

Where strictness of grammar does not weaken expression, it should be attended to . . . .   But where, by small grammatical negligence, the energy of an idea is condensed, or a word stands for a sentence, I hold grammatical rigor in contempt.
    Thomas Jefferson

Adjectives do most of the work, smuggling in actual information under the guise of normal journalism. Thus the use of soft-spoken (mousy), loyal (dumb), high-minded (inept), hardworking (plodding), self-made (crooked), and pragmatic (totally immoral).
    John Leo, "Journalism for the Lay Reader," *Time*

A man's grammar, like Caesar's wife, must not only be pure, but above suspicion of impurity.
    Edgar Allan Poe, *Marginalia*

As to the adjective: when in doubt, strike it out.
    Mark Twain, *Pudd'nhead Wilson's Calendar*

Pick adjectives as you would a diamond or a mistress.
    Stanley Walker

GROUP

I want to be part of the herd . . . but at the edge of it looking over their shoulders.
    Mac Baird

It may be laid down as an axiom that a man who does not live the life of the mob will not think its thoughts either.
    Lewis Browne

One dog barks at something, and a hundred bark at the sound.
    Chinese proverb

A group is subject to the truly magical power of words.
    Sigmund Freud

One can stand still in a flowing stream, but not in a world of men.
    Japanese proverb

What makes a multitude of individuals a society rather than a crowd is a commonly held ideal. While such an ideal is always a fiction, . . . it is men's ability to believe in such fictions that enables them to act together as part of a group.
    Melvin Lyon, *Symbol and Idea in Henry Adams*

I likened you to those I saw you with.
    Maltese proverb

I don't care to belong to a club that accepts people like me as members.
Groucho Marx

A conference is just an admission that you want somebody to join you in your troubles.
Will Rogers

Rubbing minds together, like striking flint and steel, can start fires of motivation.
Auren Uris

People very rarely think in groups; they talk together, they exchange information, they adjudicate, they make compromises. But they do not think; they do not create.
William H. Whyte, Jr., *The Organization Man*

H

HAPPINESS

True happiness arises from . . . the friendship and conversation of a few select companions.
    Joseph Addison

I had a pleasant time with my mind, for it was happy.
    Louisa May Alcott

Happiness is not a destination. Happiness is a process.
    Aristotle

To be happy we must not be too concerned with others.
    Albert Camus, *The Fall*

On the whole, the happiest people seem to be those who have no particular cause for being happy except that they are so.
    William R. Inge

When one door of happiness closes another opens; but often we look so long at the closed door that we do not see the one which has been opened for us.
    Helen Keller

Most folks are about as happy as they make up their minds to be.
    Abraham Lincoln

I cannot help being happy. I've struggled against it but to no good. Apart from an odd five minutes here and there, I have been happy all my life. There is, I am well aware, no virtue whatever in this. It results from a combination of heredity, health, good fortune, and shallow intellect.
    Arthur Marshall, *Taking Liberties*

The hours that make us happy make us wise.
  John Masefield

Ask yourself whether you are happy and you cease to be so.
  John Stuart Mill, *Autobiography*

Unquestionably, it is possible to do without happiness; it is done involuntarily by nineteen-twentieths of mankind.
  John Stuart Mill, *Utilitarianism*

The small share of happiness attainable by man exists only insofar as he is able to cease to think of himself.
  Theodor Reik, *Of Love and Lust*

I do not know what your destiny will be, but one thing I know is that those of you who will be happy will have found a way to serve.
  Albert Schweitzer

I'm not an unhappy person. I'm a happy person with problems.
  Lilless McPherson Shilling

I know what happiness is, for I have done good work.
  Robert Louis Stevenson

HEALTH COMMUNICATION

Refuse to be ill. Never tell people you are ill; never own it to yourself. Illness is one of those things which a man should resist on principle at the onset.
  Edward George Bulwer-Lytton

Thousands upon thousands of persons have studied disease. Almost no one has studied health.
  Adelle Davis

Health is not a condition of matter, but of mind.
  Mary Baker Eddy, *Science and Health*

Establishing and maintaining open lines of communication about communicable disease is a vital way of countering ignorance and meeting our moral obligation.
  Linda K. Fuller, *Communicating about Communicable Diseases*

Doctors think a lot of patients are cured who have simply quit in disgust.
  Don Herold

The average patient looks upon the average doctor very much as the noncombatant

looks upon the troops fighting on his behalf. The more trained men there are between his body and the enemy the better.
    Rudyard Kipling

The ultimate indignity is to be given a bedpan by a stranger who calls you by your first name.
    Maggie Kuhn

Other books have been written by men physicians . . . . One would suppose in reading them that women possess but one class of physical organs, and that these are always diseased. Such teaching is pestiferous, and tends to cause and perpetuate the very evils it professes to remedy.
    Mary Livermore

One of the first duties of the physician is to educate the masses not to take medicine.
    Sir William Osler

All sorts of bodily diseases are produced by half-used minds.
    George Bernard Shaw

Heaven defend me from a busy doctor.
    Welsh proverb

HISTORY

Historical fiction is not only a respectable literary form: it is a standing reminder of the fact that history is about human beings.
    Helen M. Cam, *Historical Novels*

History will be kind to me for I intend to write it.
    Winston Churchill

History is written by the winners.
    Alex Haley

The only thing we learn from history is that people don't learn from history.
    Georg Wilhelm Friedrich Hegel

Very few things happen at the right time and the rest do not happen at all. The conscientious historian will correct these defects.
    Herodotus

Journalism allows its readers to witness history; fiction gives its readers an opportunity to live it.
    John Hersey

HUMOR

There are two things that should never be researched. One of them is what makes people laugh. The other is the love-making habits of consenting adults. In some cases, it's the same thing.
Erma Bombeck

A little levity will save many a good heavy thing from sinking.
Samuel Butler, II

The most difficult character in comedy is the fool, and he who plays the part must be no simpleton.
Miguel de Cervantes

Men will confess to treason, murder, arson, false teeth, or a wig. How many of them will own up to a lack of humor?
Frank Moore Colby, *The Colby Essays*

The chief difference between American humor and English humour is the way they spell it.
William Cole

A sense of humor . . . is not so much the ability to appreciate humorous stories as it is the capacity to recognize the absurdity of the positions one gets into from time to time, together with skill in retreating from them with dignity.
Dana L. Farnsworth

Mirth defuses rage. Anger demands a serious attitude, but humor banishes the tightness and severity necessary for anger. If mirth is experienced, rage is impossible.
William Fry

Common humor is very basic, isn't it? At both the [Washington] *Post* and *Newsweek* there's a rather great, healthy irreverence that makes working a lot of fun.
Katharine Graham

Humor very often cuts the knot of serious questions more trenchantly and successfully than severity.
Horace, *Satires*

Humor is laughing at what you haven't got when you ought to have it.
Langston Hughes, *The Book of Negro Humor*

I did not intend to write a funny book, at first. I did not know I was a humorist. I have never been sure about it. In the middle ages, I should probably have gone about preaching and got myself burnt or hanged.
Jerome K. Jerome, *My Life and Times*

The humorist runs with the hare; the satirist hunts with the hounds.
    Ronald A. Knox

Humor simultaneously wounds and heals, indicts and pardons, diminishes and enlarges; it constitutes inner growth at the expense of outer gain, and those who possess and honestly practice it make themselves more through a willingness to make themselves less.
    Louis Kronenberger, *Company Manners*

The teller of a mirthful tale has latitude allowed him. We are content with less than absolute truth.
    Charles Lamb, *The Last Essays of Elia*

Yet I admit we have to make a pretense at humor in moments of trial. It is a sort of survival quality that came down with us through the ages that we must take adversity with a smile or a joke. Tell any man that he has lost his job, and his "reaction," as they say in college, will be to make some kind of joke about having lots of time now for golf.
    Stephen Leacock, *The Saving Grace of Humor*

Think of what would happen to us in America if there were no humorists; life would be one long Congressional Record.
    Thomas L. Masson

Dying's tough, but it's not as tough as comedy.
    A.E. Matthews, said on his deathbed

The humorist has a good eye for the humbug; he does not always recognize the saint.
    W. Somerset Maugham, *The Summing Up*

What is learned with humor is learned well.
    Marshall McLuhan

Humor can allow me to kick stronger. If you envelop the challenge with humor you can go farther than if you have a straight face. I use it to push people. It's part of my style.
    Salvador Minuchin

The test of a real comedian is whether you laugh at him before he opens his mouth.
    George Jean Nathan, *American Mercury*

Comedy, we may say, is society protecting itself--with a smile.
    J.B. Priestley, *George Meredith*

The worst in life, we are told, is compatible with the best in art. So too the worst in

life is compatible with the best in humor.
   Agnes Repplier, *In Pursuit of Laughter*

Humor restores our perspective . . . . Humor has been called the bullet-proof vest that protects against the ravages of negative emotions.
   Vera Robinson

Everything is funny as long as it is happening to somebody else.
   Will Rogers, *The Illiterate Digest*

Give me the truth. I'll exaggerate it and make it funny.
   Will Rogers

The reason that there are so few women comics is that so few women can bear being laughed at.
   Anna Russell, in London *Sunday Times*

When a thing is funny, search it for a hidden truth.
   George Bernard Shaw

I like a man who talks me to death, provided he is amusing; it saves so much trouble.
   Mary Shelley

The surest mark of inner adequacy is the operation of a sense of humor.
   T.V. Smith

They don't seem to write . . . comedy anymore--just a series of gags.
   Barbara Stanwyck

Humor is the sense of the Absurd which is despair refusing to take itself seriously.
   Arland Ussher

The word humor, according to the Oxford Dictionary, originally meant moisture or juice and only fairly recently, that is to say from the 17th century, came to mean that quality of action, speech, or writing which excites amusement, or the faculty of perceiving what is ludicrous or amusing. As anyone who has experienced the lubricating effect of even a small joke in a household knows, humor still has an element of juice. It keeps life from drying up, gives it freshness and flavor.
   Elizabeth Gray Vining

All the world over, the most good-natured find enjoyment in those who miss trains or sit down on frozen pavements.
   Dame Rebecca West

I

IDEAS

Not to engage in the pursuit of ideas is to live like ants instead of like men. The ant can live without ideas because the whole course of its life is fixed. But man has the freedom--and therefore the necessity--to choose and to choose in terms of ideas.
    Mortimer J. Adler

Nothing is more dangerous than an idea if it's the only one you have.
    Alain, *Propos sur la religion*

Every man with an idea has at least two or three followers.
    Brooks Atkinson, *Once around the Sun*

An idea not capable of realization is an empty soap bubble.
    Berthold Auerbach, *Sträflinge*

Who can mistake great thoughts?
They seize upon the mind--arrest, and search,
And shake it.
    Philip James Bailey, *Festus: A Village Feast*

If you see a good idea, steal it.
    Coleman Bender

What divides men is less a difference in ideas than a likeness in pretensions.
    Pierre-Jean de Béranger

A fact in itself is nothing. It is valuable only for the idea attached to it, or for the proof which it furnishes.
    Claude Bernard, *Introduction to the Study of Experimental Medicine*

Borrowed thoughts, like borrowed money, only show the poverty of the borrower.
Countess of Blessington

One can live in the shadow of an idea without grasping it.
Elizabeth Bowen, *The Heat of the Day*

There is no adequate defense, except stupidity, against the impact of a new idea.
Percy W. Bridgman, *The Intelligent Individual and Society*

A new idea is delicate. It can be killed by a sneer or a yawn; it can be stabbed to death by a quip and worried to death by a frown on the right man's brow.
Charles Brower

Every new idea has something of the pain and peril of childbirth about it.
Samuel Butler, II, *The Note-Books of Samuel Butler*

Thought once awakened does not again slumber.
Thomas Carlyle, *On Heroes and Hero Worship*

The ideas I stand for are not mine. I borrowed them from Socrates. I swiped them from Chesterfield. I stole them from Jesus. And I put them in a book. If you don't like their rules, whose would you use?
Dale Carnegie

There are well-dressed foolish ideas just as there are well-dressed fools.
Sébastien-Roch Nicolas de Chamfort

Hang ideas! They are tramps, vagabonds, knocking at the back-door of your mind, each taking a little of your substance, each carrying away some crumb of that belief in a few simple notions you must cling to if you want to live decently and would like to die easy.
Joseph Conrad, *Lord Jim*

An idea is more than information; it is information with legs on it. It is headed somewhere.
Edgar Dale

What moves men of genius, or rather, what inspires their work, is not new ideas, but their obsession with the idea that what has already been said is still not enough.
Eugène Delacroix, *Journal*

A source of our errors is, that we attach thoughts to words which do not express them with accuracy.
René Descartes, *Principles of Philosophy*

As the fletcher makes straight his arrow, a wise man makes straight his trembling and unsteady thought, which is difficult to guard, difficult to hold back.
Dhammapada

Neither man nor nation can exist without a sublime idea.
Fyodor Dostoevsky

Some writers agree that ideas come from God, who spreads idea dust each evening. The ideas sift down about our heads like diamond chips. The fact that some of them come at inadvertent times makes me suspect that God has a great sense of humor.
Bill Downey, *Right Brain . . . Write On!*

As certainly as water falls in rain on the tops of mountains and runs down into the valleys, plains, and pits, so does thought fall first on the best minds, and run down, from class to class, until it reaches the masses, and works revolutions.
Ralph Waldo Emerson

You can kill a man but you can't kill an idea.
Medgar Evers

If I carried all the thoughts of the world in my hand, I would take care not to open it.
Bernard Fontenelle

Clothe an idea in words and it loses its freedom of movement.
Egon Friedell

My ideas have undergone a process of emergence by emergency. When they are needed badly enough, they are accepted.
R. Buckminster Fuller

The idea is the old age of the spirit and the disease of the mind.
Edmond and Jules de Goncourt, *Journal*

All ideas are to some extent inevitably subversive . . . . Christianity was subversive to paganism.
Albert Guerard, *Testament of a Liberal*

You are never quite at ease about a new idea born in your mind, for you do not know in what storms of contradiction it may involve you.
Jean Guibert, *On Kindness*

Beware of people carrying ideas. Beware of ideas carrying people.
Barbara Grizzuti Harrison

Ideas move fast when their time comes.
Carolyn Heilbrun, *Toward a Recognition of Androgyny*

When a thought takes one's breath away, a lesson on grammar seems an impertinence.
　　Thomas Wentworth Higginson, *Poems by Emily Dickinson*

Where did ideas come from? This one had leaped at him when he'd been exhausted, AWOL from his search.
　　Laura Z. Hobson, *Gentleman's Agreement*

Many ideas grow better when transplanted into another mind than in the one where they sprang up.
　　Oliver Wendell Holmes, Jr.

A man's mind stretched to a new idea never goes back to its original dimensions.
　　Oliver Wendell Holmes, Sr.

Ideas are born, they struggle, triumph, change, and they are transformed; but is there a dead idea which in the end does not live on, transformed into a broader and clearer goal?
　　Eugenio María de Hostos

There is one thing stronger than all the armies in the world: and that is an idea whose time has come.
　　Victor Hugo

Every new idea is obscure at first. It is or it wouldn't be new.
　　Robert Irwin

Great ideas need landing gear as well as wings.
　　C.D. Jackson

The very idea that there is another idea is something gained.
　　Richard Jefferies, *The Story of My Heart*

To say that an idea is fashionable is to say, I think, that it has been adulterated to a point where it is hardly an idea at all.
　　Murray Kempton, *Part of Our Time*

A man may die, nations may rise and fall, but an idea lives on. Ideas have endurance without death.
　　John F. Kennedy

Ideas shape the course of history.
　　John Maynard Keynes

We do not sell ideas if they are not good. Ideas are not salami.
　　Nikita Khrushchev

Every good thought you think is contributing its share to the ultimate result of your life.
   Grenville Kleiser

Thoughts, like fleas, jump from man to man. But they don't bite everybody.
   Stanislaw Lec, *Unkempt Thoughts*

Just as our eyes need light in order to see, our minds need ideas in order to conceive.
   Nicolas Malebranche, *Recherche de la vérité*

A single idea, if it is right, saves us the labor of an infinity of experiences.
   Jacques Maritain, *Reflections on America*

An idea isn't responsible for the people who believe in it.
   Don Marquis

In our popular discussions, unwise ideas must have a hearing as well as wise ones, dangerous ideas as well as safe, un-American as well as American.
   Alexander Meiklejohn

My guess is that well over eighty percent of the human race goes through life without having a single original thought.
   H.L. Mencken

A society made up of individuals who were capable of original thought would probably be unendurable. The pressure of ideas would simply drive it frantic.
   H.L. Mencken, *Minority Report*

Great ideas are not charitable.
   Henry de Montherlant, *Le maître de Santiago*

Profundity of thought belongs to youth, clarity of thought to old age.
   Friedrich Nietzsche, *Miscellaneous Maxims and Opinions*

You cannot put a rope around the neck of an idea; you cannot put an idea up against a barrack-square wall and riddle it with bullets; you cannot confine it in the strongest prison cell that your slaves could ever build.
   Sean O'Casey, *Death of Thomas Ashe*

The best way to have a good idea is to have lots of ideas.
   Linus Pauling

We find it hard to believe that other people's thoughts are as silly as our own, but they probably are.
   James Harvey Robinson, *The Mind in the Making*

He is the greatest artist who has embodied, in the sum of his works, the greatest number of the greatest ideas.
John Ruskin

Men can live without air for a few minutes, without water for about two weeks, without food for about two months--and without a new thought for years on end.
Kent Ruth

He who cannot change the very fabric of his thought will never be able to change reality.
Anwar el-Sadat, *In Search of Identity*

Thought is an infection. In the case of certain thoughts it becomes an epidemic.
Wallace Stevens, *Opus Posthumous*

That fierce light which beats upon a throne
And blackens every blot.
Alfred, Lord Tennyson, dedication of *Idylls of the King*

The most powerful factors in the world are clear ideas in the minds of energetic men of good will.
J. Arthur Thomson

No man can establish title to an idea--at the most he can only claim possession. The stream of thought that irrigates the mind of each of us is a confluent of the intellectual river that drains the whole of the living universe.
Maurice Valency, introduction to *Jean Giraudoux: Four Plays*

I not only use all the brains I have, but all I can borrow.
Woodrow Wilson

All the really good ideas I ever had came to me while I was milking a cow.
Grant Wood

The chaos of our society is the product of the dishevelment of our ideas.
Philip Wylie, *Generation of Vipers*

ILLUSION

Beware the light at the end of the tunnel. It could be a freight train coming the other way.
Bear Bryant, former football coach of the University of Alabama

Beware of illusions! What do you mean? Some of my best friends are illusions. Been sustaining me for years.
Norma Jean Harris (Sheila Ballantyne)

Obsessed by a fairy tale, we spend our lives searching for a magic door and a lost kingdom of peace.
Eugene O'Neill, *More Stately Mansions*

Things are not always what they seem.
Phaedrus

IMAGE

A picture is worth ten thousand words.
Frederick R. Barnard, *Printers' Ink*

Trying to be fascinating is an asinine position to be in.
Katharine Hepburn

A career is born in public--talent in privacy.
Marilyn Monroe

It is only the shallow people who do not judge by appearances.
Oscar Wilde

IMAGINATION

What is now proved was once only imagin'd.
William Blake, *The Marriage of Heaven and Hell*

I never saw a moor,
I never saw the sea,
Yet know I how the heather looks,
And what a wave must be.
Emily Dickinson

I used to lie awake as a child and get more entertainment and terror out of blank walls and plain furniture than most children could find in a toy-store.
Charlotte Perkins Gilman, *The Yellow Wall-Paper*

I don't understand the process of imagination--though I know that I am very much at its mercy. I feel that these ideas are floating around in the air and they pick me to settle upon. The ideas come to me; I don't produce them at will. They come to me in the course of a sort of controlled daydream, a directed reverie.
Joseph Heller, in *Writers at Work*

Imagination has more charms in writing than in speaking. It must fold its wings when it enters a salon.
Prince de Ligne, *Mes écarts*

It is the extreme concreteness of a child's imagination which enables him, not only to take from each book exactly what he requires--people, or genii, or tables and chairs--but literally to furnish his world with them.

Iris Origo, *Images and Shadows*

So you see, imagination needs moodling--long, inefficient, happy idling, dawdling, and puttering.

Brenda Ueland

If you can imagine it, you can achieve it.
If you can dream it, you can become it.

William A. Ward

INDEX

Sir Frederick Pollock used to say that a man who would publish a book without an index ought to be banished ten miles beyond Hell where the Devil himself could not go because of the stinging nettles.

Roscoe Pound

A book without an index is like a mind without a memory.

Ancient proverb

Speech is the index of the mind.

Seneca

INFORMATION

We have smothered ourselves, buried ourselves, in the vast heap of information which all of us have and none of us has.

Gamaliel Bradford

Information is the currency of democracy.

Ralph Nader

He who cares more for information than for inspiration prefers elevators to wings.

J.B. Opdycke, *Amor Vitaque*

INTERNATIONAL COMMUNICATION

In Hollywood, they bring you ice-cold Coke to show you're a regular guy. In England they bring you milky tea to show you're one of the chaps. In France, it's champagne if you're really *sympathique*. But in Italy they bring you nothing--they are too busy kissing your arms.

Gina Lollobrigida

There should be no inferiors and no superiors for true world friendship.
Carlos P. Romulo

The motion picture industry has provided a window on the world, and the colonized nations have looked through that window and have seen the things of which they have been deprived. It is perhaps not generally realized that a refrigerator can be a revolutionary symbol--to a people who have no refrigerators.
Achmed Sukarno

We shall never be able to remove suspicion and fear as potential causes of war until communication is permitted to flow, free and open, across international boundaries.
Harry S. Truman

I can get a better grasp of what is going on in the world from one good Washington dinner party than from all the background information NBC piles on my desk.
Barbara Walters

INTERVIEWING

Listening to someone talk isn't at all like listening to their words played over on a machine. What you hear when you have a face before you is never what you hear when you have before you a winding tape.
Oriana Fallaci, *The Egotists*

You can interview me all you want; just don't ask me any questions.
Tom Robbins

Wait for those unguarded moments. Relax the mood and, like the child dropping off to sleep, the subject often reveals his truest self.
Barbara Walters

INTIMACY

It is in opposition (the disputed territory of the argument, the battle for self-definition that goes on beneath the words) . . . that intimacy takes place.
Nadine Gordimer

It is much easier to tell intimate things in the dark.
William McFee, *Casuals of the Sea*

Ask yourself whether you are happy and you cease to be so.
John Stuart Mill, *Autobiography*

INTRODUCTION

It's always nice to be introduced by someone whose paycheck you sign.
James B. Edwards

The assumption is that you have something you want to say and that someone, or many people, want to hear your message.
Linda K. Fuller, *Communicating Comfortably*

I want a recording of that introduction. It was tremendous. In fact, I think we should hold a minute of awed silence.
Richard Griffith, on responding to an introduction

I plan to start my talk by running through a disjointed and time consuming introduction.
James Hopper

My father would have appreciated that introduction, but only my mother would have believed it.
Lyndon B. Johnson

Making an introduction is something like building a bridge. An effective bridge has to span the gulf and reach both sides. If it fails to reach either side, the traveler is sure to fall in the abyss below.
Daisy Jones

J

JARGON

Incomprehensible jargon is the hallmark of a profession.
  Kingman Brewster

Professional jargon is unpleasant. Translating it into English is a bore. I narrow-mindedly outlawed the word "unique." Practically every press release contains it. Practically nothing ever is.
  Fred Hechinger

Men love jargon. It is so palpable, tangible, visible, audible; it makes so obvious what one has learned; it satisfies the craving for results. It is impressive for the uninitiated. It makes one feel that one belongs. Jargon divides men into Us and Them.
  Walter Kaufmann

Gobbledygook: Talk or writing which is long, pompous, vague, involved, usually with Latinized words. It is also talk or writing which is merely long, even though the words are fairly simple, with repetition over and over again, all of which could have been said in a few words.
  Maury Maverick

Jargon allows us to camouflage intellectual poverty with verbal extravagance.
  David Pratt

In our Victorian dislike of the practice of calling a spade a bloody shovel, it is not necessary to go to the opposite extreme of calling it an agricultural implement.
  Robert W. Seton-Watson

JOKES

If Adam came on earth again the only thing he would recognize would be the old jokes.
    Thomas Robert Dewar

Th' las' man that makes a joke owns it.
    Finley Peter Dunne, *Mr. Dooley's Opinions*

A difference of taste in jokes is a great strain on the affections.
    George Eliot

The jests of the rich are ever successful.
    Oliver Goldsmith, *The Vicar of Wakefield*

More is often taught by a jest than by the most serious teaching.
    Baltasar Gracian, *The Art of Worldly Wisdom*

If you think before you speak, the other fellow gets in his joke first.
    Edgar Watson Howe

A civil servant doesn't make jokes.
    Eugene Ionesco

He that jokes confesses.
    Italian proverb

Nothing reveals a man's character better than the kind of joke at which he takes offense.
    Georg C. Lichtenberg

The joke hit my head and came out of the voice box (without any thought of whether it was appropriate or not--without any editing).
    Baird Oldfield

A jest loses its point when he who makes it is the first to laugh.
    Friedrich von Schiller, *Fiesco*

For every ten jokes, thou hast got an hundred enemies.
    Laurence Sterne, *Tristram Shandy*

A good joke, like a good song, may be a perfect work of art.
    B.H. Streeter

Times change: the farmer's daughter now tells jokes about the traveling salesman.
    Carey Williams

JOURNALISM

Journalism is literature in a hurry.
    Matthew Arnold

Journalism has already come to be the first power in the land.
    Samuel Bowles

It's all storytelling, you know. That's what journalism is all about.
    Tom Brokaw

Journalism largely consists in saying "Lord Jones Dead" to people who never knew Lord Jones was alive.
    G.K. Chesterton, *The Wisdom of Father Brown*

Journalism consists in buying white paper at two cents a pound and selling it at ten cents a pound.
    Charles A. Dana

Journalism is in fact history on the run.
    Thomas Griffith

Journalism can never be silent: that is its greatest virtue and greatest fault. It must speak, and speak immediately, while the echoes of wonder, the claims of triumph, and the signs of horror are still in the air.
    Henry Anatole Grunwald

News work is highly addictive. It is the cocaine of crafts.
    William F. Kerby, *A Proud Profession: Memoirs of a Wall Street Journal Reporter*

Writing for a newspaper is like running a revolutionary war; you go into battle not when you are ready but when action offers itself.
    Norman Mailer, *The Presidential Papers*

The only qualities for real success in journalism are ratlike cunning, a plausible manner, and a little literary ability . . . . The capacity to steal other people's ideas and phrases--that one about ratlike cunning was invented by my colleague Murray Sayle--is also invaluable.
    Nicholas Tomalin

Journalism is the ability to meet the challenge of filling space.
    Dame Rebecca West

Rock journalism is people who can't write interviewing people who can't talk for

people who can't read.
Frank Zappa, in Linda Botts, *Loose Talk*

JOURNALISTS

Trying to be a first-rate reporter on the average American newspaper is like trying to play Bach's St. Matthew Passion on a ukulele: The instrument is too crude for the work, for the audience, and for the performer.
Ben Bagdikian

A reporter discovers, in the course of many years of interviewing celebrities, that most actors are more attractive behind a spotlight than over a spot of tea.
Phyllis Battelle

War correspondents . . . see a great deal of the world. Our obligation is to pass it on to others.
Margaret Bourke-White

Journalists are interesting. They just aren't as interesting as the things they cover.
Nora Ephron

Find a hard-boiled journalist and you find a thwarted idealist.
Russell Green

If I have lived by any maxim as a reporter, it was that every person is an expert on the circumstances of his life.
Joseph Lelyveld, *Move Your Shadow: South Africa, Black and White*

A good reporter cannot afford to be cynical; a good reporter cannot afford to be skeptical.
Curtis MacDougall, recalled on his death

If Saint Paul were to come back to our world in the flesh, he would become a newspaperman.
Abbé Michonneau

A journalist is basically a chronicler, not an interpreter of events. Where else in society do you have the license to eavesdrop on so many different conversations as you have in journalism? Where else can you delve into the life of our times? I consider myself a fortunate man to have a forum for my curiosity.
Bill Moyers

I ain't no lady. I'm a newspaperwoman.
Hazel Brannon Smith

A newspaper reporter is related to a telephone as a musician is related to a piano.
　　James B. Stewart, on the difficulty of reporting from India

The function of a good reporter is not to cover a story, but to uncover it.
　　Herbert Bayard Swope

Most journalists are restless voyeurs who see the warts on the world, the imperfections in people and places . . . . Gloom is their game, the spectacle their passion, normality their nemesis.
　　Gay Talese, *The Kingdom and the Power*

The only authors whom I acknowledge as American are the journalists. They, indeed, are not great writers, but they speak the language of their countrymen, and make themselves heard by them.
　　Alexis de Tocqueville

When a reporter sits down at the typewriter, he's nobody's friend.
　　Theodore H. White

K

KINDNESS

Shall we make a new rule of life from tonight: always to be a little kinder than necessary?
    Sir James M. Barrie

More flies are taken with a drop of honey, than a tun of vinegar.
    Sir Henry George Bohn, *A Handbook of Proverbs*

One of the most difficult things to give away is kindness--it usually is returned.
    Cort R. Flint

Let us be kinder to one another.
    Aldous Huxley's last words

Part of kindness is loving people more than they deserve.
    Joseph Joubert, *Pensées*

In this world, you must be a bit too kind in order to be kind enough.
    Pierre Marivaux

If there is any kindness I can show, or any good thing I can do to any fellow human being, let me do it now, and not deter or neglect it, as I shall not pass this way again.
    William Penn

Men are cruel, but Man is kind.
    Rabindranath Tagore, *Stray Birds*

KNOWLEDGE

He who knows useful things, not many things, is wise.
    Aeschylus, *Fragments*

There are some people that if they don't know, you can't tell 'em.
    Louis Armstrong

Men can know with the heart and not only with the mind.
    Ben Zion Bokser, *From the World of the Cabbalah*

Knowledge is increasing faster than we can distribute it. We increase knowledge at electronic speed, distribute it with a horse and buggy.
    Edgar Dale

A man should keep his little brain attic stocked with all the furniture that he is likely to use, and the rest he can put away in the lumber-room of his library, where he can get it if he wants it.
    Sir Arthur Conan Doyle, "Five Orange Pips," *The Adventures of Sherlock Holmes*

Never try to tell everything you know. It may take too short a time.
    Norman Ford, *Headmasters Courageous*

If you have knowledge, let others light their candles by it.
    Margaret Fuller

No knowledge is so easily found as when it is needed.
    Robert Henri, *The Art Spirit*

Amongst all things, knowledge is truly the best thing; from its not being liable ever to be stolen, from its not being purchasable, and from its being imperishable.
    Hitopadesa

Our knowledge grows in *spots*. The spots may be large or small, but the knowledge never grows all over: some old knowledge always remains what it was . . . . Our minds grow in spots; and like grease-spots, the spots spread. But we let them spread as little as possible: we keep unaltered as much of our old knowledge, as many of our old prejudices and beliefs, as we can. We patch and tinker more than we renew.
    William James, *Pragmatism*

You can know ten things by learning one.
    Japanese proverb

He who does not know one thing knows another.
    Kenyan proverb

To know is not to know, unless some one else has known that I know.
    Lucilius, *Satires*

Far better to know one thing thoroughly,
Than to be superficially dressed up with many.
    Menander, *Fragments*

Learned men are the cisterns of knowledge, not the fountain-heads.
    James Northcote, *Table-Talk*

Half of our knowledge we must snatch, not take.
    Alexander Pope, *Moral Essays*

L

LANGUAGE

Language was not given to man: he seized it.
Louis Aragon, *Le Libertinage*

Language is the mother, not the handmaiden, of thought; words will tell you things you never thought or felt before.
W.H. Auden

By its very looseness, by its way of evoking rather than defining, suggesting rather than saying, English is a magnificent vehicle for emotional poetry.
Max Beerbohm, *And Even Now*

Every living language, like the perspiring bodies of living creatures, is in perpetual motion and alteration; some words go off, and become obsolete; others are taken in, and by degrees grow into common use; or the same word is inverted to a new sense and notion, which in tract of time makes as observable a change in the air and features of a language, as age makes in the lines and mien of a face.
Richard Bentley, *A Dissertation upon the Epistles of Phalaris*

A man's language is an unerring index of his nature.
Laurence Binyon

The liberation of language is rooted in the liberation of ourselves.
Mary Daly

I recognize but one mental acquisition as a necessary part of the education of a lady or gentleman, namely, an accurate and refined use of the mother tongue.
Charles W. Eliot

Language is a city to the building of which every human being brought a stone.
Ralph Waldo Emerson

Language is fossil poetry.
  Ralph Waldo Emerson, "The Poet," *Essays: Second Series*

The trouble with the English language is that it is no longer English.
  Peter Enahoro, *How to Be a Nigerian*

To work through an interpreter is like hacking one's way through a forest with a feather.
  James Evans

I am aware that many object to the severity of my language; but is there no cause for severity? I will be as harsh as truth, and as uncompromising as justice. On this subject I do not wish to think, or speak, or write, with moderation. No! no! Tell a man whose house is on fire to give a moderate alarm; tell him to moderately rescue his wife from the hands of the ravisher; tell the mother to gradually extricate her babe from the fire into which it has fallen; but urge me not to use moderation in a cause like the present.
  William Lloyd Garrison, *The Liberator*

Astrological language is a golden cord that binds us to a dim past while it prepares us for an exciting future of planetary explorations.
  Linda Goodman

Every age has a language of its own; and the difference in the words is often far greater than in the thoughts. The main employment of authors, in their collection capacity, is to translate the thought of other ages into the language of their own.
  Augustus and Julius C. Hare, *Guesses at Truth*

English is a funny language. A fat chance and a slim chance are the same thing.
  Jack Herbert

Language is a living thing. We can feel it changing. Parts of it become old: they drop off and are forgotten. New pieces bud out, spread into leaves, and become big branches, proliferating.
  Gilbert Highet, *Explorations*

Language is by its very nature a communal thing; that is, it expresses never the exact thing but a compromise--that which is common to you, me, and everybody.
  Thomas Ernest Hulme, *Speculations*

To learn a second language you must murder it.
  Otto Jespersen

Language is the dress of thought.
  Samuel Johnson

In human relations a little language goes farther than a little of almost anything else. Whereas one language now often makes a wall, two can make a gate.
Walter V. Kaulfers

The way to learn a language is to breathe it in. Soak it up! Live it!
Doris Lessing

It is remarkable how very debased the language has become in a short period in America.
Frederick Marryat, *A Diary in America*

Such is the character of human language, that no word conveys to the mind, in all situations, one single definitive idea; and nothing is more common than to use words in a figurative sense.
John Marshall

When an age is in throes of profound transition, the first thing to disintegrate is language.
Rollo May, *Power and Innocence*

Language--a form of organized stutter.
Marshall McLuhan

Language is the light of the mind.
John Stuart Mill

Language is by all odds the most subtle and powerful technique we have for controlling other people.
George A. Miller

The only language men ever speak perfectly is the one they learn in babyhood, when no one can teach them anything!
Maria Montessori, *The Absorbent Mind*

Language may die at the hands of the schoolmen: it is regenerated by the poets.
Emmanuel Mounier, *Be Not Afraid*

The English language has a number of words and expressions which by general consent are "fighting words" when said without a disarming smile.
Frank Murphy

Language makes culture, and we make a rotten culture when we abuse words.
Cynthia Ozick, in *The First Ms. Reader*

A foreign tongue is spread not by fire and the sword but by its own richness and superiority.
Alexander Pushkin

Only where there is language is there world.
Adrienne Rich

I cannot learn languages; men of ordinary capacity can learn Sanskrit in less time than it takes me to buy a German dictionary.
George Bernard Shaw

Language was given to man to conceal his thoughts.
Stendhal

The world was made before the English language, and seemingly upon a different design.
Robert Louis Stevenson

I see no sense in "faking" conversation for the sake of teaching language. It's stupid and deadening to pupil and teacher. Talk should be natural and have for its object an exchange of ideas.
Anne Sullivan, in Helen Keller, *The Story of My Life*

Ours is a precarious language, as every writer knows, in which the merest shadow line often separates affirmation from negation, sense from nonsense, and one sex from the other.
James Thurber, *Lanterns and Lances*

A pinch of probably is worth a pound of perhaps.
James Thurber

Language is the expression of ideas, and if the people of one country cannot preserve an identity of ideas they cannot retain an identity of language.
Noah Webster, *An American Dictionary of the English Language*

A language is a dialect that has an army and a navy.
Max Weinreich, in Leo Rosten, *The Joys of Yiddish*

Die Grenzen meiner Sprache bedeuten die Grenzen meiner Welt. (The limits of my language mean the limits of my world.)
Ludwig Wittgenstein, *Tractatus Logico-Philosophicus*

LAUGHTER

It is bad to suppress laughter. It goes back down and spreads to your hips.
Fred Allen

Men will let you abuse them if only you will make them laugh.
    Henry Ward Beecher, *Proverbs from Plymouth Pulpit*

Nobody ever died of laughter.
    Max Beerbohm

Laughter is the corrective force which prevents us from becoming cranks.
    Henri Bergson

Laughter is the shortest distance between two people.
    Victor Borge

Of all days, the day on which one has not laughed is surely the most wasted.
    Sébastien-Roch Nicolas de Chamfort, *Maximes et pensées*

A human being should beware how he laughs, for then he shows all his faults.
    Ralph Waldo Emerson, *Journals*

Fun gives you a forcible hug, and shakes laughter out of you, whether you will or no.
    David Garrick

Laughter is a tranquilizer with no side effects.
    Arnold Glasgow

There is nothing in which people more betray their character than in what they laugh at.
    Goethe, *Elective Affinities*

I work with tears and raging, all the cathartic processes, but laughter is the way in, and it's a very powerful one.
    Dr. Annette Goodheart

If you don't learn to laugh at trouble, you won't have anything to laugh at when you grow old.
    Edgar Watson Howe

Laughter is the sun that drives winter from the human face.
    Victor Hugo

'Tis the loud laugh bespeaks the vacant mind.
    James Joyce, *Ulysses*, echoing Oliver Goldsmith

If you're not allowed to laugh in heaven, I don't want to go there.
    Martin Luther

A laugh's the wisest, easiest answer to all that's queer.
    Herman Melville, *Moby Dick*

In a comedy, laughs don't hurt.
    David Picker

One inch of joy surmounts of grief a span,
Because to laugh is proper to the man.
    François Rabelais, *Gargantua and Pantagruel*

We are in the world to laugh. In purgatory or in hell we shall no longer be able to do so. And in heaven it would not be proper.
    Jules Renard, *Journal*

We are all here for a spell. Get all the good laughs you can.
    Will Rogers

If you can't laugh at yourself, make fun of other people.
    Bobby Slayton

The world loved man when he smiled. The world became afraid of him when he laughed.
    Rabindranath Tagore, *Stray Birds*

A good laugh is sunshine in a house.
    William Makepeace Thackeray

I was irrevocably betrothed to laughter, the sound of which has always seemed to me the most civilized music in the world.
    Sir Peter Ustinov, *Dear Me*

We are always more disposed to laugh at nonsense than at genuine wit; because the nonsense is more agreeable to us, being more conformable to our natures.
    Marguerite de Valois

LEADERSHIP

The leader appears as master of the situation.
    William Albig

He is not the best statesman who is the greatest doer, but he who sets others doing with the greatest success.
    Anonymous

To be a leader of men one must turn one's back on men.
    Havelock Ellis

I suppose that leadership at one time meant muscle; but today it means getting along with people.
Indira Gandhi

LEARNING

Be eager for learning, even if it comes from the snout of a hog.
Arabic proverb

To be learning something new is ever the chief pleasure of mankind.
Aristotle

We are trying to overcome our limitations in order, patiently. We don't tackle flying through rock until a little later in the program.
Richard Bach, *Jonathan Livingston Seagull*

In seed time learn, in harvest teach, in winter enjoy.
William Blake, *The Marriage of Heaven and Hell*

We can prevent people from learning, but we can't make them unlearn.
Ludwig Börne, *Aphorismen und Fragmente*

Never learn anything until you find you have been made uncomfortable for a long time by not knowing it.
Samuel Butler, II, *The Way of All Flesh*

Learning is the art of ignoring.
Elias Canetti

Learning is a treasure that follows its owner everywhere.
Chinese proverb

Learning is like rowing upstream: not to advance is to drop back.
Chinese proverb

Personally I'm always ready to learn, although I do not always like being taught.
Winston Churchill

Learn as though you would never be able to master it; hold it as though you would be in fear of losing it.
Confucius, *Analects*

He who is afraid of asking is ashamed of learning.
Danish proverb

Learning is the eye of the mind.
>   Thomas Draxe, *Bibliotheca Scholastica Instructissima*

Learning is heavy, and yet it waieth not; it is fayre, and yet fewe seeke it; sweet, but few will taste of her.
>   John Florio, *Firste Fruites*

Learning in old age is like writing on sand; learning in youth is like engraving on stone.
>   Solomon Ibn Gabirol, *Choice of Pearls*

I never met a man so ignorant that I could not learn something from him.
>   Galileo, *Dialogues concerning Two New Sciences*

Learning by study must be won;
'Twas ne'er entail'd from son to son.
>   John Gay, "The Pack Horse and the Carrier," *Fables*

That which any one has been long learning unwillingly, he unlearns with proportionable eagerness and haste.
>   William Hazlitt, *The Plain Speaker*

No man deeply engaged in serious work has time to learn.
>   Joseph Hergesheimer

The mind grows by what it feeds on.
>   Josiah Holland

If you are a lover of instruction, you will be well instructed.
>   Isocrates, *Ad Demonicum*, inscribed over his school in Athens

What we first learn we best ken.
>   James Kelly, *Scottish Proverbs*

Learning must be sought; it will not come of itself.
>   Simeon ben Lakish, *Midrash Mishle*

Give up learning, and put an end to your troubles.
>   Lao-Tse, *Tao Te Ching*

I would walk twenty miles to listen to my worst enemy if I could learn something.
>   Gottfried Wilhelm von Leibniz

He who would learn to fly one day must first learn to stand and walk and run and climb and dance: one cannot fly into flying.
Friedrich Nietzsche, *Thus Spake Zarathustra*

Do not waste the hours of daylight in listening to that which you may read by night.
Sir William Osler

A person who wants to learn will always find a teacher.
Persian proverb

Too much rigidity on the part of teachers should be followed by a brisk spirit of insubordination on the part of the taught.
Agnes Repplier, *Points of View*

O! this learning, what a thing it is.
William Shakespeare, *Taming of the Shrew*

You cannot learn to skate without being ridiculous . . . . The ice of life is slippery.
George Bernard Shaw, *Fanny's First Play*, introduction

The perfect method of learning is analogous to infection. It enters and spreads.
Leo Stein, *Journey into the Self*

So much has already been written about everything that you can't find out anything about it.
James Thurber, *Lanterns and Lances*

The only things worth learning are the things you learn after you know it all.
Harry S. Truman

You must fuse at white heat the several particles of your learning into an element so ductible and so strong that nothing can destroy it without destroying you.
Owen D. Young

LETTERS

Correspondence is equal to half a meeting in person.
Arabic proverb

Nine-tenths of the letters in which people speak unreservedly of their inmost feelings are written after ten at night.
Thomas Hardy

I have received no more than one or two letters in my life that were worth the postage.
Henry David Thoreau

LIBRARY

There are times when I think the ideal library is composed solely of reference books. They are like understanding friends--always ready to meet your mood, always ready to change the subject when you have had enough of this or that.
J. Donald Adams

People can lose their lives in libraries; they ought to be warned.
Saul Bellow

An ordinary man can . . . surround himself with two thousand books . . . and thenceforward have at least one place in the world in which it is possible to be happy.
Augustine Birrell

I have always imagined that Paradise will be a kind of library.
Jorge Luis Borges

Being a writer in a library is rather like being a eunuch in a harem.
John Braine

The library is not a shrine for the worship of books. It is not a temple where literary incense must be burned or where one's devotion to the bound book is expressed in ritual. A library, to modify the famous metaphor of Socrates, should be the delivery room for the birth of ideas, a place where history comes to life.
Norman Cousins

A book is a fragile creature, it suffers the wear of time, it fears rodents, the elements, and clumsy hands . . . . So the librarian protects the books not only against mankind but also against nature and devotes his life to this war with the forces of oblivion.
Umberto Eco, *The Name of the Rose*

History records how the living ideas of civilization were saved and nourished behind a wall of books. Our libraries today serve the same cause, for the defenders of freedom must remain strong in mind and heart. From the famous metropolitan libraries of America to the modest bookmobiles that serve our rural areas, books guard the wisdom of the past and kindle the ideas of tomorrow.
Dwight D. Eisenhower

Books are a delightful society. If you go into a room filled with books, even without taking them down from their shelves, they seem to speak to you, to welcome you.
William E. Gladstone

A library is thought in cold storage.
Herbert Samuel, *A Book of Quotations*

LIFE

We're born princes and the civilizing process turns us into frogs.
Eric Berne

No two human beings have made, or ever will make, exactly the same journey in life.
Sir Arthur Keith

Life is a foreign language; all men mispronounce it.
Christopher Morley, *Thunder on the Left*

The life committed to nothing larger than itself is a meager life indeed.
Martin Seligman

The game of life is a game of boomerangs. Our thoughts, deeds, and words return to us sooner or later with astounding accuracy.
Florence Scovel Shinn

The more I see of man . . . the more I like dogs.
Madame de Staël

The mass of men lead lives of quiet desperation.
Henry David Thoreau

Nowadays most men lead lives of noisy desperation.
James Thurber, *Further Fables for Our Time*

The world is a comedy to those that think, a tragedy to those that feel.
Horace Walpole

LISTENING

To talk to someone who does not listen is enough to tense the devil.
Pearl Bailey, *Talking to Myself*

Two great talkers will not travel far together.
George Borrow, *Lavengro*

Beware of the man who goes to cocktail parties not to drink but to listen.
Pierre Daninos

He listens to good purpose who takes note.
Dante, "Inferno," *The Divine Comedy*

To do all the talking and not be willing to listen is a form of greed.
Democritus of Abdera

Speak your truth quietly and clearly; and listen to others, even the dull and ignorant; they too have their story.
   Max Ehrmann, *Desiderata*

Nature has given man one tongue and two ears, that we may hear twice as much as we speak.
   Epictetus, *Fragments*

Everything has been said already; but as no one listens, we must always begin again.
   André Gide

Never speak of yourself to others; make them talk about themselves instead: therein lies the whole art of pleasing. Everyone knows it and everyone forgets it.
   Edmond and Jules de Goncourt, *Idées et sensations*

Learning is easier gotten by the ears than by the eyes.
   Stefano Guazzo, *Civil Conversation*

There are people who instead of listening to what is being said to them are already listening to what they are going to say themselves.
   Albert Guinon

The funny thing about human beings is that we tend to respect the intelligence of, and eventually to like, those who listen attentively to our ideas even if they continue to disagree with us.
   S.I. Hayakawa

It takes a great man to make a good listener.
   Sir Arthur Helps, *Brevia*

No man would listen to you talk if he didn't know it was his turn next.
   Edgar Watson Howe

Look out fer th' feller who lets you do all th' talkin'.
   Kin Hubbard, *Abe Martin's Primer*

The only way to entertain some folks is to listen to them.
   Kin Hubbard

Wherefore, my beloved brethren, let every man be swift to hear, slow to speak, slow to wrath.
   James 1:19

No one cares to speak to an unwilling listener. An arrow never lodges in a stone: often it recoils upon the sender of it.
   Saint Jerome, *Letters*

Give us grace to listen well.
John Keble

Wisdom is the reward you get for a lifetime of listening when you'd have preferred to talk.
Doug Larson

The opposite of talking isn't listening. The opposite of talking is waiting.
Fran Lebowitz

What a mercy it would be if we were able to open and close our ears as easily as we open and close our eyes!
Georg C. Lichtenberg

One must talk little, and listen much.
Mauritanian proverb

My father used to say to me: "Son, you do all right in this world if you just remember that when you talk you are only repeating what you already know--but if you listen you may learn something."
J.P. McEvoy, *Charlie Would Have Loved This*

No one really listens to anyone else, and if you try it for a while you'll see why.
Mignon McLaughlin

A good listener is not only popular everywhere, but after a while, he knows something.
Wilson Mizner

We'll talk without listening to each other; that is the best way to get along.
Alfred de Musset

Listen, or thy tongue will keep thee deaf.
Native American proverb

People will listen a great deal more patiently while you explain your mistakes than when you explain your successes.
Wilbur N. Nesbit

If in all our practices of life we could learn to listen . . . ; if we could grasp what the other persons are saying as they themselves understand what they are saying, the major hostilities of life would disappear for the simple reason that misunderstanding would disappear.
Harry Overstreet

The grace of listening is lost if the listener's attention is demanded, not as a favor, but as a right.
Pliny the Younger

Know how to listen, and you will profit even from those who talk badly.
Plutarch

Think twice before you speak--and you'll find everyone talking about something else.
Francis Rodman

The most precious thing a man can lend is his ears.
Dagobert D. Runes, *Treasury of Thought*

Hear twice before you speak once.
Scottish proverb

Give it an understanding, but no tongue.
William Shakespeare, *Hamlet*

To listen is an effort, and just to hear is no merit. A duck hears also.
Igor Stravinsky

No syren did ever so charm the ear of the listener, as the listening ear has charmed the soul of the syren.
Sir Henry Taylor, *The Statesman*

He began to realize the deep truth that no one, broadly speaking, ever wishes to hear what you have been doing.
Angela Thirkell

But no one would possibly listen to her. No one ever listened to one unless one said the wrong thing.
Sylvia Townsend Warner

A good listener tries to understand thoroughly what the other person is saying. In the end he may disagree sharply, but before he disagrees, he wants to know exactly what it is he is disagreeing with.
Kenneth A. Wells, *Guide to Good Leadership*

The reason why we have two ears and only one mouth is that we may listen more and talk less.
Zeno

LITERATURE

It is one of the paradoxes of American literature that our writers are forever looking back with love and nostalgia at lives they couldn't wait to leave.
Anatole Broyard

Literature is the art of writing something that will be read twice; journalism what will be grasped at once.
Cyril Connolly, *Enemies of Promise*

Preaching is fatal to art in literature.
Stephen Crane

Literature is a transmission of power. Textbooks and treatises, dictionaries and encyclopedias, manuals and books of instruction--they are communications; but literature is a power line, and the motor, mark you, is the reader.
Charles P. Curtis

What is so wonderful about great literature is that it transforms the man who reads it towards the condition of the man who wrote.
E.M. Forster, *Two Cheers for Democracy*

Great literature is simply language charged with meaning to the utmost possible degree.
Ezra Pound, *How to Read*

Literature is news that *stays* news.
Ezra Pound, *ABC of Reading*

Literature is an occupation in which you have to keep proving your talent to people who have none.
Jules Renard

Literature: proclaiming in front of everyone what one is careful to conceal from one's immediate circle.
Jean Rostand, *Journal d'un caractère*

The illusion of art is to make one believe that great literature is very close to life, but exactly the opposite is true. Life is amorphous, literature is formal.
Françoise Sagan, in *Writers at Work*

LOVE

There is a silence, born of love, which expresses everything.
Count Vittorio Alfieri

Absence makes the heart grow fonder.
  Thomas Haynes Bayly

The word *love* has by no means the same sense for both sexes, and this is one cause of the serious misunderstandings that divide them.
  Simone de Beauvoir

L'amour vient de l'aveuglement,
L'amitié de la connaissance.
(Love comes from blindness,
 Friendship from knowledge.)
  Comte de Bussy-Rabutin

The way to love anything is to realize it might be lost.
  G.K. Chesterton

Real loving is walking side-by-side in day-by-day living.
  Mary Evans

Two persons love in one another the future good which they aid one another to unfold.
  Margaret Fuller

It is easier to love humanity as a whole than to love one's neighbor.
  Eric Hoffer

The supreme happiness in life is the conviction that we are loved.
  Victor Hugo, *Les misérables*

Love has as few problems as a motor car. The only problems are the driver, the passengers, and the road.
  Franz Kafka

He drew a circle that shut me out--
Heretic, rebel, a thing to flout.
But Love and I had the wit to win:
We drew a circle that took him in.
  Edwin Markham

Love is what happens to men and women who don't know each other.
  W. Somerset Maugham

To be able to say how much you love is to love but little.
  Petrarch

Loving is not just caring deeply; it's, above all, understanding.
  Françoise Sagan

Love does not consist in gazing at each other but in looking outward in the same direction.
Antoine de Saint-Exupéry, *Wind, Sand, and Stars*

Love is not love which alters when it alteration finds.
William Shakespeare, *Sonnet 16*

Love is but the discovery of ourselves in others, and the delight in the recognition.
Alexander Smith

Laurel is green for a season, and love is sweet for a day;
But love grows bitter with treason, and laurel outlives not May.
Algernon Charles Swinburne, "Hymn to Proserpine"

He alone may chastise who loves.
Rabindranath Tagore, *The Crescent Moon*

If love is the answer, could you please rephrase the question?
Lily Tomlin

You must be as clearsighted when you are loved as when you are hated. This love is only an advance payment for what they expect of you.
Yevgeny Yevtushenko, *A Precocious Autobiography*

LYING

Clever liars give details, but the cleverest don't.
Anonymous

A little inaccuracy saves a world of explanation.
C.E. Ayers

Who lies for you will lie against you.
Bosnian proverb

The world wants to be deceived.
Sebastian Brandt, *Ship of Fools*

The most terrible of lies is not that which is uttered but that which is lived.
W.G. Clarke

It takes a wise man to handle a lie; a fool had better remain honest.
Norman Douglas

Lying is an indispensable part of making life tolerable.
Bergen Evans

We lie loudest when we lie to ourselves.
    Eric Hoffer

He who permits himself to tell a lie once finds it much easier to do it a second and a third time till at length it becomes habitual.
    Thomas Jefferson

It is always the best policy to speak the truth--unless, of course, you are an exceptionally good liar.
    Jerome K. Jerome, *The Idler*

There is nothing so pathetic as a forgetful liar.
    F.M. Knowles, *A Cheerful Year Book*

There are times when lying is the most sacred of duties.
    Eugène Labiche, *Les vivacités du Capitaine Tic*

Lying increases the creative faculties, expands the ego, lessens the friction of social contacts . . . . It is only in lies, whole-heartedly and bravely told, that human nature attains through words and speech the forbearance, the nobility, the romance, the idealism, that--being what it is--it falls so short of in fact and in deed.
    Clare Boothe Luce

The biggest liar in the world is They Say.
    Douglas Malloch

If one is to be called a liar, one may as well make an effort to deserve the name.
    A.A. Milne, *The Sunny Side*

Mendacem memorem esse oportere. (A liar needs a good memory.)
    Quintilian, *Institutes of Oratory*

Repetition does not transform a lie into a truth.
    Franklin D. Roosevelt, radio address

To tell a falsehood is like the cut of a sabre; for though the wound may heal, the scar of it will remain.
    Sa'di, *Gulistan*

People lie because they don't remember clear what they saw.
People lie because they can't help making a story better than it was the way it happened.
    Carl Sandburg, *The People, Yes*

The liar's punishment is not in the least that he is not believed but that he cannot

believe anyone else.
    George Bernard Shaw

A lie never lives to be old.
    Sophocles

There is no lie that many men will not believe; there is no man who does not believe many lies; and there is no man who believes only lies.
    John Sterling

A lie is an abomination unto the Lord, and a very present help in trouble.
    Adlai Stevenson, speech

Ours is an age in which partial truths are tirelessly transformed into total falsehoods and then acclaimed as revolutionary revelations.
    Thomas Szasz, *The Second Sin*

A lie can travel half way around the world while the truth is putting on its shoes.
    Mark Twain

M

MARRIAGE

In every house of marriage there's room for an interpreter.
   Stanley Kunitz

Most of the time in married life is taken up by talk.
   Friedrich Nietzsche

In order to keep something sacred here below, it would be better if a marriage had one slave, instead of two strong-willed people.
   Madame de Staël, *Germany*

The married state is . . . the completest image of heaven and hell we are capable of receiving in this life.
   Sir Richard Steele

The best part of married life is the fights. The rest is only so-so.
   Thornton Wilder, *The Matchmaker*

MEANING

Take care of the sense and the sounds will take care of themselves.
   Lewis Carroll, *Alice's Adventures in Wonderland*

Meanings are discovered, not invented.
   Viktor Frankl, *The Will to Meaning*

The quest for certainty blocks the search for meaning. Uncertainty is the very condition to impel man to unfold his powers.
   Erich Fromm, *Man for Himself*

There is no wing like meaning.
　　Wallace Stevens, *Opus Posthumous*

MEMORY

God gave us our memories so that we might have roses in December.
　　Sir James M. Barrie

Memory is the thing you forget with.
　　Alexander Chase

A short pencil is better than a long memory.
　　Hiram Curry

Memory is the personal journalism of the soul.
　　Richard Schickel, *Time*

There's hope a great man's memory may outlive his life half a year.
　　William Shakespeare, *Hamlet*

When I was young I could remember anything, whether it had happened or not.
　　Mark Twain

MEN

The advertising media in this country continuously inform the American male of his need for indispensable signs of his virility.
　　Frances M. Beal

One good thing about being a man is that men don't have to talk to each other.
　　Peter Cocotas

My theory is that men are no more liberated than women.
　　Indira Gandhi

MONEY

Money will say more in one moment than the most eloquent lover in years.
　　Henry Fielding, *The Miser*

Of all the icy blasts that blow on love, a request for money is the most chilling and havoc-wreaking.
　　Gustave Flaubert

There's no money in poetry, but then there's no poetry in money either.
    Robert Graves

All fair words make me look to my purse.
    George Herbert, *Jacula Prudentum*

According to your purse, govern your mouth.
    Italian proverb

The two most beautiful words in the English language are: "Check enclosed."
    Dorothy Parker

When money speaks, the truth is silent.
    Russian proverb

It is difficult to get a man to understand something when his salary depends upon his not understanding it.
    Upton Sinclair

MUSIC

Music washes away from the soul the dust of everyday life.
    Berthold Auerbach

Composers should write tunes that chauffeurs and errand boys can whistle.
    Sir Thomas Beecham

Every composer knows the anguish and despair occasioned by forgetting ideas which one has not time to write down.
    Hector Berlioz

The popular song is America's greatest ambassador.
    Sammy Cahn

Music is well said to be the speech of angels.
    Thomas Carlyle

Musick is almost as dangerous as Gunpowder; and it may be requires looking after no less than the *Press* or the *Mint*. 'Tis possible a publick Regulation might not be amiss.
    Jeremy Collier

Music hath charms to soothe a savage breast,
To soften rocks, or bend a knotted oak.
    William Congreve, *The Mourning Bride*

I think popular music in this country is one of the few things in the 20th century that have made giant strides in reverse.
    Bing Crosby

Opera is when a guy gets stabbed in the back and, instead of bleeding, he sings.
    Ed Gardner, on "Duffy's Tavern," 1940s radio program

Music is Love in search of a word.
    Sidney Lanier, *The Symphony*

But to me the actual sound of the words is all-important; I feel always that the words complete the music and must never be swallowed up in it. The music is the shining path over which the poet travels to bring his song to the world.
    Lotte Lehmann

Music is the universal language of mankind.
    Henry Wadsworth Longfellow

Musick, the Mosaique of the Air.
    Andrew Marvell, *Musicks Empire*

The grandeur of man lies in song, not in thought.
    François Mauriac, *Second Thoughts*

Without music life would be a mistake.
    Friedrich Nietzsche, *The Twilight of the Idols*

Music is your own experience, your thoughts, your wisdom. If you don't live it, it won't come out of your horn.
    Charlie Parker

God, pitying the toils which our race is born to undergo, gave us the gift of song.
    Plato

Music is the moonlight in the gloomy night of life.
    Jean Paul Richter, *Titan*

These songs are to Negro culture what the works of great poets are to English culture: They are the soul of the race made manifest.
    Paul Robeson

Give me a laundry-list and I'll set it to music.
    Gioacchino Rossini

Music is "Ordered Sound."
    Harold Samuel

Jazz will endure as long as people hear it through their feet instead of their brains.
  John Philip Sousa

Jazz is the folk music of the machine age.
  Paul Whiteman

N

NAMES

Sticks and stones will break my bones, but names will never hurt me.
    English proverb

Nicknames stick to people, and the most ridiculous are the most adhesive.
    Thomas C. Haliburton

What's in a name? That which we call a rose by any other name would smell as sweet.
    William Shakespeare, *Romeo and Juliet*

NEWS

Harmony seldom makes a headline.
    Silas Bent, *Strange Bedfellows*

All I have to do to get a story on the front page of every one of AP's 2,000 clients is to mention in the lead a treatment for piles, ulcers, or sexual impotence--three conditions that every telegraph editor has, or is worried about.
    Alton Blakeslee

News is the first rough draft of history.
    Benjamin Bradlee

What the good Lord lets happen I am not ashamed to print in my paper.
    Charles A. Dana

[Television] has created a nation of news junkies who tune in every night to get their fix on the world.
    Robert MacNeil, *Time*

What you *see* is news, what you *know* is background, and what you *feel* is opinion.
    Lester Markel

News is as hard to hold as quicksilver, and it fades more rapidly than any morning-glory.
    Stanley Walker, *City Editor*

NEWSPAPERS

From the American newspapers, you'd think America was populated solely by naked women and cinema stars.
    Lady Astor

A newspaper is a circulating library with high blood pressure.
    Arthur "Bugs" Baer

He who is without a newspaper is cut off from his species.
    Phineas T. Barnum

A newspaper is lumber made malleable. It is ink made into words and pictures. It is conceived, born, grows up, and dies of old age in a day.
    Jim Bishop, *Quill*

The only reason this country is different from any place else is that once in a great while, this huge, snobbish, generally untalented news reporting business stops covering stories of interest only to itself and actually serves the public.
    Jimmy Breslin

A newspaper is always a weapon in somebody's hands.
    Claud Cockburn, *In Time of Trouble*

Call it vanity, call it arrogant presumption, call it what you wish, but I would grope for the nearest open grave if I had no newspaper to work for, no need to search for and sometimes find the winged word that just fits, no keen wonder over what each unfolding day may bring.
    Bob Considine, *It's All News to Me*

Newspapers are the world's mirrors.
    James Ellis

Every good newspaper is muckraking to some degree. It's part of our job. Where there's muck, we ought to rake it.
    James P. Gannon

Never argue with people who buy ink by the gallon.
    Tommy Lasorda

Any man with ambition, integrity--and $10,000,000--can start a daily newspaper.
    Henry Morgan

Newspapers are read at the breakfast and dinner tables. God's great gift to man is appetite. Put nothing in the paper that will destroy it.
    William Rockhill Nelson

We look like television in print.
    Allen Neuharth, *USA Today* founder

A dilemma has to get up pretty early in the morning to fool the *New York Times*.
    Edwin Newman

Never believe in mirrors or newspapers.
    John Osborne, *The Hotel in Amsterdam*, play

Let me make the newspapers and I care not what is preached in the pulpit or what is enacted in Congress.
    Wendell Phillips

Les journaux sont les cimetières des idées. (Newspapers are the cemeteries of ideas.)
    Pierre-Joseph Proudhon

Our republic and its press will rise or fall together.
    Joseph Pulitzer

More than print and ink, a newspaper is a collection of fierce individualists who somehow manage to perform the astounding daily miracle of merging their own personalities under the discipline of the deadline and retain the flavor of their own minds in print.
    Arthur Ochs Sulzberger

I buy newspapers to make money to buy more newspapers to make more money.
    Lord Thomson of Fleet (Roy Herbert Thomson)

If some great catastrophe is not announced every morning, we feel a certain void. "Nothing in the paper today," we sigh.
    Paul Valéry

Newspaper reading is an activity that leads to gradual loss of memory, since most people read the newspapers with the subconscious wish of trying to forget as fast as possible all they read.
    S.G. Warburg

I want to tell you what a newspaper means. It's a serious, sacred business. The least

smell of corruption, fear, or favoritism must never creep into its news columns . . . .
A newspaper, like Caesar's wife, must be above suspicion. Avoid even the
appearance of evil.
  Joseph Ward

They kill good trees to put out bad newspapers.
  James G. Watt, U.S. Secretary of the Interior, *Newsweek*

For forty years he has carried out, rather literally, the dictum of Mr. Dooley that the
mission of a modern newspaper is to "comfort the afflicted and afflict the comfortable."
  John K. Winkler, *W.R. Hearst*

NONVERBAL COMMUNICATION

For half a million years people have talked with head, face, hands, and body--and you
cannot abolish the habits of a half a million years.
  William Norwood Brigance

Facial expression is human experience rendered immediately visible.
  Edmund Carpenter

A smile appeared upon her face as if she'd taken it directly from her handbag and
pinned it there.
  Loma Chandler

The teeth are smiling, but is the heart?
  Congolese proverb

He might have brought an action against his countenance for libel and recovered heavy
damages.
  Charles Dickens

They might not need me; but they might.
I'll let my head be just in sight;
A smile as small as mine might be
Precisely their necessity.
  Emily Dickinson

It is surely better to be arrogant than to look it. The arrogant character insults you only
now and then; the arrogant look insults you continually.
  Denis Diderot, *Rameau's Nephew*

One's eyes are what one is, one's mouth is what one becomes.
  John Galsworthy

Your body is the harp of the soul. And it is yours to bring forth from it sweet music or confused sounds.
    Kahlil Gibran

Who can refute a sneer?
    William Paley, *The Principles of Moral and Political Philosophy*

If a man takes off his sunglasses, I can hear him better.
    Hugh Prater

I'll speak to thee in silence.
    William Shakespeare, *Cymbeline*

There was speech in their dumbness, language in their very gesture.
    William Shakespeare, *The Winter's Tale*

It was better not to speak, nor let your face or eyes show what you were feeling, because if people didn't know how you felt about them, or things, or maybe thought you had no feeling at all, they couldn't hurt as much, only a little.
    Frances Silverberg

O

OBSERVATION

You can observe a lot just by watching.
   Yogi Berra

A nose that can see is worth two that sniff.
   Eugene Ionesco

Hearing a hundred times is not as good as seeing once.
   Japanese proverb

The eyes are in the head for a reason.
   Ad Reinhardt, *Art in America*

OPEN-MINDEDNESS

Open-mindedness is not the same as empty-mindedness. To hang out a sign saying "Come right in; there is no one at home" is not the equivalent of hospitality.
   John Dewey, *Democracy and Education*

A foolish consistency is the hobgoblin of little minds.
   Ralph Waldo Emerson, "Self-Reliance," *Essays: First Series*

Each mind is pressed, and open every ear, to hear new tidings, though they no way joy us.
   Edward Fairfax

A closed mind is a dying mind.
   Edna Ferber

An open mind, like an open window, should be screened to keep the bugs out.
   Virginia Hutchinson

The closed mind, if closed long enough, can be opened by nothing short of dynamite.
   Gerald W. Johnson

If you keep your mind sufficiently open people will throw a lot of rubbish into it.
   William A. Orton

OPINIONS

Opinion is the main thing which does good or harm in the world. It is our false opinions of things which ruin us.
   Marcus Aurelius, *Meditations*

The oppression of any people for opinion's sake has rarely had any other effect than to fix those opinions deeper, and render them more important.
   Hosea Ballou

The absurd man is he who never changes his opinions.
   Auguste Barthélemy

The antiquity and general acceptance of an opinion is no assurance of its truth.
   Pierre Bayle, *Thoughts on the Comet*

The man who never alters his opinion is like standing water, and breeds reptiles of the mind.
   William Blake, *The Marriage of Heaven and Hell*

If in the last few years you hadn't discarded a major opinion or acquired a new one, check your pulse. You may be dead.
   Gelett Burgess

Circumstances are the creators of most men's opinions.
   A.V. Dicey

The only sin which we never forgive in each other is difference of opinion.
   Ralph Waldo Emerson

Stay at home in your mind. Don't recite other people's opinions.
   Ralph Waldo Emerson, "Social Aims," *Letters and Social Aims*

Tomorrow a stranger will say with masterly good sense precisely what we have thought and felt all the time, and we shall be forced to take with shame our own opinion from another.
   Ralph Waldo Emerson

Your opinion of others is apt to be their opinion of you.
   B.C. Forbes, *Epigrams*

Men who borrow their opinions can never repay their debts.
Lord Halifax, *Miscellaneous Thoughts and Reflections*

Opinions cannot survive if one has no chance to fight for them.
Thomas Mann, *The Magic Mountain*

So many men, so many opinions.
Terence, *Phormio*

A man of discernment . . . knows both his own view and that of others.
Zohar, *The Book of Splendor*

ORIGINALITY (see also CREATIVITY)

Originality does not consist of inventing a new language, but in expressing in the accepted language all possible new and personal thoughts.
René Dumesnil

Originality exists in every individual because each of us differs from the others. We are all primary numbers divisible only by ourselves.
Jean Guitton

Originality is simply a pair of fresh eyes.
Thomas Wentworth Higginson

What is originality? Undetected plagiarism.
William R. Inge

Originality is the art of concealing your source.
Franklin P. Jones

Originality does not consist in saying what no one has ever said before, but in saying exactly what you think yourself.
James Stephens

P

PATIENCE

Patience is a most necessary quality for business; many a man would rather you heard his story than granted his request.
    Lord Chesterfield

A handful of patience is worth more than a bushel of brains.
    Dutch proverb

Lack of pep is often mistaken for patience.
    Kin Hubbard

How poor are they that have not patience!
What wound did ever heal but by degrees?
    William Shakespeare, *Othello*

PEACE

They shall beat their swords into ploughshares, and their spears into pruninghooks: Nation shall not lift up sword against nation; neither shall they learn war any more.
    Isaiah 2:4

To the person who shall have done the best work for fraternity among nations, for the abolition or reduction of standing armies and promotion of peace congresses.
    Alfred Nobel

Peace is when time doesn't matter as it passes by.
    Maria Schell

Peace won by compromise is usually a short-lived achievement.
    Winfield Scott

PERFECTION

Perfection irritates as well as it attracts, in fiction as in life.
> Louis Auchincloss, *Pioneers and Caretakers: A Study of Nine American Women Novelists*

Trifles make perfection, and perfection is no trifle.
> Michelangelo

Whoever thinks a faultless piece to see,
Thinks what ne'er was, nor is, nor e'er shall be.
> Alexander Pope, "An Essay on Criticism"

Perfection is such a nuisance that I often regret having cured myself of tobacco.
> Émile Zola

PERSISTENCE

Nothing in the world can take the place of persistence. Talent will not; nothing is more common than unsuccessful men with talent. Genius will not; unrewarded genius is almost a proverb. Education will not; the world is full of educated derelicts. Persistence and determination alone are omnipotent.
> Calvin Coolidge

The best way out is always through.
> Robert Frost

The force of the waves is in their perseverance.
> Gila Guri

Everything's hard when you first try.
> Paz Shilling, eight years old

PERSUASION

Writing good editorials is chiefly telling the people what they think, not what you think.
> Arthur Brisbane

People are more willing to be convinced by the calm perusal of an argument than in a personal discussion.
> Emily Collins

The best cause requires a good pleader.
> Dutch proverb

Anyone who has been cajoled, trapped, or persuaded into any kind of promise, usually looks upon himself more as a victim than as a criminal, when he succumbs to fate.
R.B. Cunninghame Graham

Several excuses are always less convincing than one.
Aldous Huxley

Well-chosen phrases are a great help in the smuggling of offensive ideas.
Vladimir Jabotinsky, *The War and the Jew*

Men may be convinced, but they cannot be pleased, against their will.
Samuel Johnson, *The Lives of the English Poets*

We may convince others by our arguments; but we can only persuade them by their own.
Joseph Joubert, *Pensées*

You have not converted a man because you have silenced him.
John Morley

In science the credit goes to the man who convinces the world, not to the man to whom the idea first occurs.
Sir William Osler

We are usually convinced more easily by reasons we have found ourselves than by those which have occurred to others.
Blaise Pascal, *Pensées*

Nothing sways the stupid more than arguments they can't understand.
Cardinal de Retz, *Mémoires*

One of the best ways to persuade others is with your ears--by listening to them.
Dean Rusk

The shepherd always tries to persuade the sheep that their interests and his own are the same.
Stendhal

To study persuasion intensively is to study human nature minutely.
Charles H. Woolberg

For God's sake don't say yes until I've finished talking.
Darryl F. Zanuck

PHOTOGRAPHY

Photography can never grow up if it imitates some other medium. It has to walk alone; it has to be itself.
  Berenice Abbott

It is my intention to present--through the medium of photography-- intuitive observations of the natural world which may have meaning to the spectators.
  Ansel Adams

I really believe there are things nobody would see if I didn't photograph them.
  Diane Arbus

Photographers are the only dictators in America.
  Celâl Bayar, President of Turkey

The photographer's palette [is] a thousand shades of gray.
  H.E. Clark

The camera is one of the greatest liars of our time.
  John Gunther

Everything is a subject. Every subject has a rhythm. To feel it is the raison d'être. The photograph is a fixed moment of such a raison d'être, which lives on in itself.
  André Kertész

The camera can be the most deadly weapon since the assassin's bullet. Or it can be the lotion of the heart.
  Norman Parkinson

The camera makes everyone a tourist in other people's reality, and eventually in one's own.
  Susan Sontag, *New York Review of Books*

Photography is a major force in explaining man to man.
  Edward Steichen

Magazine photography is the mural painting of modern times.
  Gene Thornton

PLAGIARISM

Goethe said there would be little left of him if he were to discard what he owed to others.
  Charlotte Cushman

The immature poet imitates; the mature poet plagiarizes.
    T.S. Eliot

I'd rather be caught holding up a bank than stealing so much as a two-word phrase from another writer; but . . . when someone has the wit to coin a useful word, it ought to be acclaimed and broadcast or it will perish.
    Jack Smith

PLAYING

Man is most nearly himself when he achieves the seriousness of a child at play.
    Heraclitus

The natural state of man is play.
    Carl Jung

In our play we reveal what kind of people we are.
    Ovid, *The Art of Love*

Avoid compulsion and let early education be a manner of amusement. Young children learn by games; compulsory education cannot remain in the soul.
    Plato

PLAY WRITING

If a playwright is funny, the English look for a serious message, and if he's serious, they look for a joke.
    Sacha Guitry

There are only two hard things to write in a play--the first act and the third act. The second act will take care of itself.
    Moss Hart

Between the writing of plays, in the vast middle of the night, when our children and their mother slept, I sat alone, and my thoughts drifted back in time, murmuring the remembrance of things past into the listening ear of silence; fashioning thoughts to unspoken words, and setting them down upon the sensitive tablets of the mind.
    Sean O'Casey

When the characters are really alive before their author, the latter does nothing but follow them in their actions, in their words, in the situations which they suggest to him.
    Luigi Pirandello, *Six Characters in Search of an Author*

You write a hit play the same way you write a flop.
    William Saroyan

When I was writing *The Shadow of the Glen* I got more aid than any learning would have given me from a chink in the floor of the old Wicklow house where I was staying, that let me hear what was being said by the servant girls in the kitchen.
John M. Synge

POETRY

It's silly to suggest the writing of poetry as something ethereal, a sort of soul-crashing emotional experience that wrings you. I have no fancy ideas about poetry. It doesn't come to you on the wings of a dove. It's something you work hard at.
Louise Bogan

Were it not for poetry, life would be a constant bleeding. Poetry grants us what nature denies us: a golden age which never rusts, a spring which never fades, unbeclouded happiness, and eternal youth.
Ludwig Börne

Written by a sponge dipped in warm milk and sprinkled with sugar.
John Ciardi, on traditional poetry for children

Poetry, like schoolboys, by too frequent and severe correction, may be cowed into dullness!
Samuel Taylor Coleridge, *Anima Poetae*

[Poetry is the] expression of the hunger for elsewhere.
Benjamin De Casseres, *The Muse of Lies*

If I read a book and it makes my whole body so cold that no fire can ever warm me, I know *that* is poetry. If I feel physically as if the top of my head were taken off, I know *that* is poetry. These are the only ways I know it. Is there any other way?
Emily Dickinson

Poetry should help, not only to refine the language of the time, but to prevent it from changing too rapidly.
T.S. Eliot, "Milton"

Like a piece of ice on a hot stove the poem must ride on its own melting.
Robert Frost, *Collected Poems*

Poetry is the renewal of words forever and ever. Poetry is that by which we live forever and ever unjaded. Poetry is that by which the world is never old.
Robert Frost

Writing free verse is like playing tennis with the net down.
Robert Frost

Poetry is the language in which man explores his own amazement.
    Christopher Fry

Every poem is in a sense a kiss bestowed upon the world, but mere kisses do not produce children.
    Goethe

The English method [of poetry] is to fill the mind with beauty; the Greek method was to set the mind to work.
    Edith Hamilton, *The Greek Way*

Experience has taught me, when I am shaving of a morning, to keep watch over my thoughts, because, if a line of poetry strays into my memory, my skin bristles so that the razor ceases to act . . . . The seat of this sensation is the pit of the stomach.
    A.E. Housman, *The Name and Nature of Poetry*

If Poetry comes not as naturally as the Leaves to a tree it had better not come at all.
    John Keats

I think Poetry should surprise by a fine excess and not by Singularity--it should strike the Reader as a wording of his own highest thoughts, and appear almost a Remembrance.
    John Keats

When power leads man toward arrogance, poetry reminds him of his limitations. When power narrows the area of man's concern, poetry reminds him of the richness and diversity of existence. When power corrupts, poetry cleanses.
    John F. Kennedy, last major public speech, Amherst College, October 26, 1963

First, I do not sit down at my desk to put into verse something that is already clear in my mind. If it were clear in my mind, I should have no incentive or need to write about it . . . .   We do not write in order to be understood; we write in order to understand.
    C. Day Lewis, *The Poetic Image*

A poem should not mean
But be.
    Archibald MacLeish, *Ars Poetica*

To this generation I would say: Memorize some bit of verse of truth or beauty.
    Edgar Lee Masters

Most people ignore most poetry
because
most poetry ignores most people.
    Adrian Mitchell, *Poems*

Poetry heals the wounds inflicted by reason.
Novalis, *Detached Thoughts*

Poetry is articulate painting, and painting is silent poetry.
Plutarch, *Moralia*

Poetry atrophies when it gets too far from music.
Ezra Pound, *How to Read*

Poetry . . . is the revelation of a feeling that the poet believes to be interior and personal--which the reader recognizes as his own.
Salvatore Quasimodo

More often than prose or mathematics, poetry is received in a hostile spirit, as if its publication were an affront to the reader.
Michael Roberts

Ordering a man to write a poem is like commanding a pregnant woman to give birth to a redheaded child. You can't do it--it's an act of God.
Carl Sandburg

Poetry is the achievement of the synthesis of hyacinths and biscuits.
Carl Sandburg, *Atlantic Monthly*

Poetry is the opening and closing of a door, leaving those who look through to guess about what is seen during a moment.
Carl Sandburg, *Atlantic Monthly*

Poetry is the record of the best and happiest moments of the happiest and best minds.
Percy Bysshe Shelley, *A Defence of Poetry*

A poem is never finished, only abandoned.
Paul Valéry

Poetry is the spontaneous overflow of powerful feelings: it takes its origin from emotion recollected in tranquility.
William Wordsworth, preface, *Lyrical Ballads*

A poet's autobiography is his poetry. Anything else can be only a footnote.
Yevgeny Yevtushenko

POETS

It is a sad fact about our culture that a poet can earn much more money writing or talking about his art than he can by practicing it.
W.H. Auden, *The Dyer's Hand*

A great poet is the most precious jewel of a nation.
Ludwig van Beethoven, letter to Bettina von Arnim

To know how to say what others only know how to think is what makes men poets or sages; and to dare to say what others only dare to think makes men martyrs or reformers--or both.
Elizabeth Charles

We all write poems; it is simply that poets are the ones who write in words.
John Fowles, *The French Lieutenant's Woman*

A man sometimes does not recognize as his own what he has written as a poet.
Victor Hugo

The poet dreams being awake. He is not possessed by his subject but has dominion over it.
Charles Lamb, *Essays of Elia*

Poets aren't very useful.
Because they aren't consumeful or very produceful.
Ogden Nash

It is the role of the poet to look at what is happening in the world and to know that quite other things are happening.
V.S. Pritchett, *The Myth Makers*

Many people like a poet just as they like their cheese: they find him good only when moldered by maggots.
Moritz Gottlieb Saphir, *Humoristische Abende*

That is what all poets do: they talk to themselves out loud; and the world overhears them.
George Bernard Shaw, *Candida*

The poet is the priest of the invisible.
Wallace Stevens, *Opus Posthumous*

A poet looks at the world as a man looks at a woman.
Wallace Stevens, *Opus Posthumous*

The poet is a man who lives at last by watching his moods. An old poet comes at last to watch his moods as narrowly as a cat does a mouse.
Henry David Thoreau, *Journal*

POLITICAL COMMUNICATION

I look forward to these confrontations with the press to kind of balance up the nice and pleasant things that come to me as President.
  Jimmy Carter

Nobody believes a rumor here in Washington until it's officially denied.
  Edward Cheyfitz

You campaign in poetry. You govern in prose.
  Mario Cuomo

Since a politician never believes what he says, he is surprised when others believe him.
  Charles de Gaulle

I should have had a circuitous answer that was a non-answer.
  Geraldine A. Ferraro

Ronald Reagan is clearly to television what Franklin Roosevelt was to radio.
  David Gergen

You wait for a gem in an endless sea of blah.
  Lawrence Grossman, on television coverage of political conventions

The press conference is a politician's way of being informative without saying anything. Should he accidentally say something, he has at his side a press officer who immediately explains it away by "clarifying" it.
  Emery Kelen, *Platypus at Large*

Politicians are the same all over. They promise to build a bridge even where there is no river.
  Nikita Khrushchev

The secret of the demagogue is to make himself as stupid as his audience so that they believe they are as clever as he.
  Karl Kraus

A politician must often talk and act before he has thought and read.
  Lord Thomas Babington Macaulay

I have never found in a long career of politics that criticism is ever inhibited by ignorance.
  Harold Macmillan, *Wall Street Journal*

America is the only country in the world where you can go on the air and kid politicians--and where politicians go on the air and kid the people.
    Groucho Marx

A politician is . . . trained in the art of inexactitude. His words tend to be blunt or rounded, because if they have a cutting edge they may later return to wound him.
    Edward R. Murrow

All my major works have been written in prison . . . . I would recommend prison not only to aspiring writers but to aspiring politicians, too.
    Jawaharlal Nehru

Your mind must always go, even while you're shaking hands and going through all the maneuvers. I developed the ability long ago to do one thing while thinking another.
    Richard M. Nixon

Never lose your temper with the press or the public is a major rule of political life.
    Christabel Parkhurst

I want my questions answered by an alert and experienced politician, prepared to be grilled and quoted--not my hand held by an old smoothie.
    William Safire

De Gaulle did not call in "writers"; the very idea is grotesque. The leader who allows others to speak for him is abdicating.
    May Sarton

The relationship between a reporter and a President is exactly the same as that between a pitcher and a batter . . . they both are trying to keep each other away.
    Merriman Smith

The hardest thing about any political campaign is how to win without proving that you are unworthy of winning.
    Adlai Stevenson

You have only three real friends: Jesus Christ, Sears, Roebuck, and Gene Talmadge.
    Eugene Talmadge, U.S. Senator, to the voters of Georgia

I have a habit of comparing the phraseology of communiques, one with another across the years, and noting a certain similarity of words, a certain similarity of optimism in the reports which followed the summit meetings, and a certain similarity in the lack of practical results during the ensuing years.
    Margaret Thatcher

The last thing a political party gives up is its vocabulary.
    Alexis de Tocqueville

Polls are like sleeping pills designed to lull the voters into sleeping on election day. You might call them "sleeping polls."

    Harry S. Truman

I've often wondered how some people in positions of this kind . . . manage without having had any acting experience.

    Barbara Walters

I am not anxious to be the loudest voice or the most popular. But I would like to think that, at a crucial moment, I was an effective voice of the voiceless, an effective hope of the hopeless.

    Whitney M. Young, Jr., *National Urban League News*

POSITIVE THINKING

Any positive thinker is compelled to see everything in the light of his own convictions.

    Antoinette Brown Blackwell

It is never too late to be what you might have been.

    George Eliot

He started to sing as he tackled the thing
That couldn't be done, and he did it.

    Edgar A. Guest

Believe you can, and you can; believe you will, and you will. See yourself achieving, and you will achieve. Never give up; giving up is like letting go of a life preserver when you are almost saved.

    Gardner Hunting

No pessimist ever discovered the secrets of the stars, or sailed to an uncharted land, or opened a new heaven to the human spirit.

    Helen Keller

I'm not going to let *that* rob me of my joy.

    Charlotte McPherson

In the long run the pessimist may be proved right, but the optimist has a better time on the trip.

    Daniel Reardon

In these times you have to be an optimist to open your eyes when you awake in the morning.

    Carl Sandburg

Possunt quia posse videntur. (They can because they think they can.)
> Virgil, *Aeneid*

POWER

Silence is power.
> African proverb

The more frugal and honest you are the less power you need.
> Maxwell Anderson

Don't let your will roar when your power only whispers.
> Thomas Fuller

The more noise a man or a motor makes the less power there is available.
> William James

The truth is that all men having power are to be mistrusted.
> James Madison

What nonsense! No one ever seduced by books? Since the invention of writing, people have been seduced by the power of the word into all kinds of virtues, follies, conspiracies, and gallantries. They have been lured to religion, urged into sins, and lured into salvation.
> Phyllis McGinley, *Ladies' Home Journal*

He that I am reading seems always to have the most force.
> Michel de Montaigne

Speak softly, and carry a big stick.
> Theodore Roosevelt

Power buries those who wield it.
> Talmud

In some ways, certain books are more powerful by far than any battle.
> Henry A. Wallace

It is generally presumed that there are four great powers which govern society--the sword, the pen, women, and money. The fifth great power is journalism.
> I.M. Wise

PRACTICE

I never practice. I always play.
> Wanda Landowska, in *An Encyclopedia of Quotations about Music*

Unused capacities atrophy, cease to be.
Tillie Olsen

The final performance, which may take a minute, has been preceded by many hours of rehearsal.
Logan Pearsall Smith

People prefer theory to practice because it involves them in no more real responsibility than a game of checkers, while it permits them to feel they're doing something serious and important.
Leo Stein, *Journey into the Self*

Practice may not make perfect, but it does make better.
Cindy Wood

PRAISE

There is no amount of praise which a man and an author cannot bear with equanimity. Some authors can even stand flattery.
Maurice Baring, *Dead Letters*

He who praises everybody, praises nobody.
James Boswell

The advantage of doing one's praising for oneself is that one can lay it on so thick and exactly in the right places.
Samuel Butler, II, *The Way of All Flesh*

If you want children to improve, let them hear the nice things you say about them to others.
Haim G. Ginott

We find it easy to believe that praise is sincere: why should anyone lie in telling us the truth?
Jean Rostand, *De la vanité*

The ego is never so intact that one can't find a hole in which to plug a little praise.
Phyllis Theroux, *Parents Magazine*

I can live for two months on a good compliment.
Mark Twain

There is nothing you can say in answer to a compliment. I have been complimented myself a great many times, and they always embarrass me--I always feel that they have not said enough.
Mark Twain, "Fulton Day, Jamestown"

Nothing is truer in a sense than a funeral oration: it tells precisely what the dead man should have been.
    Louis Gustave Vapereau

PREJUDICE

Racism is the snobbery of the poor.
    Raymond Aron

A prejudice is a vagrant opinion without visible means of support.
    Ambrose Bierce, *The Devil's Dictionary*

Being a star has made it possible for me to get insulted in places where the average Negro could never *hope* to go and get insulted.
    Sammy Davis, Jr., *Yes I Can*

Prejudice, which sees what it pleases, cannot see what is plain.
    Aubrey de Vere

I am free of all prejudice. I hate everyone equally.
    W.C. Fields

I hang onto my prejudices; they are the testicles of my mind.
    Eric Hoffer, *Before the Sabbath*

A great many people think they are thinking when they are merely rearranging their prejudices.
    William James

In overcoming prejudice, working together is even more effective than talking together.
    Ralph W. Sockman

It is never too late to give up our prejudices.
    Henry David Thoreau

Prejudice is an opinion without judgment.
    Voltaire

PREPARATION

If you wish me to speak for an hour, give me ten minutes to prepare. If, however, you want me to speak for ten minutes, give me a month.
    Winston Churchill

I did not speak often, and never without preparation.
    Sir Edward Clarke

I have made it a fixed rule to spend one hour in preparation for every minute I am to speak--five minutes, five hours.
    William DeWitt Hyde

First, go into your bathroom, take off your clothes, and step into a nice hot shower. With the water going off full blast, open your mouth and say in a normal tone of voice, "Good evening, folks!"
    Art Linkletter

Chance favors the prepared mind.
    Louis Pasteur

If you don't prepare for a speech, you are letting people hear your first draft.
    Lilless McPherson Shilling

If you rehearse in the car, you don't get any argument.
    Bob Snyder

Of course, sometimes it is not possible to prepare an address fully, but it is much better to do so even if you intend to speak extemporaneously.
    Robert A. Taft

There is something about me that thinks you're not ready unless you've been in a tizzy. You need a certain amount of tizzy.
    Martha Tumblin

No man not inspired can make a good speech without preparation.
    Daniel Webster

PROBLEMS

There is no new knowledge without a new problem.
    Leo Baeck, *The Interrelations of Judaism, Science, Philosophy, and Ethics,* lecture

Problems are messages.
    Shakti Gawain

Crisis reveals character. It also creates character.
    Carol Gilligan

Mistakes are a fact of life. It is the response to error that counts.
Nikki Giovanni

Failure doesn't last forever.
Linda Gottlieb

The best remedy for disturbances is to let them run their course, for so they quiet down.
Baltasar Gracian

In my experience, the worst thing you can do to an important problem is discuss it.
Simon Gray, *Otherwise Engaged*

Do you know what *really* would be a marvelous invention? A remote control device for life. Whenever you found yourself in an unpleasant situation, you could pull out your remote control and switch around until you found a situation you liked better.
Lewis Grizzard

To live is to have problems and so to solve problems is to grow intellectually.
J.P. Guilford

Fortunately, psychoanalysis is not the only way to resolve inner conflicts. Life itself remains a very effective therapist.
Karen Horney

When you are in trouble, people who call to sympathize are really looking for the particulars.
Edgar Watson Howe, *Country Town Sayings*

We all live behind bars, which we carry around with us.
Franz Kafka

I learned much from my teachers, more from my books, and most from my troubles.
Isaac Kaminer, *Baraitot de Rabbi Yitzhak*

When written in Chinese, the world *crisis* is composed of two characters--one represents danger and one represents opportunity.
John F. Kennedy

Problems are the price of progress--don't bring me anything but problems.
Charles Kettering

In crises the most daring course is often the safest.
Henry A. Kissinger

If you have problems, let me know. I may not have a solution, but I have been working on my empathy for a long time.
    Forrest Lang

Mishaps are like knives, that either serve or cut us, as we grasp them by the blade or the handle.
    James Russell Lowell

Man has to suffer. When he has no real afflictions, he invents some.
    José Martí, *Adulterous Thoughts*

Life would be dull and colorless but for the obstacles that we have to overcome and the fights that we have to win.
    Jawaharlal Nehru

Learn to accept in silence the minor aggravations, cultivate the gift of taciturnity, and consume your own smoke with an extra draught of hard work.
    Sir William Osler

The basic problem most people have is that they're doing nothing to solve their basic problem.
    Bob Richardson

When you live next to the cemetery, you can't weep for everyone.
    Russian proverb

We can't wait for the storm to blow over; we've got to learn to work in the rain.
    Pete Silas, Chairman, Phillips Petroleum

Nobody knows the trouble I've seen--and most of it never happened.
    Mark Twain

PROFANITY

Oaths are but words, and words are but wind.
    Samuel Butler, *Hudibras*

Vulgarity is the garlic in the salad of taste.
    Cyril Connolly

Swearing was invented as a compromise between running away and fighting.
    Finley Peter Dunne, *Mr. Dooley's Opinions*

There are worse words than cuss words; there are words that hurt.
    Tillie Olsen

Unto the lewd all things are lewd.
    Theodore Schroeder, *A Challenge to Sex Censors*

In certain trying circumstances, urgent circumstances, desperate circumstances, profanity furnishes a relief denied even to prayer.
    Mark Twain

PRONUNCIATION

If you take care to pronounce correctly the words usually mispronounced, you may have the self-love of the purist, but you will not sell any goods.
    George Ade, *Fables in Slang*

He pronounced some of his words as if they were corks being drawn out of bottles.
    Winston Graham

PROPAGANDA

There is no need for propaganda to be rich in intellectual content.
    Paul Joseph Goebbels

The great masses of the people . . . will more easily fall victims to a great lie than to a small one.
    Adolf Hitler

Much of what has been achieved by the art of education in the nineteenth century has been frustrated by the art of propaganda in the twentieth.
    Harold J. Laski, *A Grammar of Politics*

A propagandist is a specialist in selling attitudes and opinions.
    Hans Speier

PROVERBS

Proverbs are short sentences drawn from long experience.
    Miguel de Cervantes

Proverbs may be called the literature of the illiterate.
    Frederick S. Cozzens

A proverb is the child of experience.
    English proverb

The maxims of men disclose their hearts.
    French proverb

A new maxim is often a brilliant error.
    Malesherbes

Almost every wise saying has an opposite one, no less wise, to balance it.
    George Santayana, *Little Essays*

The proverbist knows nothing of the two sides of a question. He knows only the roundness of answers.
    Karl Shapiro, *The Bourgeois Poet*

PUBLICITY

The price of justice is eternal publicity.
    Arnold Bennett, *Things That Have Interested Me*

I have often wondered if newspaper publicity would not have had thirteen original colonies fighting among themselves if we had been present at their conference at the time of the Revolution.
    William Hard

Of course I'm a publicity hound. Aren't all crusaders? How can you accomplish anything unless people know what you're trying to do?
    Vivien Kellems

Publicity is to a contemporaneous culture what the great public monuments and churches and buildings of state are to more traditional societies, an instrument of solidarity; but because publicity is only generalized gossip of the in-group, the solidarity it creates is synthetic.
    Christopher Lasch

I don't care if you criticize us, agree with us, or disagree with us. Just mention us, that is all we ask.
    David Owen

My advice to any diplomat who wants to have a good press is to have two or three kids and a dog.
    Carl Rowan

PUBLIC OPINION

The daily press has more power in the shaping of public opinion than any other force in America.
    Jerome D. Barnum

Every man speaks of public opinion, and means by public opinion, public opinion minus his opinion.
G.K. Chesterton, *Heretics*

The people are a many-headed beast.
Horace, *Epistles*

Opinion surveys are people who don't matter reporting on opinions that do matter.
John A. Lincoln

No one ever went broke underestimating the taste of the American public.
H.L. Mencken

Today's public opinion, though it may appear as light as air, may be tomorrow's legislation--for better or for worse.
Earl Newsome

In America, public opinion is the leader.
Frances Perkins

Private opinion is weak, but public opinion is almost omnipotent.
Harriet Beecher Stowe

PUBLIC RELATIONS

Public relations is the attempt, by information, persuasion, and adjustment, to engineer public support for an activity, cause, movement, or institution.
Edward L. Bernays

Shakespeare, in the familiar lines, divided great men into three classes: those born great, those who achieve greatness, and those who have greatness thrust upon them. It never occurred to him to mention those who hire public relations experts and press secretaries to make themselves look great.
Daniel J. Boorstin

I have found it [public relations] to be the craft of arranging truths so that people will like you. Public-relations specialists make flower arrangements of the facts, placing them so that the wilted and less attractive petals are hidden by sturdy blooms.
Alan Harrington

Public relations doesn't mean treating the public like relations.
Ronald C. Henderson

The businessman only wants two things said about his company--what he pays his public-relations people to say and what he pays his advertising people to say. He

doesn't like anybody ever to look above, beyond, or over that.
  Don S. Hewitt, producer of *60 Minutes*

Planned public relations is usually a stepchild of conflict.
  Kinsey M. Robinson

PUBLISHING

Posterity--what you write for after being turned down by publishers.
  George Ade

The printing press is either the greatest blessing or the greatest curse of modern times, one sometimes forgets which.
  Sir James M. Barrie, *Sentimental Tommy*

I wonder whether what we are publishing now is worth cutting down trees to make paper for the stuff.
  Richard Brautigan

I am a publisher--a hybrid creature: one part star-gazer, one part gambler, one part businessman, one part midwife, and three parts optimist.
  Cass Canfield, recalled on his death

The day of the printed word is far from ended. Swift as is the delivery of the radio bulletin, graphic as is television's eyewitness picture, the task of adding meaning and clarity remains urgent. People cannot and need not absorb meanings at the speed of light.
  Erwin Canham, editor, *Christian Science Monitor*

The Printing press may be strictly denominated a Multiplication Table as applicable to the mind of man. The art of printing is a multiplication of mind.
  Richard Carlile

There is nothing much wrong with American newspapers today except us publishers.
  John Cowles

A publisher lives by what he feels. Authors do too, but authors are blind moles working their solitary way along their individual tunnels; the publisher is like the Pied Piper of Hamelin, piping his way along a path he wants them to follow.
  Lovat Dickson

Publishers are all cohorts of the devil; there must be a special hell for them somewhere.
  Goethe

I do not think publishing is hard work. I like publishing because it is possible to survive one's mistakes.
    Michael Joseph

No author dislikes to be edited as much as he dislikes not to be published.
    Russell Lynes

Publishing a volume of verse is like dropping a rose petal down the Grand Canyon and waiting for the echo.
    Don Marquis

Getting published is like eating peanuts. Once you start you can't stop.
    Mary Maxwell

Gutenberg made everybody a reader. Xerox makes everybody a publisher.
    Marshall McLuhan, interview in the *Washington Post*

Though an angel should write, still 'tis devils must print.
    Thomas Moore

Printing is the adjunct of civilization, for through it we receive the bulk of the world's intelligence. It is the chief means in the transmission of knowledge from age to age and era to era. It is the art that preserves all others.
    Catherine Talbott

The trouble with the publishing business is that too many people who have half a mind to write a book do so.
    William Targ

PUNCTUATION

No iron can stab the heart with such force as a period put just at the right place.
    Isaac Babel

One who uses many periods is a philosopher; many interrogations, a student; many exclamations, a fanatic.
    J.L. Basford

PUNS

Hanging is too good for a man who makes puns. He should be drawn and quoted.
    Fred Allen

A man who would make so vile a pun would not scruple to pick a pocket.
    John Dennis

I never knew an enemy to puns who was not an ill-natured man.
  Charles Lamb

May my last breath be drawn through a pipe and exhaled in a pun.
  Charles Lamb

A pun is a pistol let off at the ear; not a feather to tickle the intellect.
  Charles Lamb, *Last Essays of Elia*

A pun is the lowest form of humor--when you don't think of it first.
  Oscar Levant

If lawyers are disbarred and clergymen defrocked, doesn't it follow that electricians can be delighted; musicians denoted; cowboys deranged; models deposed; tree surgeons debarked, and dry cleaners depressed?
  Virginia Ostman

Of puns it has been said that they who most dislike them are least able to utter them.
  Edgar Allan Poe

Q

QUESTIONS

Hypothetical questions get hypothetical answers.
    Joan Baez, *Daybreak*

Young Rabi . . . went to the public schools and stood at the top of his class with little effort. He remembers vividly how his mother would tirelessly inquire, "Did you ask any good questions in school today?"
    Frances Bellow

Better ask twice than lose your way once.
    Danish proverb

A timid question will always receive a confident answer.
    Charles J. Darling, *Scintillae Juris*

Hasty questions require slow answers.
    Dutch proverb

A fool may ask more questions in an hour than a wise man can answer in seven years.
    English proverb

A wise man's question contains half the answer.
    Solomon Ibn Gabirol, *Choice of Pearls*

Why do people always expect authors to answer questions? I am an author because I want to *ask* questions. If I had answers I'd be a politician.
    Eugene Ionesco

Some questions just don't have answers.
    Francis Jenkins

The way a question is asked limits and disposes the ways in which any answer to it--right or wrong--may be given.
    Susanne K. Langer

It is easier to judge a person's mental capacity by his questions than by his answers.
    Duc de Levis, *Maxims*

The scientist is not a person who gives the right answers; he's the one who asks the right questions.
    Claude Lévi-Strauss, *Le cru et le cuit*

Man will not live without answers to his questions.
    Hans Morgenthau

A question is a trap and an answer is your foot in it.
    John Steinbeck

There are no foolish questions and no man becomes a fool until he has stopped asking questions.
    Charles Steinmetz

I feel very strongly about putting questions; it partakes too much of the style of the day of judgment. You start a question, and it's like starting a stone. You sit quietly on top of a hill; and away the stone goes, starting others.
    Robert Louis Stevenson, *The Strange Case of Dr. Jekyll and Mr. Hyde*

Better ask ten times than go astray once.
    Yiddish proverb

QUOTATIONS

One must be a wise reader to quote wisely and well.
    A. Bronson Alcott

Quotations are a columnist's bullpen. Stealing someone else's words frequently spares the embarrassment of eating your own.
    Peter Anderson

The surest way to make a monkey of a man is to quote him.
    Robert Benchley, *My Ten Years in a Quandry*

Quoting: The act of repeating erroneously the words of another.
    Ambrose Bierce, *The Devil's Dictionary*

Next to being witty yourself, the best thing is being able to quote another's wit.
    Christian N. Bovee

To quote copiously and well requires taste, judgement, and erudition, a feeling for the beautiful, an appreciation of the noble, and a sense of the profound.
  Christian N. Bovee

They lard their lean books with the fat of others' works.
  Robert Burton, *The Anatomy of Melancholy*

Appropriate things are meant to be appropriated.
  Samuel Butler

For quotable good things, for pregnant aphorisms, for touchstones of ready application, the opinions of the English judges are a mine of instruction and a treasury of joy.
  Benjamin N. Cardozo

A quote is a personal possession and you have no right to change it.
  Ray Cave

Most anthologists . . . of quotations are like those who eat cherries . . . first picking the best ones and winding up by eating everything.
  Sébastien-Roch Nicolas de Chamfort, *Maximes et pensées*

I have always been very struck by the advantage enjoyed by people who lived at an earlier period of the world than one's own. They had the first opportunity of saying the right thing. Over and over again it had happened to me to think of something which I thought was worth saying, only to find that it had been already exploited, and very often spoiled, before I had an opportunity of saying it.
  Winston Churchill

It is a good thing for an uneducated man to read books of quotations.
  Winston Churchill, *My Early Life*

The wisdom of the wise and the experience of the ages are perpetuated by quotation.
  Benjamin Disraeli

By necessity, by proclivity, and by delight, we all quote.
  Ralph Waldo Emerson

The next thing to saying a good thing yourself is to quote one. All minds quote.
  Ralph Waldo Emerson

Next to the originator of a good sentence is the first quoter of it.
  Ralph Waldo Emerson, *Letters and Social Aims*

Stay at home in your mind. Don't recite other people's opinions. I hate quotations.

Tell me what you know.
>   Ralph Waldo Emerson, *Journals*

If you quote, do not be too nice in your quotation, nor correct a man if he misquotes slightly.
>   Clifton Fadiman

I think we must . . . quote whenever we feel that the allusion is interesting or helpful or amusing.
>   Clifton Fadiman

To each reader those quotations are agreeable that neither strike him as hackneyed nor rebuke his ignorance.
>   H.W. Fowler

A writer expresses himself in words that have been used before because they give his meaning better than he can give it himself, or because they are beautiful or witty, or because he expects them to touch a chord of association in his reader, or because he wishes to show that he is learned and well read.
>   H.W. Fowler, "Quotation," *A Dictionary of Modern English Usage*

When a thing has been said, and well said, have no scruple: Take it and copy it.
>   Anatole France

Nothing gives an author so much pleasure as to find his works respectfully quoted by other learned authors.
>   Benjamin Franklin

Stronger than an army is a quotation whose time has come.
>   W.I.E. Gates

Apt quotations carry convictions.
>   William E. Gladstone

Quotations (such as have point and lack triteness) from the great old authors are an act of filial reverence on the part of the quoter, and a blessing to a public grown superficial and external.
>   Louise Imogen Guiney, *Scribner's Magazine*

Have you ever observed that we pay much more attention to a wise passage when it is quoted than when we read it in the original author?
>   Philip G. Hamerton

This is not the age of pamphleteers. It is the age of the engineers. The speak-gap is mightier than the pen. Democracy will not be salvaged by men who talk fluently,

debate forcefully, and quote aptly.
    Lancelot Hogben, *Science for the Citizen*

Every quotation contributes something to the stability or enlargement of the language.
    Samuel Johnson

I will not say that he willfully misquotes, but he does fail to quote accurately.
    Abraham Lincoln

I quote others only in order to better express myself.
    Michel de Montaigne

The difference between my quotations and those of the next man is that I leave out the inverted commas.
    George Moore

There are two kinds of marriages--where the husband quotes the wife, or where the wife quotes the husband.
    Clifford Odets

Many excelled me: I know it.
Yet I am quoted as much as they.
    Ovid's epitaph

A book that furnishes no quotations is, *me judice*, no book--it is a play thing.
    Thomas Love Peacock

Misquotation is, in fact, the pride and privilege of the learned. A widely read man never quotes accurately, for the rather obvious reason that he read too widely.
    Hesketh Pearson, *Common Misquotations*

When you see yourself quoted in print and you're sorry you said it, it suddenly becomes a misquotation.
    Laurence J. Peter

A fine quotation is a diamond on the finger of a witty person, but a pebble in the hands of a fool.
    Joseph Roux, *Meditations of a Parish Priest*

To say that anything was a quotation was an excellent method, in Eleanor's eyes, for withdrawing it from discussion.
    Saki (H.H. Munro)

He that lays down precepts for the governing of our lives and moderating our passions, obliges humanity, not only in the present, but in all future generations.
    Seneca

I often quote myself; it adds spice to my conversation.
George Bernard Shaw

It is little service to the reader to print windy, dozen-page letters of no high quality when a few quoted phrases and a sentence of summary would have conveyed the nature of most of them.
John Skow

To be occasionally quoted is the only fame I care for.
Alexander Smith

It is better to be quotable than to be honest.
Tom Stoppard

He read to learn, and not to quote; to digest and master, and not merely to display.
Joseph Story

For in New York as in the rest of the country famous remarks are very seldom quoted correctly.
Simeon Strunsky, *No Mean City*

She quoted a friend who used to say any advice is good as long as it is strong enough.
Alice B. Toklas

In the dying world I come from quotation is a national vice. No one would think of making an after-dinner speech without the help of poetry. It used to be the classics, now it's lyric verse.
Evelyn Waugh, *The Loved One*

Now we sit through Shakespeare in order to recognize the quotations.
Orson Welles

Everything of importance has been said before by somebody who did not discover it.
Alfred North Whitehead

Most people are other people. Their thoughts are someone else's opinions, their lives a mimicry, their passions a quotation.
Oscar Wilde, *De Profundis*

The nice thing about quotes is that they give us a nodding acquaintance with the originator, which is often socially impressive.
Kenneth Williams, *Acid Drops*

Some for renown, on scraps of learning dote.
And think they grow immortal as they quote.
Edward Young, *Love of Fame*

R

RADIO

Radio brings you information at the speed of light, but it has not increased the speed of thought by a single m.p.h. In the wake of sensation, wisdom still plods in the dust far to the rear.
John Crosby

If liberty is to flourish, a government should never be allowed to force people to listen to any radio program.
William O. Douglas

Radio is the manly art of shouting brave words into a defenseless microphone.
Peter Lind Hayes

It [radio] came from nowhere, blazed up like a brush fire, pulled us together at the bottom of the Depression, held us together through a war, galloped up to the brink of television, and fell over dead.
Sam Moore

Radio has succumbed to its first enemy: it has become static.
Gilbert Seldes, *The Great Audience*

The ideal voice for radio may be defined as having no substance, no sex, no owner, and a message of importance to every housewife.
Harry V. Wade

READERS

Readers are plentiful; thinkers are rare.
Harriet Martineau

Every reader reads himself. The writer's work is merely a kind of optical instrument that makes it possible for the reader to discern what, without this book, he would perhaps never have seen in himself.

Marcel Proust, *Within a Budding Grove*

Care should be taken, not that the reader *may* understand, but that he *must* understand.

Quintilian, *Institutes of Oratory*

Everybody else is working to change, persuade, tempt, and control them. The best readers come to fiction to be free of all that noise.

Philip Roth, in *Writers at Work*

Along with responsible newspapers we must have responsible *readers*. No matter how conscientiously the publisher and his associates perform their work, they can do only half the job. Readers must do the rest. The fountain serves no useful purpose if the horse refuses to drink.

Arthur Hays Sulzberger

READING

I took a course in speed reading, learning to read straight down the middle of the page, and I was able to go through *War and Peace* in twenty minutes. It's about Russia.

Woody Allen

Repeat reading for me shares a few things with hot-water bottles and thumb-sucking: comfort, familiarity, the recurrence of the expected.

Margaret Atwood

Superficial the reading of grown men in some sort must ever be; it is only once in a lifetime that we can know the passionate reading of youth.

Walter Bagehot, *Literary Studies*

To read without reflecting is like eating without digesting.

Edmund Burke

It is more profitable to reread some old books than to read new ones, just as it is better to repair and add to an old temple than to build one entirely new.

Chang Chao, *Yumengying*

There is a great deal of difference between an eager man who wants to read a book and the tired man who wants a book to read.

G.K. Chesterton

A man may as well expect to grow stronger by always eating as wiser by always reading.

Jeremy Collier

The man who reads only for improvement is beyond the hope of much improvement before he begins.
    Jonathan Daniels

Why are we reading, if not in hope that the writer will magnify and dramatize our days, will illuminate and inspire us with wisdom, courage, and the hope of meaningfulness, and press upon our minds the deepest mysteries, so we may feel again their majesty and power?
    Annie Dillard

Reading, to most people, means an ashamed way of killing time disguised under a dignified name.
    Ernest Dimnet, *The Art of Thinking*

Read only brief or systematic books, one at a time, and books beautifully written, on fine paper and attractively bound. Read in an attractive room, and from time to time let your eyes gaze upon beautiful objects so that you will come to love what you read.
    Profiat Duran, *Maaseh Ephod*

One always tends to overpraise a long book, because one has got through it.
    E.M. Forster, *Abinger Harvest*

You may have tangible wealth untold:
Caskets of jewels and coffers of gold.
Richer than I you can never be--
I had a Mother who read to me.
    Strickland Gillilan, "The Reading Mother," in *The Best Loved Poems of the American People*

Reading is a joy, but not an unalloyed joy. Books do not make life easier or more simple, but harder and more interesting.
    Harry Golden, *So What Else Is New?*

I have not placed reading before praying because I regard it as more important, but because in order to pray aright, we must understand what we are praying for.
    Angelina Grimké

The art of reading is to skip judiciously.
    Philip G. Hamerton, *The Intellectual Life*

In a very real sense, people who have read good literature have lived more than people who cannot or will not read . . . . It is not true that we have only one life to live; if we can read, we can live as many more lives and as many kinds of lives as we wish.
    S.I. Hayakawa

All that wearies profoundly is to be condemned for reading. The mind profits little by what is termed heavy reading.
    Lafcadio Hearn, *On Reading in Relation to Literature*

Every man who knows how to read has it in his power to magnify himself, to multiply the ways in which he exists, to make his life full, significant, and interesting.
    Aldous Huxley

The end of reading is not more books but more life.
    Holbrook Jackson

People seldom read a book which is given to them. The way to spread a work is to sell it at a low price.
    Samuel Johnson

I am a part of all that I have read.
    John Kieran

Where do I find all the time for not reading so many books?
    Karl Kraus, *Aphorisms and More Aphorisms*

And does anyone seriously believe that a half-hour dramatization on television of some historical event or some current problem actually can convey as much as could be learned in the same time by reading twenty or thirty pages of a well-written composition? The truth is that most of the "modern" methods of communication are inefficient, wasteful, and inadequate when addressed to anyone competent to read.
    Joseph Wood Krutch

What is reading but silent conversation?
    Walter Savage Landor, *Imaginary Conversations*

Until I feared I would lose it, I never loved to read. One does not love breathing.
    Harper Lee, *To Kill a Mockingbird*

Some people read because they are too lazy to think.
    Georg C. Lichtenberg

Reading books in one's youth is like looking at the moon through a crevice; reading books in middle age is like looking at the moon in one's courtyard; and reading books in old age is like looking at the moon on an open terrace. This is because the depth of benefits of reading varies in proportion to the depth of one's own experience.
    Lin Yutang

If fiction is to help at all in the process of living, it is by illuminating its conflicts and its ambiguities. We read to find out more about what it is like to be a human being,

not to be told how to be one.
    Penelope Lively

Have you ever rightly considered what the mere ability to read means? That it is the key which admits us to the whole world of thought and fancy and imagination? To the company of saint and saga, of the wisest and the wittiest at their wisest and wittiest moment? That it enables us to see with the keenest eyes, hear with the finest ears, and listen to the sweetest voices of all time?
    James Russell Lowell

Only one hour in the normal day is more pleasurable than the hour spent in bed with a book before going to sleep, and that is the hour spent in bed with a book after being called in the morning.
    Rose Macaulay

The pleasure of all reading is doubled when one lives with another who shares the same books.
    Katherine Mansfield

There are people who read too much: the bibliobibuli. I know some who are constantly drunk on books, as other men are drunk on whiskey or religion. They wander through this most diverting and stimulating of worlds in a haze, seeing nothing and hearing nothing.
    H.L. Mencken, *Minority Report*

What I mean by reading is not skimming, not being able to say as the world saith, "Oh, yes, I've read that!," but reading again and again, in all sorts of moods, with an increase of delight every time, till the thing read has become a part of your system and goes forth along with you to meeting any new experience you may have.
    Charles Edward Montague, *A Writer's Notes on His Trade*

Love of reading enables a man to exchange the wearisome hours of life which come to every one, for hours of delight.
    Montesquieu

There is hardly any grief that an hour's reading will not dissipate.
    Montesquieu, *Mes pensées*

It is one of the oddest things in the world that you can read a page or more and think of something utterly different.
    Christian Morgenstern, *Aphorisms*

There is danger in reading bad books, but also greater danger in not reading good ones.
    John Courtney Murray

Just the knowledge that a good book is waiting one at the end of a long day makes that day happier.

Kathleen Norris, *Hands Full of Living*

Reading is the sole means by which we slip, involuntarily, often helplessly, into another's skin, another's voice, another's soul.

Joyce Carol Oates

Reading isn't an occupation we encourage among police officers. We try to keep the paper work down to a minimum.

Joe Orton, *Loot*, play

Whoever would know himself, let him open a book.

Jean Paulham, *Elements*

No man can read with profit that which he cannot learn to read with pleasure.

Noah Porter, *Books and Reading*

When you read, *read*! Too many students just half read. I never read without summarizing--and so understanding what I read. The art of memory is the art of understanding.

Roscoe Pound

We must form our minds by reading deep rather than wide.

Quintilian, *Institutes of Oratory*

Life being very short, and the quiet hours of it few, we ought to waste none of them in reading valueless books.

John Ruskin, *Sesame and Lilies*

There are two motives for reading a book: one, that you enjoy it; the other, that you can boast about it.

Bertrand Russell

To expect a man to retain everything that he has ever read is like expecting him to carry about in his body everything that he has ever eaten.

Arthur Schopenhauer, *Parerga and Paralipomena*

Language is the soul of the intellect, and reading is the essential process by which that intellect is cultivated beyond the commonplace experiences of everyday life.

Charles Scribner

Sir, he hath never fed of the dainties that are bred in a book.
He hath not eat paper, as it were; he hath not drunk ink:

His intellect is not replenished; he is only an animal,
Only sensible in the duller parts.
  William Shakespeare, *Love's Labour's Lost*

If a man has read a great number of books, and does not think things through, he is only a bookcase.
  Shu Shuehmou

People say that life is the thing, but I prefer reading.
  Logan Pearsall Smith, *Trivia*

Reading is seeing by proxy.
  Herbert Spencer, *The Study of Sociology*

Reading is to the mind what exercise is to the body.
  Sir Richard Steele, *Tatler*

My education was the liberty I had to read indiscriminately and all the time, with my eyes hanging out.
  Dylan Thomas

Book love . . . is your pass to the greatest, the purest, and the most perfect pleasure that God has prepared for His creatures.
  Anthony Trollope

The man who does not read good books has no advantage over the man who can't read them.
  Mark Twain

Thanks to my friends for their care in my breeding,
Who taught me betimes to love working and reading.
  Isaac Watts, *The Sluggard*

My mother read to me in the big bedroom in the mornings, when we were in her rocker together, which ticked in rhythm as we rocked, as though we had a cricket accompanying the story.
  Eudora Welty

Who knows if Shakespeare might have thought less if he had read more?
  Edward Young

REJECTION

It circulated for five years, through the halls of fifteen publishers, and finally ended up with Vanguard Press, which, as you can see, is rather deep into the alphabet.
  Patrick Dennis, on *Auntie Mame*

To read some magazines makes one wonder what the editor has rejected.
  Farmer's Almanac

Some writers enclose a stamped, self-addressed envelope for the manuscript to come
back in; this is too much of a temptation to the editor.
  Ring Lardner

RELATIONSHIPS

Please all, and you will please none.
  Aesop

Relationships are only as alive as the people engaging in them.
  Donald B. Ardell

If you don't like someone, the way he holds his spoon will make you furious; if you do
like him, he can turn his plate over into your lap and you won't mind.
  Irving Becker

In reconciling one human to another, the one who forgives restores the integrity of
being.
  Jacqueline Collins

An intense, one-to-one involvement is as socially conditioned as a hamburger and a
malt.
  Marie Edwards

It is always disagreeable when a person we consider our inferior likes or loathes the
same things we do, thereby becoming our equal.
  Maxim Gorky

People who cannot bear to be alone are generally the worst company.
  Albert Guinon

The eye of a needle is not too narrow to hold two friends that agree; the breadth of the
world is not sufficiently wide to contain in its fold two foes.
  Shekel Ha-Kodesh

What is important to a relationship is a harmony of emotional roles and not too great
a disparity in the general level of intelligence.
  Mirra Komarovsky

We are almost always bored by the very people by whom it is vital not to be bored.
  François de La Rochefoucauld, *Maxims*

We read that we ought to forgive our enemies; but we do not read that we ought to forgive our friends.
Cosimo de' Medici

No individual is isolated. He who is sad, saddens others.
Antoine de Saint-Exupéry

Only the brave know how to forgive.
Laurence Sterne, *Sermons*

If you want a person's faults, go to those who love him. They will not tell you, but they know.
Robert Louis Stevenson

We live in a time of fast food, fast relationships.
Brenda Tolomen

The best index to a person's character is (a) how he treats people who can't do him any good, and (b) how he treats people who can't fight back.
Abigail Van Buren

Seek acquaintance with the wise, intimacy with the good.
Xiphilinus

RESEARCH

A drug is a substance which when injected into a guinea pig produces a scientific paper.
Anonymous

Basic research is when I'm doing what I don't know I'm doing.
Wernher von Braun

The average Ph.D. thesis is nothing but a transference of bones from one graveyard to another.
J. Frank Dobie

The way to do research is to attack the facts at the point of greatest astonishment.
Celia Green

What is research but a blind date with knowledge?
Will Henry

The ink of the scholar is more sacred than the blood of the martyr.
Mohammed

Inquiry is a duty, and error in research is not a sin.
Benjamin ben Moses Nahawendi, *Sefer Dinim* (Book of Rules)

No one but the author is interested in a long list of references stuck onto the end of an article like barnacles on a ship's bottom.
Editor, *New England Journal of Medicine*, 1964

A scholar knows no boredom.
Jean Paul Richter, *Hesperus*

Research is when you study and write--a lot.
Paz Shilling, four years old

The primary reason to publish is because the future of the profession depends on it.
Margretta M. Styles

The ambitious teacher can only rise in the academic bureaucracy by writing at complicated length about writing that has already been much written about.
Gore Vidal, *Matters of Fact and of Fiction*

REVISION

There is no such thing as good writing. There is only good rewriting.
Louis D. Brandeis

I like to rewrite. Once it is all down then you've got it trapped. I have never rewritten anything that I didn't believe was improved when I was done.
Barnaby Conrad, in Bill Downey, *Right Brain . . . Write On!*

I keep going over a sentence. I nag it, gnaw it, pat and flatter it.
Janet Flanner (Genêt)

I have never been good at revising. I always thought I made things worse by recasting and retouching. I never knew what was meant by choice of words. It was one word or none.
Robert Frost

There are days when the result is so bad that no fewer than five revisions are required. In contrast, when I'm greatly inspired, only four revisions are needed.
John Kenneth Galbraith

I ordinarily write three or four handwritten pages and then rework them for two hours. I can work for four hours, or forty-five minutes. It's not a matter of time. I set a realistic objective: How can I inch along to the next paragraph? Inching is what it is. It's not: How can I handle the next chapter? How can I get to the next stage in a way that I like? I think about that as I walk the dog or walk the twenty minutes from my apartment to the studio where I work.

> Joseph Heller, in *Writers at Work*

You must make frequent use of the eraser if you want to write something that deserves a second reading.

> Horace, *Satires*

Read over your compositions and, when you meet a passage which you think is particularly fine, strike it out.

> Samuel Johnson

Writing without feedback is like going though a tunnel without headlights on.

> Jan Keller

If it sounds like writing, I rewrite it.

> Elmore Leonard

Together they wiggle each word like a loose tooth, to see which, if any, will fall out.

> Barbara Melville

I have written--often several times--every word I have ever published. My pencils outlast their erasers.

> Vladimir Nabokov

I believe in impulse and naturalness, but followed by discipline in the cutting.

> Anaïs Nin

I can't write five words but that I change seven.

> Dorothy Parker, in *Writers at Work*

I've made it a practice to do all my first drafts on the backs of circulars or old correspondence or something like that so I can't submit them. Then I revise, as often as necessary. When I find I'm having trouble now I'll put an old manuscript in the typewriter and just do rough drafts for awhile on the back as roughly and crudely as necessary. Then I go back and rewrite that part. That seems to have kept me from any prolonged blocks in the last few years. Nobody's going to see it but me, and I suspend criticism. I just plunge ahead and put down whatever occurs to me . . . . I can always change it, but meanwhile I've managed to get a little further along.

> Frederick Pohl

I conscientiously tried [rewriting], but found that my first draft was almost always better than my second. This discovery has saved me an immense amount of time. I do not, of course, apply it to the substance, but only to the form.

> Bertrand Russell, "How I Write"

Rewriting is when playwriting really gets to be fun . . . . In baseball, you only get three swings and you're out. In rewriting, you get almost as many swings as you want and you know, sooner or later, you'll hit the ball.

   Neil Simon

Do not be afraid of the possibility that what you write will fail to live up to your expectations, or those of the school teacher on your shoulder. Anything you write can be changed. Anything you write can be thrown away. You have nothing to lose. But if you write nothing in the first place, you have nothing to gain, nothing to change. Most professional writers rewrite and rewrite. They would never publish their first drafts, and they would never publish at all if they did not write their first drafts.

   Frank Smith, *Writing and the Writer*

As a general rule, run your pen through every other word you have written; you have no idea what vigor it will give your style.

   Sydney Smith, in Lady Holland, *A Memoir of the Reverend Sydney Smith*

Blot out, correct, insert, refine,
Enlarge, diminish, interline;
Be mindful, when invention fails,
To scratch your head, and bite your nails.

   Jonathan Swift, "On Poetry"

Not that the story need be long, but it will take a long while to make it short.

   Henry David Thoreau

I am an obsessive rewriter, doing one draft and then another and another, usually five. In a way, I have nothing to say, but a great deal to add.

   Gore Vidal

RHETORIC

Rhetoric is the art of ruling the minds of men.

   Plato

If rhetoric teaches nothing else, she requires that her student make up his mind, that he take decision only after search and full inquiry, that he speak from his convictions with all the skill he can acquire.

   Karl R. Wallace

We must ask of rhetoric that it lend a hand in freeing us from the forces that have brutalized us.

   Otis M. Walter

RISK TAKING

All things are difficult before they are easy.
John Morley

Nothing would be done at all, if a man waited till he could do it so well that no one could find fault with it.
Cardinal John Henry Newman

If you climb to the top of Mount Everest, you know you've accomplished something; if you get to the top of some grassy knoll, the feeling isn't there.
William Nolen, *The Making of a Surgeon*

He who never makes mistakes makes nothing.
Eric Partridge

S

SATIRE

The job of satire is to frighten and enlighten.
    Richard Condon

A satirist is a man who discovers unpleasant things about himself and then says them about other people.
    Peter McArthur

The boldest way, if not the best,
To tell men freely of their foulest faults,
To laugh at their vain deeds and vainer thoughts.
    John Sheffield, *Essay on Satire*

Satire is a sort of glass, wherein beholders do generally discover everybody's face but their own.
    Jonathan Swift, *The Battle of the Books*

SCIENCE

Every great scientific truth goes through three stages. First, people say it conflicts with the Bible. Next, they say it has been discovered before. Lastly, they say they have always believed it.
    Louis Agassiz, in Bennett Cerf, *The Laugh's on Me*

Along come the scientists and make the words of our fathers into folklore.
    S.Y. Agnon

That is the essence of science: ask an impertinent question, and you are on the way to the pertinent answer.
    Jacob Bronowski, *The Ascent of Man*

Every great advance in science has issued from a new audacity of imagination.
    John Dewey, *The Quest for Certainty*

Nothing in science has any value to society if it is not communicated.
    Anne Roe, *The Making of a Scientist*

SCREENWRITING

I write scripts to serve as skeletons awaiting the flesh and sinew of images.
    Ingmar Bergman

Hollywood . . . scripts . . . a medium where both syntax and the language itself were subjected to horrid mutilation by young men who thought of themselves as writers and who proved it by the enormous salaries they received from those higher up who were even less knowledgeable of the mother tongue.
    Bessie Breuer

You sell a screenplay like you sell a car. If someone drives it off a cliff, that's it.
    Rita Mae Brown

If my books had been any worse, I should not have been invited to Hollywood, and if they had been any better, I should not have come.
    Raymond Chandler

In Hollywood, writers are considered only the first drafts of human beings.
    Frank Deford

The honors Hollywood has for the writer are as dubious as tissue-paper cuff links.
    Ben Hecht

I'm a Hollywood writer; so I put on a sports jacket and take off my brain.
    Ben Hecht

Remember the pungent analysis given by a young poet of the state of mind that permeates the authors in the capital of filmdom. "The films take our best ideas," he said. "We work like slaves, inventing, devising, changing, to please the morons who run this game. We spend endless hours in search of novel ideas, and in the end, what do we get for it?. . . A lousy fortune!"
    Alexander King, *Rich Man, Poor Man, Freud, and Fruit*

SECRETS

Three may keep a secret, if two of them are dead.
    Benjamin Franklin, *Poor Richard's Almanack*

If you would wish another to keep your secret, first keep it yourself.
    Seneca

To whom you tell your secrets, to him you resign your liberty.
    Spanish proverb

SELF

Seriously to contemplate one's abject personal triteness is probably the most painful act a man can perform.
    Robert M. Adams, *Bad Mouth*

You grow up the day you have your first real laugh--at yourself.
    Ethel Barrymore

O, would the Lord the gift to gie us
to see ourselves as others see us.
    Robert Burns, "To a Louse"

Man will become better when you show him what he is like.
    Anton Chekhov

Nothing is so easy as to deceive one's self; for what we wish, that we readily believe.
    Demosthenes, *Third Olynthiac*

Be yourself; who else is better qualified?
    Frank J. Giblin, II

The ancient sage who concocted the maxim, "Know Thyself" might have added, "Don't Tell Anyone!"
    H.F. Henrichs

Don't compromise yourself. You are all you've got.
    Janis Joplin

Character, like a photograph, develops in darkness.
    Yousuf Karsh

I think self-awareness is probably the most important thing towards being a champion.
    Billie Jean King

Knowing others is wisdom.
Knowing the self is enlightenment.
    Lao-Tse, *Tao Te Ching*

When one is a stranger to oneself then one is estranged from others too.
   Anne Morrow Lindbergh, *Gift from the Sea*

To have a quiet mind is to possess one's mind wholly; to have a calm spirit is to possess one's self.
   Hamilton Mabie

And this above all: to thine own self be true. And it must follow as the night the day, thou canst not then be false to any man.
   William Shakespeare, *Hamlet*

We know what we are but not what we may be.
   William Shakespeare, *Hamlet*

Somebody's boring me . . . . I think it's me.
   Dylan Thomas

If a man does not keep pace with his companions, perhaps it is because he hears a different drummer. Let him step to the music which he hears, however measured or far away.
   Henry David Thoreau

Trying to define yourself is like trying to bite your own teeth.
   Alan Watts

SELF-ESTEEM

Nothing is a greater impediment to being on good terms with others than being ill at ease with yourself.
   Honoré de Balzac

A strong sense of identity gives man an idea he can do no wrong; too little accomplishes the same.
   Djuna Barnes, *Nightwood*

I know merit; those praising me are right.
   Pierre Corneille

I felt so tall within--I felt as if the power of the nation was with me.
   Frederick Douglass

Discouragement is simply the despair of wounded self-love.
   François Fénelon

You have no idea what a poor opinion I have of myself--and how little I deserve it.
   W.S. Gilbert

Self-respect cannot be hunted. It cannot be purchased. It is never for sale. It cannot be fabricated out of public relations: it comes to us when we are alone, in quiet moments, in quiet places, when we suddenly realize that knowing the good, we have done it; knowing the beautiful, we have served it; knowing the truth, we have spoken it.

Alfred Whitney Griswold

He who undervalues himself is justly undervalued by others.

William Hazlitt, "On the Knowledge of Character"

How a man feels about himself is often more critical to his success than what he is objectively.

Harry Levinson

All you need is to tell a man that he is no good ten times a day, and very soon he begins to believe it himself.

Lin Yutang, *With Love and Irony*

If you love yourself meanly, childishly, timidly, even so shall you love your neighbor.

Maurice Maeterlinck, *Wisdom and Destiny*

The most difficult secret for a man to keep is his own opinion of himself.

Marcel Pagnol

No one can make you feel inferior without your consent.

Eleanor Roosevelt, *This Is My Story*

Self-respect will keep a man from being abject when he is in the power of enemies, and will enable him to feel that he may be in the right when the world is against him.

Bertrand Russell, *Authority and the Individual*

Public opinion is a weak tyrant compared with our own private opinion. What a man thinks of himself, that it is which determines, or rather indicates, his fate.

Henry David Thoreau, *Walden*

If I only had a little humility, I would be perfect.

Ted Turner

A man cannot be comfortable without his own approval.

Mark Twain, "What Is Man?"

SILENCE

An inability to stay quiet is one of the most conspicuous failings of mankind.

Walter Bagehot

Let no one tell me that silence gives consent, because whoever is silent dissents.
    Maria Isabel Barreno

Drawing on my fine command of language, I said nothing.
    Robert Benchley

God has given to man a cloak whereby he can conceal his ignorance, and in this cloak he can enwrap himself at any moment, for it always lies near at hand. This cloak is silence.
    Bhartrihari, *The Niti Sataka*

Silence is one of the hardest things to refute.
    Josh Billings

If a thing goes without saying, let it.
    Jacob Braude, *Treasury of Wit and Humor*

If we have not quiet in our minds, outward comfort will do no more for us than a golden slipper on a gouty foot.
    John Bunyan

Silence is sometimes the severest criticism.
    Charles Buxton

Speech is silvern. Silence is golden.
    Thomas Carlyle, *Sartor Resartus*

Silence is the cruelty of the provincial.
    Coco Chanel

The first virtue, son, if thou wilt learn,
Is to restrain and keep well thy tongue.
    Geoffrey Chaucer, *The Manciple's Tale*

Silence is the unbearable repartee.
    G.K. Chesterton

Silence is a true friend who never betrays.
    Confucius

If you don't say anything, you won't be called on to repeat it.
    Calvin Coolidge

I have noticed that nothing I never said ever did me any harm.
    Calvin Coolidge

Adults don't want equality. They want quiet.
    Bill Cosby

Silence is sweeter than speech.
    Dinah Mulock Craik

Let thy speech be better than silence, or be silent.
    Dionysius the Elder

What is the use of speech? Silence were fitter:
Lest we should still be wishing things unsaid.
    Ernest Dowson

A time to rend, and a time to sew; a time to keep silence, and a time to speak.
    Ecclesiastes 3:7

Blessed is the man who, having nothing to say, abstains from giving us wordy evidence of the fact.
    George Eliot, *The Impressions of Theophrastus Such*

Silence gives consent.
    Oliver Goldsmith, *The Good-natured Man*

Silence is argument carried on by other means.
    Ernesto "Che" Guevara

The temple of our purest thoughts is silence.
    Sarah J. Hale

Some persons talk simply because they think sound is more manageable than silence.
    Margaret Halsey

Next to entertaining or impressive talk, a thorough-going silence manages to intrigue most people.
    Florence Hurst Harriman

Words would have been as presumptuous as an embrace: yet the inadequacy of silence was painful.
    Shirley Hazzard

The beginning of wisdom is silence.
    Hebrew proverb

A man is known by the silence he keeps.
    Oliver Herford

Think twice before you speak and then say it to yourself.
Elbert Hubbard

Very often the quiet fellow has said all he knows.
Kin Hubbard

Silence gives consent, or a horrible feeling that nobody's listening.
Franklin P. Jones

You will find that deep place of silence right in your room, your garden, or even your bathtub.
Elisabeth Kübler-Ross

It is a great misfortune neither to have enough wit to talk well nor enough judgment to be silent.
Jean de La Bruyère

Silence is the wit of fools.
Jean de La Bruyère, *Characters*

People who make no noise are dangerous.
Jean de La Fontaine, *Fables*

With virtue and quietness one may conquer the world.
Lao-Tse

It is never so difficult to speak as when we are ashamed of our silence.
François de La Rochefoucauld, *Maxims*

Keep quiet and people will think you are a philosopher.
Latin proverb

He who, silent, loves to be with us, and who loves us in our silence, has touched one of the keys that warm hearts.
Johann Kaspar Lavater

There are very few people who don't become more interesting when they stop talking.
Mary Lowry

To communicate through silence is a link between the thoughts of man.
Marcel Marceau

The deepest feeling always shows itself in silence;
not in silence, but restraint.
Marianne Moore

If you keep your mouth shut, you will never put your foot in it.
   Austin O'Malley

Look wise; say nothing, and grunt. Speech was given to conceal thought.
   Sir William Osler

What silences we keep, year after year,
With those who are most near to us,
And dear!
   Nora Perry

Into the closed mouth the fly does not get.
   Philippine proverb

Even a fool, when he holdeth his peace, is counted wise; and he that shutteth his lips
is esteemed a man of understanding.
   Proverbs 17:28

Whoso keepeth his mouth and his tongue keepeth his soul from troubles.
   Proverbs 21:23

I regret often that I have spoken; never that I have been silent.
   Publilius Syrus, *Sententiae*

Of a distinguished general it was said that "he could hold his tongue in eight
languages."
   Jean Paul Richter

To say the right thing at the right time, keep still most of the time.
   John W. Roper

Judicious silence is far preferable to the truth roughly told.
   St. Francis de Sales

It is difficult to keep quiet if you have nothing to do.
   Arthur Schopenhauer

Wise men say nothing in dangerous times.
   John Selden

I believe in the discipline of silence, and could talk for hours about it.
   George Bernard Shaw

The cruelest lies are often told in silence.
   Robert Louis Stevenson, *Virginibus Puerisque*

For words divide and rend;
But silence is most noble till the end.
    Algernon Charles Swinburne

You can only improve on saying nothing by saying nothing often.
    Frank Tyger

Don't talk unless you can improve the silence.
    Vermont proverb

He knew the precise psychological moment when to say nothing.
    Oscar Wilde, *The Picture of Dorian Gray*

Silence is the ultimate eloquence of sorrow.
    William Winter

It was one of those parties where you cough twice before you speak, and then decide
not to say it after all.
    P.G. Wodehouse

SIMPLICITY

The most difficult thing in the world is to make things simple enough, and enticing
enough, to cause readers to turn the page.
    Helen Gurley Brown

The composing room has an unlimited supply of periods available to terminate short,
simple sentences.
    Turner Catledge, former Managing Editor, *New York Times*

Genius is the ability to reduce the complicated to the simple.
    C.W. Ceram

To be simple is the best thing in the world; to be modest is the next best thing. I am
not sure about being quiet.
    G.K. Chesterton, *All Things Considered*

Make everything as simple as possible, but not simpler.
    Albert Einstein

I would never use a long word where a short one would answer the purpose. I know
there are professors in this country who "ligate" arteries. Other surgeons only tie them,
and it stops the bleeding just as well.
    Oliver Wendell Holmes, Sr.

Don't, Sir, accustom yourself to use big words for little matters.
Samuel Johnson

The greatest things gain by being expressed simply; they are spoiled by emphasis. But one must say trifling things nobly, because they are supported solely by expression, tone, and manner.
Jean de La Bruyère, *Characters*

Thou canst not adorn simplicity. What is naked or defective is susceptible of decoration; what is decorated is simplicity no longer.
Walter Savage Landor, *Imaginary Conversations*

To write simply is as difficult as to be good.
W. Somerset Maugham

Remember, few people are fooled by fancy language. It's been a long time since I've heard anyone say, "I can't understand what he is saying; he must be highly intelligent."
Douglas Mueller

Speak properly, and in as few words as you can, but always plainly; for the end of speech is not ostentation, but to be understood.
William Penn, *More Fruits of Solitude*

I never write *metropolis* for seven cents because I can get the same price for *city*. I never write *policeman* because I can get the same money for *cop*.
Mark Twain

Executives at every level are prisoners of the notion that a simple style reflects a simple mind. Actually, a simple style reflects hard work and hard thinking.
William K. Zinsser

SINCERITY

The secret of success is sincerity: once you can fake that, you've got it made.
Jean Giraudoux

The most exhausting thing in life is being insincere.
Anne Morrow Lindbergh

If you have to make an unpopular speech, give it all the sincerity you can muster; that's the only way to sweeten it.
Cardinal de Retz, *Mémoires*

It is dangerous to be sincere unless you are also stupid.
George Bernard Shaw, *Man and Superman*

A little sincerity is a dangerous thing, and a great deal of it is absolutely fatal.
Oscar Wilde, "The Critic as Artist"

It isn't always your words that others listen to, but the strength and sincerity behind them. When a sincere man speaks, the world moves.
Paramahansa Yogananda

SLANDER

The proper way to check slander is to despise it; attempt to overtake and refute it, and it will outrun you.
Saint Augustine

There are different ways of assassinating a man--by pistol, sword, poison, or moral assassination. They are the same in their results except that the last is more cruel.
Napoléon Bonaparte, *Maxims*

The slanderer is like one who flings dust at another when the wind is contrary; the dust returns on him who threw it.
Buddha

The more implausible a slander is, the better fools remember it.
Casimir Delavigne

He who blackens others does not whiten himself.
German proverb

A single sentence sometimes casts an odium on a man's character that years of integrity will not efface.
Jean-Jacques Rousseau

An irresponsible reporter in front of a typewriter can do more damage than a drunken surgeon swinging a knife in the operating room.
Damon Runyon

The worthiest people are frequently attacked by slander, as we generally find that to be the best fruit which the birds have been pecking at.
Jonathan Swift

It takes your enemy and your friend, working together, to hurt you to the heart: the one to slander you and the other to get the news to you.
Mark Twain

To persevere in one's duty and be silent is the best answer to calumny.
George Washington, farewell address, 1796

SLANG

Slang has no country, it owns the world . . . . It is the voice of the god that dwells in the people.
Ralcy Husted Bell, *The Mystery of Words*

Slang, which used to be the toy or tool of the immature and the less educated, now salts--and sometimes sours--the speech of the better educated as well.
Theodore M. Bernstein

Slang is . . . vigorous and apt. Probably most of our vital words were once slang; one by one timidly made sacrosanct in spite of ecclesiastical and other wraths.
John Galsworthy, *Castles in Spain and Other Screeds*

Slang is a poor-man's poetry.
John Moore

Slang is the vengeance of the anonymous masses for the linguistic thralldom imposed on them by the educated classes.
Mario Pei

Slang is a language that rolls up its sleeves, spits on its hands, and goes to work.
Carl Sandburg, *New York Times*

SLOGANS

A good catchword can obscure analysis for fifty years.
Johan Huizinga, *The Waning of the Middle Ages*

I never met a man I didn't like.
Will Rogers

There's a difference between a philosophy and a bumper sticker.
Charles M. Schulz

Man is a creature who lives not upon bread alone, but primarily by catchwords.
Robert Louis Stevenson

SOLITUDE

People who take time to be alone usually have depth, originality, and quiet reserve.
John Miller

All man's troubles come from not knowing how to sit still in one room.
Blaise Pascal, *Pensées*

In solitude especially do we begin to appreciate the advantage of living with someone who knows how to think.
    Jean-Jacques Rousseau, *Confessions*

Language has created the word *loneliness* to express the pain of being alone, and the word *solitude* to express the glory of being alone.
    Paul Tillich

Loneliness can be conquered only by those who can bear solitude.
    Paul Tillich

SPEAKERS

The best orator is one who can make men see with their ears.
    Arabic proverb

The Speaker's eye: the most elusive organ that Nature ever created.
    Stanley Baldwin

Lecturer: One with his hand in your pocket, his tongue in your ear, and his faith in your patience.
    Ambrose Bierce, *The Devil's Dictionary*

You can't usually tell whether a man is a finished speaker until he sits down.
    Jacob Braude

An orator is a good man who is skilled in speaking.
    Cato the Elder

All the great speakers were bad speakers at first.
    Ralph Waldo Emerson

The commencement speaker represents the continuation of a barbaric custom that has no basis in logic. If the state of oratory that inundates our educational institutions during the month of June could be transformed into rain for Southern California, we should all be happily awash or waterlogged.
    Samuel Gould

Every speaker has a mouth; an arrangement rather neat.
Sometimes it's filled with wisdom. Sometimes it's filled with feet.
    Robert Orben

Although the aim of a sculptor is to convince us that he is a sculptor, the aim of an orator is to convince us he is not an orator.
    George Will

An orator must . . . cheer his guests, and . . . make them take pleasure, with hearing of things wittily devised, and pleasantly set forth.
Thomas Wilson

SPEAKING AND PUBLIC SPEAKING

Accustomed as I am to public speaking, I know the futility of it.
Franklin Pierce Adams

The brain starts working the moment you are born and never stops until you stand up to speak in public.
Anonymous

Speeches grow and mature. They need time to ripen, and they require constant cultivation. Some people find this incredible. "Good speakers," they argue, "can talk off the cuff." That notion, of course, is sheer fantasy.
J. Jeffrey Auer

So much to say. And so much not to say! Some things are better left unsaid. But so many unsaid things can become a burden.
Virginia Mae Axline

Every man speaks more virtuously than he either thinks or acts.
Sir Francis Bacon

First I tell them what I am going to tell them; then I tell them; and then I tell them what I've told them.
Hilaire Belloc, in Hesketh Pearson, *Lives of the Wits*

Speaking without thinking is shooting without aiming.
W.G. Benham, *Benham's Book of Quotations, Proverbs, and Household Words*

First have something to say, second say it, third stop when you have said it, and finally give it an accurate title.
Josh Billings

I do not object to people looking at their watches when I am speaking. But I strongly object when they start shaking them to make sure they are still going.
Lord Birkett

All the ends of speaking are reducible to four: every speech being intended to enlighten the understanding, to please the imagination, to move the passion, or to influence the will. Any one discourse admits only one of these ends as the principal.
George Campbell, *The Philosophy of Rhetoric*

Birds are entangled by their feet, and men by their tongues.
Jacob Cats, *Moral Emblems*

It isn't the first-hand information that makes the best speech, but the second-hand timing.
Hal Chadwick

Oratory is the power to talk people out of their sober and natural opinions.
Paul Chatfield

Talk doesn't cook rice.
Chinese proverb

To talk much and arrive nowhere is the same as climbing a tree to catch a fish.
Chinese proverb

I was having emergency surgery this morning. Has that one already been used?
Michael Crouch, on arriving late to a lecture

Speak boldly, and speak truly,
Shame the devil.
John Fletcher

Half the world is composed of people who have something to say and can't, and the other half who have nothing to say and keep on saying it.
Robert Frost

A blockhead is as ridiculous when he talketh, as is a goose when it flieth.
Lord Halifax

If you haven't struck oil in your first three minutes, *stop boring*!
George Jessel

Stand up straight. Talk out boldly. And sit down quickly.
Martin Luther

You say, to start with, you have laryngitis;
Stop right there, Maximus, and you'll delight us.
Marcus Valerius Martial, *Epigrammata*

Before a man speaks it is always safe to assume that he is a fool. After he speaks, it is seldom necessary to assume it.
H.L. Mencken, *A Mencken Chrestomathy*

In speech-making, as in life, not failure, but low aim, is crime.
Wayland Maxfield Parrish

If thou thinkest twice before thou speakest once, thou wilt speak twice the better for it.
   William Penn, *Some Fruits of Solitude*

My father gave me these hints on speech-making: "Be sincere, be brief . . . be seated."
   James Roosevelt

A paper that is read is like a kiss on the telephone--pleasant, but not the real thing. I'm now going to talk on the telephone.
   Albert Sabin

I know enough not to argue with lunch so I'll be brief.
   Stanley Schuman

I learnt to speak as men learn to skate or to cycle--by doggedly making a fool of myself until I got used to it. Then I practised it in the open air--at the street corner, in the market square, in the park--the best school.
   George Bernard Shaw, "Who I Am, and What I Think"

Put human interest into your talk. It is a universal truism that people are interested in *people* rather than things. To inject human interest, talk about people with whom your listeners can identify themselves.
   Harry Simmons

I am most fond of talking and thinking; that is to say, talking first and thinking afterwards.
   Osbert Sitwell

A speech without a specific purpose is like a journey without a destination.
   Ralph C. Smedley

Even if you're presenting the same speech for the fortieth time, it should never be thought of as a repetition, but as a recreation.
   Dorrine Anderson Turecamo, *The Toastmaster*

It usually takes more than three weeks to prepare a good impromptu speech.
   Mark Twain

SPEAKING ANXIETY

If you have the shaky hand syndrome, guard against taking a drink of water. No audience wants to see whitecaps in your glass.
   Steve Allen

Stage fright: the good news is, you will get over it. More good news: the worst

moments usually occur just before your entrance or introduction. There is something about hearing your own voice and seeing that the audience does not stand up and leave the room that restores your confidence.
Steve Allen

When I found out I had to give this talk, I thought about committing suicide; but with my luck, it'd probably be a temporary solution.
Ned Cassem

As babies, when we uttered our first "goo-goos," the people around us delightedly encouraged us to continue. Our earliest experiences with verbal communication are extremely positive. What happens, then, that huge national surveys show more people are afraid of public speaking than anything else, including death and disease?
Linda K. Fuller, in Linda K. Fuller and Lilless M. Shilling, *Commununicating Comfortably*

It's all right to have butterflies in your stomach. Just get them to fly in formation.
Rob Gilbert

My talk takes eighteen minutes if I'm relaxed and thirteen minutes if I'm nervous.
Mary Nolan Hall

I'm surprised that the phobia surrounding Public Speaking is at the top of the list of those things we all agonize over . . . . I'm convinced the fear is not so much a phobia as it is an excuse we often use for our own unwillingness to *try*.
Rod McKuen

One of life's terrors for the uninitiated is to be asked to make a speech.
George Plimpton

Many a piece did I commit to memory and rehearse in my room, over and over, yet when the day came to hear declamations, when my name was called, and I saw all eyes turned to me, I could not raise myself from my seat.
Daniel Webster

SPEECH

The shortest distance between two jokes makes a perfect speech.
O.A. Battista

Better pointed bullets than pointed speeches.
Otto von Bismarck-Schönhausen

Good talk needs invisible but skilled direction.
Brand Blanshard

Talk is cheap, but you can't buy it back.
  William Blatt

I am well aware that an after-dinner speech which is very short to him who makes it is often very long to those who have to listen to it.
  Joseph H. Choate

A dog is not considered a good dog because he is a good barker. A man is not considered a good man because he is a good talker.
  Chuang Tzu

For it is by this one gift that we are most distinguished from brute animals, that we converse together, and can express our thoughts.
  Cicero, *De Oratore*

You cannot believe, unless you pay close attention, how many devices nature has wrought for us to use in speech. For in the first place an artery stretches from the lungs to the inner part of the mouth, whereby the voice, starting from the mind, is caught up and uttered. Then the tongue is situated in the mouth and fenced about with teeth; it shapes and limits unduly loud sounds, and when it strikes the teeth and other parts of the mouth makes the sound of the voice distinct and clipped; and so we Stoics usually compare the tongue to the pick, the teeth to the strings, the nostrils to the sounding board which echoes to the string in music.
  Cicero, *On the Nature of the Gods*

Talk ought always to run obliquely, not nose to nose with no chance of mental escape.
  Frank Moore Colby, *The Colby Essays*

Let your speech be alway with grace, seasoned with salt, that ye may know how ye ought to answer every man.
  Colossians 4:6

As a vessel is known by the sound, whether it be cracked or not; so men are proved, by their speeches, whether they be wise or foolish.
  Demosthenes

The talk of a fool is like a heavy pack on a journey.
  Ecclesiasticus

The true use of speech is not so much to express our wants as to conceal them.
  Oliver Goldsmith, *The Bee*

The summary on the next lecture is one quick piece of advice: if anyone ever asks you to do a lecture on it, immediately say *no*.
  Ben Goodman

The best impromptu speeches are the ones written well in advance.
  Ruth Gordon

Logos dunastes megas. (Speech is a mighty ruler.)
  Gorgias of Leontini, *Helena*

A lecture is an occasion when you numb one end to benefit the other.
  John Gould

A pest is a man who can talk like an encyclopedia--and does.
  Oliver Herford

The dumbness in the eyes of animals is more touching than the speech of men; but the dumbness in the speech of men is more agonizing than the dumbness in the eyes of animals.
  Hindu proverb

All epoch-making revolutionary events have been produced not by written but by spoken word.
  Adolf Hitler

Talking is like playing on the harp; there is as much in laying the hands on the strings to stop their vibration as in twanging them to bring out their music.
  Oliver Wendell Holmes, Sr., *The Autocrat of the Breakfast Table*

And endless are the modes of speech, and far extends from side to side the field of words.
  Homer

None of the things which are done with intelligence are done without the aid of speech.
  Isocrates

Even so the tongue is a little member, and boasteth great things. Behold, how great a matter a little fire kindleth.
  James 3:5

The tongue is more to be feared than the sword.
  Japanese proverb

Remember that your tongue is in a wet place and likely to slip.
  Margaret Blair Johnstone

A speech is a solemn responsibility. The man who makes a bad thirty-minute speech to two hundred people wastes only a half hour of his own time. But he wastes one

hundred hours of the audience's time--more than four days--which should be a hanging offense.
    Jenkin Lloyd Jones

In the commerce of speech use only coins of gold and silver.
    Joseph Joubert

Most people tire of a lecture in ten minutes; clever people can do it in five. Sensible people never go to lectures at all.
    Stephen Leacock, *Laugh with Leacock*

Man has great power of speech, but the greater part thereof is empty and deceitful. The animals have little, but that little is useful and true; and better is a small and certain thing than a great falsehood.
    Leonardo da Vinci, *Notebooks*

A people's speech is the skin of its culture.
    Max Lerner, *America as a Civilization*

Thy speech betrayeth thee.
    Matthew 26:73

Be skillful in speech, that you may be strong.
    Merikare

If you your lips would keep from slips,
Five things observe with care;
To whom you speak, of whom you speak,
And how, and when, and where.
    W.E. Norris

One way of looking at speech is to say it is a constant stratagem to cover nakedness.
    Harold Pinter

Every speech ought to be put together like a living creature, with a body of its own, so as to be neither without head nor without feet, but to have both a middle and extremities, described proportionately to each other and to the whole.
    Plato

Speech is a mirror of the soul. As a man speaks, so he is.
    Publilius Syrus

The only difference between man and beasts is Syntax.
    Herbert Read

Mend your speech a little,
Lest it may mar your fortunes.
    William Shakespeare, *King Lear*

Speak the speech, I pray you, as I pronounced it to you, trippingly on the tongue; but if you mouth it, as many of your players do, I had as lief the town-crier spoke my lines. Nor do not saw the air too much with your hand, thus; but use all gently: for in the very torrent, tempest, and--as I may say--whirlwind of passion, you must acquire and beget a temperance, that may give it smoothness. O! it offends me to the soul to hear a robustious periwig-pated fellow tear a passion to tatters, to very rags, to split the ears of the groundlings, who for the most part are capable of nothing but inexplicable dumb-shows and noise. I would have such a fellow whipped for o'erdoing Termagant; it out-herods Herod: pray you, avoid it.
    William Shakespeare, *Hamlet*

There was a flavor of pleasure in his speech, like a teacher who is confident and precise upon some difficulty his class has raised.
    C.P. Snow

I sometimes marvel at the extraordinary docility with which Americans submit to speeches.
    Adlai Stevenson

Speech is a faculty given to man to conceal his thoughts.
    Charles-Maurice de Talleyrand

There is nothing can't be made worse by telling.
    Terence

Every man is born with the faculty of reason and the faculty of speech, but why should he be able to speak before he has anything to say?
    Benjamin Whichcote, *Moral and Religious Aphorisms*

All the skills of speech are of no use if our words are insincerely spoken.
    Wesley Wiksell

SPELLING

I take a very old-fashioned view of the importance of spelling and grammar. I don't care tuppence for imaginative stories that are badly spelt in poorly constructed sentences with no observable punctuation.
    Robert Burchfield

Nothing you can't spell will ever work.
    Will Rogers

I don't see any use in spelling a word right, and never did. I mean I don't see any use in having a uniform and arbitrary way of spelling words. We might as well make all our clothes alike and cook all dishes alike.
  Mark Twain

English orthography satisfies all the requirements of the canons of reputability under the law of conspicuous waste. It is archaic, cumbrous, and ineffective; its acquisition consumes much time and effort; failure to acquire it is easy of detection.
  Thorstein Veblen, *The Theory of the Leisure Class*

It is a pity that Chawcer, who had geneyus, was so unedicated; he's the wuss speller I know of.
  Artemus Ward (Charles Farrar Browne)

SPORTS

I don't communicate with players. I tell them what to do. I don't understand the meaning of communication.
  Paul Richards, Chicago White Sox manager

I like to get where the cabbage is cooking and catch the scents.
  Red Smith, on covering sports events, *Newsweek*

I always turn to the sports section first. The sports section records people's accomplishments; the front page nothing but man's failures.
  Earl Warren, former Chief Justice of the U.S. Supreme Court

It's what you learn after you know it all that counts.
  John Wooden, *They Call Me Coach*

STATISTICS

Then there is the man who drowned crossing a stream with an average depth of six inches.
  W.I.E. Gates

I am one of the unpraised, unrewarded millions without whom Statistics would be a bankrupt science. It is we who are born, who marry, who die, in constant ratio.
  Logan Pearsall Smith

There are three kinds of lies--lies, damned lies, and statistics.
  Mark Twain

Do not put your faith in what statistics say until you have carefully considered what they do not say.
  William W. Watt

STORIES

We live immersed in narrative, recounting and reassessing the meaning of our past actions, anticipating the outcome of our future projects, situating ourselves at the intersection of several stories not yet completed.
Peter Brooks, *Reading for the Plot*

The American imagination releases itself very easily in the short story--and has done so since the beginning of our national history.
Henry Seidel Canby

There are only two or three human stories, and they go on repeating themselves as fiercely as if they had never happened before.
Willa Cather

It may be possible in novel writing to present characters successfully without telling a story; but it is not possible to tell a story successfully without presenting characters.
Wilkie Collins

Cut off a person from all contact with tales and he will assuredly begin to invent some --probably about himself.
A.E. Coppard

Anecdotes are sometimes the best vehicles of truth, and if striking and appropriate, are often more impressive and powerful than argument.
Tryon Edwards

Stories today are told by multinational conglomerates with nothing to tell but lots to sell.
George Gerbner, on "storytelling"

I have learned in my 30-odd years of serious writing only one sure lesson: stories, like whiskey, must be allowed to mature in the cask.
Sean O'Faolain, *Atlantic Monthly*

In telling a story, it should be just true enough to be interesting, but not true enough to be tiresome.
Saki (H.H. Munro)

My theory is that people who don't like detective stories are anarchists.
Rex Stout

STYLE

A good style must, first of all, be clear. It must not be mean or above the dignity of the

subject. It must be appropriate.
Aristotle, *Rhetoric*

People think I can teach them style. What stuff it all is! Have something to say, and say it as clearly as you can. That is the only secret of style.
Matthew Arnold

The higher up you go, the more mistakes you're allowed. Right at the top, if you make enough of them, it's considered to be your style.
Fred Astaire

Style in writing is something like style in a car, a woman, or a Greek temple--the ordinary materials of this world so poised and perfected as to stand out from the landscape and compel a second look, something that hangs in the reader's mind, like a vision.
Sheridan Baker, *The Practical Stylist*

It is easy to be heavy; hard to be light.
G.K. Chesterton, *Orthodoxy*

You wouldn't say an ax handle has style to it. It has beauty, and appropriateness of form, and a "this-is-how-it-should-be-ness." But it has no style because it has no mistakes. Style reflects one's idiosyncrasies. Your personality is apt to show more to the degree that you did not solve the problem than to the degree that you did.
Charles Eames

"Style" is an expression of individualism mixed with charisma. Fashion is something that comes after style.
John Fairchild, publisher of *Women's Wear Daily*

The greatest possible mint of style is to make the words absolutely disappear into the thought.
Nathaniel Hawthorne

In stating as fully as I could how things really were, it was often very difficult and I wrote awkwardly and the awkwardness is what they called my style.
Ernest Hemingway

Style is self-plagiarism.
Alfred Hitchcock

A strict and succinct Style is that, where you can take away nothing without loss, and that loss to be manifest.
Ben Jonson, *Explorata*

A good style should show no sign of effort. What is written should seem a happy accident.
  W. Somerset Maugham, *The Summing Up*

Style is the hallmark of a temperament stamped upon the material at hand.
  André Maurois, *The Art of Writing*

Style might be described as that aspect of a piece of writing that we *perceive* but do not *observe*, what we respond to in writing without being aware of it.
  Louis T. Milic, *Stylists on Style*

The very many decisions that add up to a style are decisions about what to say, as well as how to say it. They reflect the [speaker's] organization of experience, his sense of life, so that the most general of his attitudes and ideas find expression just as characteristically in his style as in his manner.
  Richard Ohmann

In saying what is obvious, never choose cunning. Yelling works better.
  Cynthia Ozick

Style is to the book what smile is to the look.
  Ivan Panin

When we see a natural style we are quite amazed and delighted, because we expected to see an author and find a man.
  Blaise Pascal, *Pensées*

Great style, if I may say so, is also modest style, is never blotchy and bloated. It rises supreme by virtue of its natural beauty.
  Petronius, *Satyricon*

True wit is Nature to advantage dress'd,
What oft was thought, but ne'er so well express'd.
  Alexander Pope, "An Essay on Criticism"

Go ahead talking about style.
You can tell where a man gets his style
Just as you can tell where Pavlova got her legs or Ty Cobb his batting eye.
Go on talking. Only don't take my style away.
  Carl Sandburg, *Saturday Review*

If you are getting the worst of it in an argument with a literary man, always attack his style. That'll touch him if nothing else will.
  J.A. Spender

Proper words in proper places, make the true definition of a style.
Jonathan Swift, letter to a young clergyman

Every style that is not boring is a good one.
Voltaire

The only real elegance is in the mind; if you've got that, the rest really comes from it.
Diana Vreeland

But the ideal style is a style that is clear,--that cannot be misunderstood; that is forcible,--that holds the attention; and that is elegant,--that is so exquisitely adapted to its purpose that you can be conscious of its elegance only by subtly feeling the wonderful ease of habitual mastery.
Barrett Wendell, *English Composition*

SUCCESS

You canna expect to be baith grand and comfortable.
Sir James M. Barrie, *The Little Minister*

Fame always brings loneliness. Success is as ice cold and lonely as the north pole.
Vicki Baum, *Grand Hotel*

One of the advantages of success is that everybody stops giving you good advice.
Bernard Buffet

Words are one of our chief means of adjusting to all the situations of life. The better control we have over words, the more successful our adjustment is likely to be.
Bergen Evans

Just do a thing and don't talk about it. That is the great secret of success.
Sarah Grand

Success is not a destination, it's a journey.
Helen Keller

Most people would succeed in small things if they were not troubled by great ambitions.
Henry Wadsworth Longfellow

Good-fellowship, unflagging, is the prime requisite for success in our society, and the man or woman who smiles only for reasons of humor or pleasure is a deviate.
Marya Mannes, *More in Anger*

Success generally depends upon knowing how long it takes to succeed.
Montesquieu

Success is a great deodorant. It takes away all your past smells.
  Elizabeth Taylor

It is a paradoxical but profoundly true and important principle of life that the most likely way to reach a goal is to be aiming not at that goal itself but at some more ambitious goal beyond it.
  Arnold J. Toynbee

Success can make you go one of two ways. It can make you a prima donna, or it can smooth the edges, take away the insecurities, let the nice things come out.
  Barbara Walters

I have learned that success is to be measured not so much by the position that one has reached in life as by the obstacles which he has overcome while trying to succeed.
  Booker T. Washington, *Up from Slavery*

Success comes to a writer, as a rule, so gradually that it is always something of a shock to him to look back and realize the heights to which he has climbed.
  P.G. Wodehouse

SYMBOLS

I think that cars today are almost the exact equivalent of the great Gothic cathedrals: I mean the supreme creation of an era, conceived with passion by unknown artists, and consumed in image if not in usage by a whole population which appropriates them as a purely magical object.
  Roland Barthes, *Mythologies*

Words after all are symbols, and the significance of the symbols varies with the knowledge and experience of the mind receiving them.
  Benjamin N. Cardozo

Words, being symbols, do not speak without a gloss.
  Felix Frankfurter

Words are the common signs that mankind make use of to declare their intention to one another.
  Lucius Lamar

One of the inadequacies of language is that sooner or later, the thing is confused with the symbol for that thing. When the mind is centered on the verbal description of something instead of the thing itself, we conclude that "pigs are rightly named, since they are such dirty animals."
  Justice Jack Pope

T

TACT

Truth or tact? You have to choose. Most times they are not compatible.
  Eddie Cantor

Tact consists in knowing how far we may go too far.
  Jean Cocteau

Frankness is the backbone of friendship--when it is covered by the flesh of tact.
  G.C. Colmore, *The Angel and the Outcast*

Some people mistake weakness for tact. If they are silent when they ought to speak and so feign an agreement they do not feel, they call it being tactful. Cowardice would be a much better name.
  Frank Medlicott

TEACHERS

A teacher affects eternity; he can never tell where his influence stops.
  Henry Brooks Adams

The true teacher defends his pupils against his own personal influence . . . . He guides their eyes from himself to the spirit that quickens him.
  A. Bronson Alcott, "Orphic Sayings" *The Dial*

Teachers, who educate children, deserve more honor than parents, who merely gave them birth; for the latter provided mere life, while the former ensure a good life.
  Aristotle

A great teacher is . . . a spark plug, not a fuel pipe.
  M.J. Berrill

We must have teachers--a heroine in every classroom.
    Fidel Castro

Teachers open the door, but you enter by yourself.
    Chinese proverb

I have learned silence from the talkative, toleration from the intolerant, and kindness from the unkind; yet strange, I am ungrateful to those teachers.
    Kahlil Gibran, *Sand and Foam*

A teacher, like a playwright, has an obligation to be interesting or, at least, brief. A play closes when it ceases to interest audiences.
    Haim G. Ginott, *Teacher and Child*

To be a teacher in the right sense is to be a learner. I am not a teacher, only a fellow student.
    Søren Kierkegaard

But there is one blanket statement which can be made about the world's schools: the teachers talk too much.
    Martin Mayer, *The Schools*

I am a teacher--I borrow from the best.
    Ron Nickel

If a doctor, lawyer, or dentist had 40 people in his office at one time, all of whom had different needs, and some of whom didn't want to be there and were causing trouble, and the doctor, lawyer, or dentist, without assistance, had to treat them all with professional excellence for nine months, then he might have some conception of the classroom teacher's job.
    Donald D. Quinn

A great teacher has always been measured by the number of his students who have surpassed him.
    Donald Robinson

The teacher who makes little or no allowance for individual differences in the classroom is an individual who makes little or no difference in the lives of his students.
    William A. Ward

The teacher, whether mother, priest, or schoolmaster, is the real maker of history.
    H.G. Wells

TEACHING

Teaching is truth mediated by personality.
>Phyllis Brooks

Don't try to teach all you know. It may satisfy you but not the student.
>Edgar Dale

When I transfer my knowledge, I teach.
When I transfer my beliefs, I indoctrinate.
>Arthur Danto

Education is a thing of which only the few are capable; teach as you will, only a small percentage will profit by your most zealous energy.
>George Gissing, *The Private Papers of Henry Ryecroft*

Good teaching is one-fourth preparation and three-fourths theatre.
>Gail Godwin

Often what we have in teaching are things that are low risk to the teacher and high risk for the learner.
>Mary Graham

We have to stop being so teacher-centered, and become student-centered. It's not what you think they need, but what they think they need. That's the functional approach.
>Mary Anne Guitar

Never impose your language on people you wish to teach.
>Abbie Hoffman, *Revolution for the Hell of It*

Everything I learn about teaching I learn from bad students.
>John Holt

Good teaching can be identified when a teacher is able to start engines. *Excellent* teaching can be identified when a teacher is able to stimulate students to start their own engines.
>J. Willis Hurst

To teach is to learn twice.
>Joseph Joubert, *Pensées*

It is repetition, like cabbage served at every meal, that wears out the school-master's life.
>Juvenal

If we succeed in giving the love of learning, the learning itself is sure to follow.
 John Lubbock, *The Pleasures of Life*

A man who knows a subject thoroughly, a man so soaked in it that he eats it, sleeps it, dreams it--this man can always teach it with success, no matter how little he knows of technical pedagogy.
 H.L. Mencken

It's one of the unforeseen disabilities of teaching as a profession that when senility sets in, it happens in public.
 Howard Numerov

Never tell people how to do things. Tell them what to do and they will surprise you with their ingenuity.
 General George S. Patton, Jr.

Men must be taught as if you taught them not,
And things unknown proposed as things forgot.
 Alexander Pope

The young man taught all he knew and more;
The middle-aged man taught all he knew;
The old man taught all that his students could understand.
 Arnold Ross

For every person wishing to teach there are thirty not wanting to be taught.
 W.C. Sellar and R.J. Yeatman, *And Now All This*

The art of teaching is the art of assisting discovery.
 Mark Van Doren

What we have loved, others will love
And we will teach them how.
 William Wordsworth

TEAMWORK

Rain does not fall on one roof alone.
 Cameroon proverb

The nice thing about teamwork is that you always have others on your side.
 Margaret Carty

When the head aches, all the members share the pain.
 Miguel de Cervantes, *Don Quixote*

On a good team there are no superstars. There are great players, who show they are great players by being able to play with others, as a team. They have the ability to be superstars, but if they fit into a good team, they make sacrifices, they do the things necessary to help the team win. What the numbers are in salaries or statistics don't matter; how they play together does.

   Red Holzman, former coach of the New York Knicks

A team effort is a lot of people doing what I say.

   Michael Winner, British film director

TECHNOLOGY

If the human race wants to go to hell in a basket, technology can help it get there by jet. It won't change the desire or the direction, but it can greatly speed the passage.

   Charles M. Allen

Ours is a world of nuclear giants and ethical infants. If we continue to develop our technology without wisdom or prudence, our servant may prove to be our executioner.

   General Omar Bradley

Technology is a way of organizing the universe so that man doesn't have to experience it.

   Max Frisch

The real danger is not that machines will begin to think like men, but that men will begin to think like machines.

   Sydney J. Harris

Technology is the most subtle and the most effective engineer of enduring social change. Its apparent neutrality is deceptive and often disarming.

   Robert MacIver

Technology dominates us all, diminishing our freedom.

   Dorothy McCall

The new electronic interdependence recreates the world in the image of a global village.

   Marshall McLuhan, *The Medium Is the Massage*

Today, thanks to technical progress, the radio and television, to which we devote so many of the leisure hours once spent listening to parlour chatter and parlour music, have succeeded in lifting the manufacture of banality out of the sphere of handicraft and placed it in that of a major industry.

   Nathalie Sarraute, *Times Literary Supplement*

The art of our era is not art, but technology.   Today Rembrandt is painting automobiles; Shakespeare is writing research reports; Michelangelo is designing more efficient bank lobbies.
Howard Sparks, *The Petrified Truth*

If automation keeps up, man will atrophy all his limbs but the push-button finger.
Frank Lloyd Wright

TELEPHONE

There is something about saying "OK" and hanging up the receiver with a bang that kids a man into feeling that he has just pulled off a big deal, even if he has only called up central to find out the correct time.
Robert Benchley

The telephone shone as brightly as a weapon kept polished by daily use.
Colette

Why is it the average man imagines that, if faced with terror on the street, he would rise to the occasion and punch out Stallone, Schwarzenegger, and the entire World Wrestling Federation .   .   . and yet when he's sitting alone in the solitude of his own apartment, he cowers and shakes at the thought of punching out seven tiny numbers on a two-pound plastic phone?
Bruce Feirstein, *Nice Guys Sleep Alone*

I don't mind being put on "hold," but I think they've got me on "ignore."
Troy Gordon

One good reason why computers can do more work than people is that they never have to stop to answer the telephone.
Ollie M. James

The telephone is the greatest nuisance among conveniences, the greatest convenience among nuisances.
Robert Lynd

TELEVISION

Television is the first truly democratic culture--the first culture available to everyone and entirely governed by what the people want.   The most terrifying thing is what people do want.
Clive Barnes

The one function that TV news performs very well is that when there is no news we give it to you with the same emphasis as if there was news.
David Brinkley

We cannot, after all, neglect to consider the challenge television has undertaken. It is more formidable by far than that of Scheherazade the slave girl, who, after all, was given a respite after her thousand and first tale. In undertaking to entertain us--indeed, to give us a choice of entertainment--every day and every night of every week of every month of every year, television has undertaken the job it simply cannot do to everyone's satisfaction.
    William F. Buckley, Jr.

Television is democracy at its ugliest.
    Paddy Chayefsky

People don't want to be umbilically connected to an electronic box.
    Paul Del Rossi

Most American television stations reproduce all night long what a Roman could have seen only in the Coliseum during the reign of Nero.
    George Faludy

We admit many characters to our living rooms via the television screen that we would never dream of letting in through the front door.
    Bonardo Forncrook

Television should be kept in its proper place--beside us, before us, but never between us and the larger life.
    Robert Fraser, *Look*

Television makes so much at its worst that it can't afford to do its best.
    Fred W. Friendly

Television enables you to be entertained in your home by people you wouldn't have in your home.
    David Frost

Today's audience knows more about what's on television than what's in life.
    Larry Gelbart

Television is like the invention of indoor plumbing. It didn't change people's habits. It just kept them inside the house.
    Alfred Hitchcock

We can put television in its proper light by supposing that Gutenberg's great invention had been directed at printing only comic books.
    Robert M. Hutchins

All television is educational television. The only question is what is it teaching?
    Nicholas Johnson, *Life*

There is no medical proof that television causes brain damage--at least from over five feet away. In fact, TV is probably the least physically harmful of all the narcotics known to man.
  Christopher Lehmann-Haupt

The closer you come to being yourself on the screen, the longer you last [because] on television there's always the risk of a quick shot in an off-guard moment, a chance insight; and if you're playing a part, you'll be exposed.
  Jack Lescoulie

Television is dope for the eyes.
  Stanley Levinson

Television is a golden goose that lays scrambled eggs; and it is futile and probably fatal to beat it for not laying caviar. Anyway, more people like scrambled eggs than caviar.
  Lee Loevinger

[Miniseries are] the video equivalent of junk food.
  John J. O'Connor

No wonder the audiences for the late-night talk shows are growing. Who can get to sleep after hearing the 11 p.m. news?
  Terrence O'Flaherty

Statistics show that many people watch our show from the bedroom . . . and people you ask into your bedroom have to be more interesting than those you ask into your living room. I kid you not!
  Jack Paar, former host of NBC TV "Tonight Show"

The size of television's footprint is as long and as wide as the country itself . . . measured by the allegiance of audiences and advertisers.
  C. Wrede Petersmeyer

No matter what the critics say, it's hard to believe that a television program which keeps four children quiet for an hour can be all bad.
  Beryl Pfizer

There has been such a mythology built up around the supposed glamour of television life that it's hard for the average person to imagine turning down anything on TV.
  Sally Quinn, *We're Going to Make You a Star*

Just think of all the commercials, old movies, Westerns, politicians, comedians, quiz shows, soap operas, and other intrusions we can keep out of our homes just by turning off one little knob.
  Fred Randall

We're in the same position as a plumber laying a pipe. We're not responsible for what goes through the pipe.
  David Sarnoff, on broadcasting

Television . . . often cannot cover the passing of the torch without fanning the flames in the process.
  Martin Schram, *New York*

Television is the bland leading the bland.
  Murray Schumach, *The Face on the Cutting Room Floor*

Television? The word is half Latin and half Greek. No good can come of it.
  C.P. Scott

When the Roman Empire was falling apart, the people were distracted and kept happy with circuses. Now we have television.
  Benjamin Spock

[Television is] a license to print money.
  Lord Thomson of Fleet (Roy Herbert Thomson)

I secretly understood: the primitive appeal of the hearth. Television is--its irresistible charm--a fire.
  John Updike, on a child doing homework near the television set

Television is educational. If it weren't for the old movies, today's kids might not know that there was a time when the Russians were the good guys and the Germans were the bad guys.
  Bill Vaughan

Television is now so desperately hungry for material that they're scraping the top of the barrel.
  Gore Vidal

When I got my first television set, I stopped caring so much about having close relationships.
  Andy Warhol, recalled on his death

I hate television; I hate it as much as peanuts, and I can't stop eating peanuts.
  Orson Welles

Television is an instrument which can paralyze this country.
  William C. Westmoreland, on Vietnam as the first war ever reported without censorship, *Time*

Getting an award from TV is like getting kissed by someone with bad breath.
 Mason Williams

TV--chewing gum for the eyes.
 Frank Lloyd Wright

The technique [of television] is wonderful. I didn't even dream it would be so good. But I would never let my children come close to the thing. It's awful what they are doing.
 Vladimir Kosma Zworykin, developer of television, at age ninety-two

THEATRE

Theatre is, of course, a reflection of life. Maybe we have to improve life before we can hope to improve theatre.
 William Inge

Everything in life is theatre.
 Margo Jones

In all ages the drama, through its portrayal of the active and suffering spirit of man, has been more closely allied than any other art to his deeper thoughts concerning his nature and his destiny.
 Ludwig Lewisohn, *The Modern Drama*

Drama--what literature does at night.
 George Jean Nathan, *Testament of a Critic*

THINKING

It takes longer to think clearly than it takes to learn rifle-shooting, round-arm bowling, or piano-playing. The great masses of people (of all classes) cannot think at all. That is why the majority never rule. They are led like sheep by the few who know that they cannot think.
 Robert Blatchford, *God and My Neighbor*

The no-mind not-thinks no-thoughts about no-things.
 Buddha

Less than fifteen per cent of the people do any original thinking on any subject . . . . The greatest torture in the world for most people is to think.
 Luther Burbank

It would be as wise and reasonable to say that it does not matter which way the rudder

swings as the ship moves, as to say that it does not matter what a man thinks.
  W.J. Dawson, *The Making of Manhood*

What was once thought can never be unthought.
  Friedrich Dürrenmatt, *The Physicists*

One must learn to think well before learning to think; afterward it proves too difficult.
  Anatole France

The proper method for hastening the decay of error is . . . by teaching every man to think for himself.
  William Godwin, *An Enquiry concerning Political Justice*

Ours is the age which is proud of machines that think, and suspicious of men who try to.
  M. Mumfort Jones

Too often we . . . enjoy the comfort of opinion without the discomfort of thought.
  John F. Kennedy

We cannot unthink unless we are insane.
  Arthur Koestler

There are two ways to slice easily through life: to believe everything or to doubt everything. Both ways save us from thinking.
  Alfred Korzybski, *Manhood of Humanity*

Where all men think alike, no one thinks very much.
  Walter Lippmann

To think is to meander from highway to byway, and from byway to alleyway, till we come to a dead end. Stopped dead in our alley, we think what a feat it would be to get out. That is when we look for the gate to the meadows beyond.
  Antonio Machado, *Juan de Mairena*

If you make people think they're thinking, they'll love you. If you really make them think, they'll hate you.
  Don Marquis

Some flabby persons try to make education painless. "Do not," they say, "ask students to learn facts, but teach them to think." O Thinking--what intellectual crimes are committed in thy name! How can a man think if he doesn't know? Charles Darwin gathered biological facts for twenty years without seeing any binding relationship. Then one day, when he was talking through an English country lane, the idea of evolution suddenly came to him. That's what thinking is--the flashing emergence of

an idea after facts have been mulled over a long time. Even then it is probably wrong. It must be well tested . . . . You cannot think with hopes and fears and ignorance, but only with a well--trained and well-filled mind.
    W.E. McNeill

Nothing ages people like not thinking.
    Christopher Morley

We become what we think about.
    Earl Nightingale

Few people think more than two or three times a year. I have made an international reputation for myself by thinking once or twice a week.
    George Bernard Shaw

He thinks things through very clearly before going off half-cocked.
    General Carl Spaatz

Sixty minutes of thinking of any kind is bound to lead to confusion and unhappiness.
    James Thurber

We think in generalities, we live in detail.
    Alfred North Whitehead

TIME

The time you enjoy wasting is not wasted time.
    Bertrand Russell

Time is a great teacher.
    Carl Sandburg

Though I am always in haste, I am never in a hurry.
    John Wesley

TRANSLATION

Reading a translation is like looking at a tapestry on the wrong side.
    Miguel de Cervantes

The art of translation lies less in knowing the other language than in knowing your own.
    Ned Rorem, *Music from Inside Out*

It were as wise to cast a violet into a crucible that you might discover the formal

principle of its colour and odour, as seek to transfuse from one language into another the creations of a poet.
Percy Bysshe Shelley, *A Defence of Poetry*

An idea does not pass from one language to another without change.
Miguel de Unamuno, *Tragic Sense of Life*

It is as impossible to translate poetry as it is to translate music.
Voltaire

TRUST

Trust ivrybody--but cut th' ca-ards.
Finley Peter Dunne, *Mr. Dooley's Opinions*

To be trusted is a greater compliment than to be loved.
George MacDonald, *The Marquis of Lossie*

Love thy neighbor, but pull not down thy hedge.
John Ray

Pray to God but keep on rowing the boat ashore.
Russian proverb

TRUTH

The truth is often a terrible weapon of aggression. It is possible to lie, and even to murder, with the truth.
Alfred Adler, *Problems of Neurosis*

The truth which makes men free is for the most part the truth which men prefer not to hear.
Herbert Agar, *A Time for Greatness*

Truth is violated by falsehood, and it may be equally outraged by silence.
Ammian

I will omit but I will not distort.
Cleveland Amory

I don't let my mouth say nothing my head can't stand.
Louis Armstrong

Truth sits on the lips of dying men.
Matthew Arnold

Remember, son, many a good story has been ruined by over-verification.
    James Gordon Bennett

He who says there is no such thing as an honest man, you may be sure is himself a knave.
    George Berkeley

When you want to fool the world, tell the truth.
    Otto von Bismarck-Schönhausen

A truth that's told with bad intent
Beats all the lies you can invent.
    William Blake

The opposite of a correct statement is a false statement. But the opposite of a profound truth may well be another profound truth.
    Niels Bohr

La verité existe; on n'invente que le mensonge. (Truth exists; only lies are invented.)
    Georges Braque

Truth gets well if she is run over by a locomotive, while error dies of lockjaw if she scratches her finger.
    William Cullen Bryant

Deviate an inch, lose a thousand miles.
    Chinese proverb

Men occasionally stumble over the truth, but most of them pick themselves up and hurry off as if nothing had happened.
    Winston Churchill

The reader deserves an honest opinion. If he doesn't deserve it, give it to him anyhow.
    John Ciardi

An intimate truth is also a universal truth.
    John Cournos

Tell the truth
But tell it slant.
    Emily Dickinson

It is the journey to the truth which convinces the traveler that he has arrived. To be dropped on the top of Mount Everest by helicopter is not to gain the glory of the peak.
    William Gass, *Habitations of the Word*

Believe those who are seeking the truth; doubt those who have found it.
    Andre Gidé

The truth is so simple that it is regarded as pretentious banality.
    Dag Hammarskjöld

I don't care what is written about me so long as it isn't true.
    Katharine Hepburn

A truth-telling woman has few friends.
    Irish proverb

And ye shall know the truth, and the truth shall make you free.
    John 8:32

Some minds remain open long enough for the truth not only to enter but to pass on through by way of a ready exit without pausing anywhere along the route.
    Elizabeth Kenny, with Martha Ostenso, *And They Shall Walk*

Truth comes in a well rubbed-down state in the form of sayings of the ancestors.
    Khati, King of ancient Egypt, *Teaching*

Truth is not a word, it is not a concept; it isn't your truth or my truth, the Christian truth and the Muslim truth. Truth, like love, has no nationality, but to love and to see truth, there must be no hate, no jealousy, no division and no anger.
    Krishnamurti

Absolute truth is incompatible with an advanced state of society.
    Joaquim Maria Machado, *Epitaph of a Small Winner*

A truth does not become greater by frequent repetition.
    Maimonides, *Tehiyat HaMethim: Responsa*

If any man seeks for greatness, let him forget greatness and ask for truth, and he will find both.
    Horace Mann

Truth could never be wholly contained in words. All of us know it: at the same moment the mouth is speaking one thing, the heart is saying another.
    Catherine Marshall

Man has no nobler function than to defend the truth.
    Ruth McKenney

Truth has no degrees. The sea has the same level at its greatest depth as that point

where it touches the shore.
 Douglas Meador

It is hard to believe that a man is telling the truth when you know that you would lie if you were in his place.
 H.L. Mencken

In every generation there has to be some fool who will speak the truth as he sees it.
 Boris Pasternak

Truth--what we think it is at any given moment of time.
 Luigi Pirandello

These Macedonians are a rude and clownish people; they call a spade a spade.
 Plutarch

He who has but a short time to live
No longer needs dissemble.
 Philippe Quinault

There can be no literary equivalent to truth.
 Laura Riding

The truth is too simple: one must always get there by a complicated route.
 George Sand, in a letter to Armand Barbes

The most striking contradiction of our civilization is the fundamental reverence for truth which we profess and the thorough-going disregard for it which we practice.
 Vilhjalmur Stefansson

Truth in her dress finds facts too tight. In fiction she moves with ease.
 Rabindranath Tagore, *Stray Birds*

If truth is beauty, how come no one has her hair done at the library?
 Lily Tomlin

I never give them hell. I just tell the truth and they think it's hell.
 Harry S. Truman

Whoever tells the truth is chased out of nine villages.
 Turkish proverb

Truth is the most valuable thing we have. Let us economize it.
 Mark Twain

The pure and simple truth is rarely pure and never simple.
   Oscar Wilde

If you do not tell the truth about yourself you cannot tell it about other people.
   Virginia Woolf, *The Moment and Other Essays*

Tell the truth, and so puzzle and confound your adversaries.
   Sir Henry Wotton

Truth is on the side of the oppressed.
   Malcolm X (Malcolm Little)

Tell the truth and run.
   Yugoslav proverb

When truth is buried, it grows, it chokes, it gathers such explosive force that on the day it breaks out, it blows everything up with it.
   Émile Zola, *J'accuse!*

V

VOCABULARY

A person with a mind tidily stocked with a rich vocabulary feels adequate; and that sense of adequacy is the sense of power.
Mauree Applegate, *Easy in English*

Your vocabulary is mean and impoverished but quite adequate to express your thoughts.
Griff Niblack

One forgets words as one forgets names. One's vocabulary needs constant fertilizing or it will die.
Evelyn Waugh, *Diaries*

VOICE

The voice is a second face.
Gerard Bauer

The Devil hath not, in all his quiver's choice,
An Arrow for the heart like a sweet voice!
Lord Byron

The organs of speech can be brought by intelligent training into a complete obedience to the will and the feelings.
Hiram Corson

There is no index of character so sure as the voice.
Benjamin Disraeli

W

WIT

Wit is a treacherous dart. It is perhaps the only weapon with which it is possible to stab oneself in one's own back.
    Geoffrey Bocca, *The Woman Who Would Be Queen*

Wit is so shining a quality that everybody admires it; most people aim at it, all people fear it, and few love it except in themselves.
    Lord Chesterfield, *Letters to His Son*

The wit we long for spoils the wit we have.
    Jean-Baptiste Gresset, *Le méchant*

You can pretend to be serious; you can't pretend to be witty.
    Sacha Guitry

A genius for repartee is a gift for saying what a wise man thinks only.
    Thomas Hardy

Wit is the salt of conversation, not the food.
    William Hazlitt, *Lectures on the English Comic Writers*

Levity is the soul of wit.
    Melville D. Landon (Eli Perkins)

Wit sometimes enables us to act rudely with impunity.
    François de La Rochefoucauld

Wit has a deadly aim and it is possible to prick a large pretense with a small pin.
    Marya Mannes, *But Will It Sell?*

One wit, like a knuckle of ham in soup, gives a zest and flavour to the dish, but more than one serves only to spoil the pottage.
     Tobias Smollett, *Humphrey Clinker*

It is as foolish to say something brilliant with intention as it is to be silent by compulsion.
     J.M. Stuart-Young, *Passion's Peril*

Wit is the power to say what everybody would like to have said, if they had happened to think of it.
     James McNeill Whistler

WOMEN

In nine cases out of ten, a woman had better show more affection than she feels.
     Jane Austen

Woman. I understand the word itself, in that sense, has gone out of the language. Where we talk of woman . . . you talk of women, and all the difference lies therein.
     Isak Dinesen

It can be less painful for a woman not to hear the strange, dissatisfied voice stirring within her.
     Betty Friedan

I may be arrested, I may be tried and thrown into jail, but I never will be silent.
     Emma Goldman

The more I see of human beings the more I believe that for most human females, their greatest love affair is with their children.
     Germaine Greer

Has any woman ever attained such greatness that, at the mention of her name, we think of the books she wrote before we think of the woman she was?
     Winfred Kirkland

The one thing a writer has to have is not balls. Nor is it even . . . a room of her own, though that is an amazing help . . . . The one thing a writer has to have is a pencil and some paper. That's enough, so long as she knows that she and she alone is in charge of that pencil, and responsible, she and she alone, for what it writes on that paper.
     Ursula K. Le Guin, "The Hand That Rocks the Cradle Writes the Book"

Women are repeatedly accused of taking things personally. I cannot see any other honest way of taking them.
     Marya Mannes

Humor is such a strong weapon, such a strong answer. Women have to make jokes about themselves, laugh about themselves, because they have nothing to lose.
    Agnes Varda

Why have they been telling us women lately that we have no sense of humor--when we are always laughing? ... And when we're not laughing, we're smiling.
    Naomi Weisstein

I am twenty-one years old and am supposed to be silent and grin like a puppet.
    Ellen West, diary entry, c. 1911

I would venture that Anon, who wrote so many poems without signing them, was often a woman.
    Virginia Woolf

A woman must have money and a room of her own if she is to write fiction.
    Virginia Woolf, *A Room of One's Own*

WORDINESS

A plurality of words does not necessarily represent a plurality of things.
    Joseph Albo, *Sefer ha-Ikkarim* (Book of Principles)

Loquacity, n. A disorder which renders the sufferer unable to curb his tongue when you wish to talk.
    Ambrose Bierce, *The Devil's Dictionary*

So much they talked, so very little said.
    Charles Churchill, *The Rosciad*

Great talkers are like leaky pitchers; everything runs out of them.
    English proverb

Let not your tongue run away with your brains.
    French proverb

Chi parla troppo non puo parlar siempre bene. (He who talks much cannot always talk well.)
    Carlo Goldoni, *Pamela*

I hate anything that occupies more space than it is worth. I hate to see a load of bandboxes go along the street, and I hate to see a parcel of big words without anything in them.
    William Hazlitt

In all abundance there is lack.
    Hippocrates, *Precepts*

A sick man that gets talking about himself, a woman that gets talking about her baby, and an author that begins reading out of his own book, never know when to stop.
    Oliver Wendell Holmes, Sr., *The Poet at the Breakfast Table*

Amplification is the vice of the modern orator. Speeches measured by the hour die by the hour.
    Thomas Jefferson

The conversation overflowed and drowned him.
    Samuel Johnson, in James Boswell, *Life of Johnson*

He talks like a watch which ticks away minutes, but never strikes the hour.
    Samuel Johnson

He can compress the most words into the smallest ideas of any man I ever met.
    Abraham Lincoln

In general those who nothing have to say
Contrive to spend the longest time in doing it;
They turn and vary it in every way,
Hashing it, stewing it, mincing it, *ragouting* it.
    James Russell Lowell, "An Oriental Apologue"

He talked and talked because he didn't know what to say.
    Dacia Maraini, *The Holiday*

We shall probably have nothing to say, but we intend to say it at great length.
    Don Marquis, *The Almost Perfect State*

The thoughtless are rarely wordless.
    Howard K. Newton

I have made this letter longer than usual, only because I have not had time to make it shorter.
    Blaise Pascal, *Provincial Letters*

Words are like leaves, and where they most abound,
Much fruit of sense beneath is rarely found.
    Alexander Pope

He that useth many words for the explaining any subject, doth, like the cuttle fish, hide himself for the most part in his own ink.
    John Ray, *On Creation*

Words are the coins making up the currency of sentences, and there are always too many small coins.
Jules Renard

Loquax magis quam facundus. (Talkative rather than eloquent.)
Sallust, *History*

He suffered occasionally from a rush of words to the head.
Herbert Samuel

Occasionally, I recognize what I call the "squid technique." The author is doubtful about his/her facts or reasoning and retreats behind a protective cloud of ink.
Doug Savile

What cracker is this same that deafs our ears
With this abundance of superfluous breath?
William Shakespeare, *King John*

Long sentences in a short composition are like large rooms in a little house.
William Shenstone, *On Writing and Books*

Loquacity storms the ear, but modesty takes the heart.
Robert South, *A Discourse against Long and Extempore Prayers*

There are few wild beasts more to be dreaded than a talking man having nothing to say.
Jonathan Swift

The trouble with me is that I like to talk too much.
William Howard Taft

In a way, the main fault of all books is that they are too long.
Marquis de Vauvenargues

The secret of being a bore is to tell everything.
Voltaire, *Sept discours en vers sur l'homme*

WORDS

No one means all he says, and yet very few say all they mean, for words are slippery and thought is viscous.
Henry Brooks Adams, *The Education of Henry Adams*

Words, when well chosen, have so great a force in them that a description often gives us more likely ideas than the sight of things themselves.
Joseph Addison, *The Spectator*

When you have spoken the word, it reigns over you. When it is unspoken, you reign over it.
    Arabic proverb

You can taste a word.
    Pearl Bailey

The written word is the link between the past and the future.
    Lincoln Barnett

All words are pegs to hang ideas on.
    Henry Ward Beecher, *Proverbs from Plymouth Pulpit*

Of what help is anyone who can only be approached with the right words?
    Elizabeth Bibesco, *Haven*

There is no means by which men so powerfully elude their ignorance, disguise it from themselves and from others as by words.
    Gamaliel Bradford

As much good-will may be conveyed in one hearty word as in many.
    Charlotte Brontë

What so wild as words are?
    Robert Browning, *A Woman's Last Word*

Definitions are a kind of scratching and generally leave a sore place more sore than it was before.
    Samuel Butler, II, *The Note-Books of Samuel Butler*

The words! I collected them in all shapes and sizes and hung them like bangles in my mind.
    Hortense Calisher, *Extreme Magic*

The smashers of language are looking for a new justice among words. It does not exist. Words are unequal and unjust.
    Elias Canetti, *The Human Province*

Guard well thy tongue, for out of it are the issues of life.
    Thomas Carlyle

"When I use a word," said Humpty Dumpty, in rather a scornful tone, "it means just what I choose it to mean--neither more nor less."
    Lewis Carroll, *Through the Looking-Glass*

Semantics teaches us to watch our prejudices, and to take our exercise in other ways than jumping to conclusions. Semantics is the propagandist's worst friend.
    Stuart Chase

Words are what hold society together.
    Stuart and Marian T. Chase

Words are the dress of thoughts, which should no more be presented in rags, tatters, and dirt, than your person would.
    Lord Chesterfield, *Letters to His Son*

Eating words has never given me indigestion.
    Winston Churchill

Short words are best and the old words when short are best of all.
    Winston Churchill

Fair words butter no parsnips.
    John Clarke, *Paroemiologia Anglo-Latina*

Some of mankind's most terrible misdeeds have been committed under the spell of certain magic words or phrases.
    James Bryant Conant

Don't talk to me of your Archimedes' lever . . . . Give me the right word and the right accent, and I will move the world.
    Joseph Conrad, *A Personal Record*

Words, like men, grow individuality; their character changes with years and with use.
    Frederick E. Crane, *Adler vs. Deegan*

Words in themselves may be harmless, while some accent and manner may make them deadly.
    Marmaduke H. Dent

A word is dead
When it is said,
Some say.
I say it just
Begins to live
That day.
    Emily Dickinson, "A Word"

Pithy sentences are like sharp nails which force truth upon our memory.
    Denis Diderot

With words we govern men.
Benjamin Disraeli

How often could things be remedied by a word. How often it is left unspoken.
Norman Douglas, *An Almanac*

You can stroke people with words.
F. Scott Fitzgerald, *The Crack-Up*

A word and a stone let go cannot be called back.
Thomas Fuller, *Gnomologia*

As long as a word remains unspoken, you are its master; once you utter it, you are its slave.
Solomon Ibn Gabirol, *Choice of Pearls*

By words we learn thoughts, and by thoughts we learn life.
Père Girard

Spinning words, we are much like the spider spinning its web out of its own body. We, however, unlike the spider, may be enmeshed in our own web.
Isaac Goldberg, *The Wonder of Words*

Words, like fashions, disappear and recur throughout English history, and one generation's phraseology, while it may seem abominably second-rate to the next, becomes first-rate to the third.
Virginia Graham

Of all cold words of tongue or pen.
The worst are these: "I knew him when--"
Arthur Guiterman, *Prophets in Their Own Country*

We have to deal with words, and there is nothing more fluid than words.
Judge Learned Hand

Words are chameleons, which reflect the color of their environment.
Judge Learned Hand, *Commissioner vs. National Carbide*

Words--so innocent and powerless as they are, as standing in a dictionary, how potent for good and evil they become, in the hands of one who knows how to combine them!
Nathaniel Hawthorne, *American Notebooks*

Words are the only things that last forever.
William Hazlitt

The tongue is not steel, yet it cuts.
George Herbert, *Jacula Prudentum*

Words are really a mask. They rarely express the true meaning; in fact, they tend to hide it.
Hermann Hesse

The tongue is no edge-tool, but yet it will cut.
John Heywood, *Proverbs*

Words are wise men's counters, they do but reckon by them; but they are the money of fools.
Thomas Hobbes, *Leviathan*

Nescit vox missa reverti. (A word once uttered can never be recalled.)
Horace, *Ars Poetica*

A word once let out of the cage cannot be whistled back again.
Horace, *Epistles*

Words are the soul's ambassadors who go
Abroad upon her errands to and fro.
James Howell

Words form the thread on which we string our experience.
Aldous Huxley, *The Olive Tree*

Words are tools which automatically carve concepts out of experience.
Julian Sorrell Huxley

A sharp tongue is the only edged tool that grows keener with constant use.
Washington Irving, "Rip Van Winkle"

Words are less needful to sorrow than to joy.
Helen Fiske Hunt Jackson

People do not have words to fit ideas that have never occurred to them.
Robert H. Jackson

Once uttered, words run faster than horses.
Japanese proverb

How forcible are right words.
Job 6:25

And now we come to the magic of words. A word, also, just like an idea, a thought, has the effect of reality upon undifferentiated minds. Our Biblical myth of creation, for instance, where the world grows out of the spoken word of the creator, is an expression of this.
    Emma Jung

Words signify man's refusal to accept the world as it is.
    Walter Kaufmann

Words are, of course, the most powerful drug used by mankind.
    Rudyard Kipling

On a winged word hath hung the destiny of nations.
    Walter Savage Landor

Value your words. Each one may be the last.
    Stanislaw Lec, *Unkempt Thoughts*

Men are ready to suffer anything from others or from heaven itself, provided that, when it comes to words, they are untouched.
    Giacomo Leopardi, *Pensieri*

My words are little jars
For you to take and put upon a shelf.
    Amy Lowell

And though the tongue has no bones, it can sometimes break millions of them.
    F.L. Lucas

Many a man's tongue broke his nose.
    Seumas MacManus, *Heavy Hangs the Golden Grain*

For by thy words thou shalt be justified, and by thy words thou shalt be condemned.
    Matthew 12:37

Spoken words are your masters.
    Moorish proverb

All words are in a sense tombs of a forgotten past.
    Ben Morrison, *Wonderful Words*

People do not want words--they want the sound of battle . . . the battle of destiny.
    Gamal Abdel Nasser

Slogans are apt to petrify man's thinking . . . every slogan, every word almost, that is

used by the socialist, the communist, the capitalist. People hardly think nowadays. They throw words at each other.
    Jawaharlal Nehru

Hot lead can be almost as effective coming from a linotype as from a firearm.
    John O'Hara

An abstract word has no "correct meaning," never has had one, never will have one, and in the nature of things never can have one. For the lawyer, semantics has no useful lesson.
    Frederick A. Philbrick

Words are the pastels of the mind.
    J.E. Pichard

Pleasant words are as a honeycomb, sweet to the soul, and health to the bones.
    Proverbs 16:24

A word fitly spoken is like apples of gold in pictures of silver.
    Proverbs 25:11

The words of his mouth were smoother than butter, but war was in his heart; his words were softer than oil, yet were they drawn swords.
    Psalms 55:21

The great disease of knowledge is that in which, starting from words, we end up with them.
    I.A. Richards

Words not only affect us temporarily; they change us, they socialize or unsocialize us.
    David Riesman, *The Lonely Crowd*

One of our defects as a nation is a tendency to use what have been called "weasel words." When a weasel sucks eggs the meat is sucked out of the egg. If you use a "weasel word" after another there is nothing left of the other.
    Theodore Roosevelt

Words are weapons, and it is dangerous in speculation, as in politics, to borrow them from the arsenal of the enemy.
    George Santayana

Syllables govern the world.
    John Selden, *Table Talk*

It's nice to know words, because then you can read--and learn.
    Paz Shilling, six years old

But a word stung him like a mosquito.
    Edith Sitwell

One must be chary of words because they turn into cages.
    Viola Spolin

Man does not live by words alone, despite the fact that sometimes he has to eat them.
    Adlai Stevenson, speech

There is no magic in words.
    Joseph Story

These words dropped into my childish mind as if you should accidentally drop a ring into a deep well. I did not think of them much at the time, but there came a day in my life when the ring was fished up out of the well, good as new.
    Harriet Beecher Stowe

When you get to the footnote at the bottom of the page, like as not all you find is *ibid*.
    Frank Sullivan

There are three things I always forget. Names, faces,--and the third I can't remember.
    Italo Svevo

Pens are most dangerous tools, more sharp by odds
Than swords, and cut more keen than whips or rods.
    John Taylor, *News from Hell, Hull, and Halifax*

Words, like Nature, half reveal
And half conceal the Soul within.
    Alfred, Lord Tennyson, "In Memoriam"

Colors fade, temples crumble, empires fall, but wise words endure.
    Edward Thorndike

What a good thing Adam had--when he said a good thing, he knew nobody had said it before.
    Mark Twain, *Notebooks*

One great use of words is to hide our thoughts.
    Voltaire

For of all sad words of tongue or pen,
The saddest are these: "It might have been!"
    John Greenleaf Whittier, "Maud Muller"

The knowledge of words is the gate to scholarship.
   Woodrow Wilson

I would hurl words into the darkness and wait for an echo. If an echo sounded, no matter how faintly, I would send other words to tell, to march, to fight.
   Richard Wright, *American Hunger*

I love smooth words, like gold-enamelled fish
Which circle slowly with a silken swish,
And tender ones, like downy-feathered birds:
Words shy and dappled, deep-eyed deer in herds.
   Elinor Wylie, "Pretty Words," *Collected Poems*

WRITERS

A professional writer is an amateur who didn't quit.
   Richard Bach, *A Gift of Wings*

I write down everything, everything, everything. Otherwise why should I write?
   Marie Konstantinouna Bashkirtseff

When I am dead, I hope it may be said:
"His sins were scarlet, but his books were read."
   Hilaire Belloc

It took me fifteen years to discover that I had no talent for writing, but I couldn't give it up because by that time I was too famous.
   Robert Benchley, in Nathaniel Benchley, *Robert Benchley*

The writer of art has in mind the psychology of his characters; the writer of trash, the psychology of his readers.
   Shlomo Bickel, *Detaln un Sach-Hakeln*

How these authors magnify their office! One dishonest plumber does more harm than a hundred poetasters.
   Augustine Birrell

When a man can observe himself suffering, and is able, later, to describe what he's gone through, that means he was born for literature.
   Édouard Bourdet, *Vient de paraître*

There is probably no hell for authors in the next world--they suffer so much from critics and publishers in this.
   Christian Nestell Bovee, *Summaries of Thought: Authors*

For your born writer, nothing is so healing as the realization that he has come upon the right word.
    Catherine Drinker Bowen

It is well to understand as early as possible in one's writing life that there is just one contribution which every one of us can make; we can give into the common pool of experience some comprehension of the world as it looks to each of us.
    Dorothea Brande, *Becoming a Writer*

But this I know: the writer who possesses the creative gift owns something of which he is not always master--something that at times strangely wills and works for itself. If the result be attractive, the world will praise you, who little deserve praise; if it be repulsive, the same world will blame you, who almost as little deserve blame.
    Emily Brontë, *Wuthering Heights*

In a mood of faith and hope my work goes on. A ream of fresh paper lies on my desk waiting for the next book. I am a writer and I take up my pen to write.
    Pearl Buck

There is only one trait that marks the writer. He is always watching. It's a kind of trick of mind and he is born with it.
    Morley Callaghan

The discipline of the writer is to learn to be still and listen to what his subject has to tell him.
    Rachel Carson

Most of the basic material a writer works with is acquired before the age of fifteen.
    Willa Cather

The faster I write the better my output. If I'm going slow I'm in trouble. It means I'm pushing the words instead of being pulled by them.
    Raymond Chandler

An original writer is not one who imitates nobody but one whom nobody can imitate.
    François-René de Chateaubriand, *The Genius of Christianity*

Those writers who have been tempted into trying to teach writing classes are not so much tempted as forced.
    John Ciardi

If writers were good businessmen, they'd have too much sense to be writers.
    Irvin S. Cobb

No writer goes the whole length with any other. Each of them shivers at the lapses of the rest, and is blind to his own. And the youngest shiver the most. And the greatest writers have them.

Ivy Compton-Burnett

In America, only the successful writer is important, in France all writers are important, in England no writer is important, and in Australia you have to explain what a writer is.

Geoffrey Cottrell

His articles are harder to read than they are to write.

Edgar Dale

Novelists, whatever else they may be besides, are also children talking to children--in the dark.

Bernard DeVoto, *The World of Fiction*

"It is only half-an-hour"--"It is only an afternoon"--"It is only an evening," people say to me over and over again; but they don't know that it is impossible to command one's self sometimes to any stipulated and set disposal of five minutes--or that the mere consciousness of an engagement will sometimes worry a whole day. These are the penalties paid for writing books. Who ever is devoted to an art must be content to deliver himself up wholly to it, and to find his recompense in it. I am grieved if you suspect me of not wanting to see you, but I can't help it; I must go my way whether or no.

Charles Dickens

Choose an author as you choose a friend.

Wentworth Dillon, *An Essay on Translated Verse*

An author who speaks about his own books is almost as bad as a mother who talks about her own children.

Benjamin Disraeli

If there is a special Hell for writers, it would be in the forced contemplation of their own works, with all the misconceptions, the omissions, the failures that any finished work of art implies.

John Dos Passos

For forty years the American press has been lying about me, and now it tries to ignore me.

Theodore Dreiser

But though personality is a skin no writer can slip, whatever he may write about: though it is a shadow which walks inexorably by his side, so also is the age he lives in.

Elizabeth Drew

All authors to their own defects are blind.
John Dryden

He who proposes to be an author should first be a student.
John Dryden

The good writer seems to be writing about himself but has his eye always on that thread of the universe which runs through himself, and all things.
Ralph Waldo Emerson

I dip my pen in the blackest ink, because I am not afraid of falling into my inkpot.
Ralph Waldo Emerson

Mother wants me to write something nice she can show to her friends.
Carol Emshwiller

If you wish to be a writer, write.
Epictetus, *Discourses*

No man can write who is not first a humanitarian.
William Faulkner

A writer needs three things, experience, observation, and imagination, any two of which, at times any one of which, can supply the lack of the others.
William Faulkner

Life can't ever really defeat a writer who is in love with writing, for life itself is a writer's lover until death--fascinating, cruel, lavish, warm, cold, treacherous, constant.
Edna Ferber, *A Kind of Magic*

I have just spent a good week, alone like a hermit, and as calm as a god. I abandoned myself to a frenzy of literature; I got up at midday, I went to bed at four in the morning. I dined with Dakno; I smoked fifteen pipes in a day; I have written *eight* pages.
Gustave Flaubert

A writer is rarely so well inspired as when he talks about himself.
Anatole France

I make it a rule to sit at my desk eight hours a day whether anything's happening or not.
Theodore Geisel (Dr. Seuss)

He that readeth good writers and pickes out their flowres for his own nose, is lyke a foole.
Stephen Gosson, "Loyterers," *The Schoole of Abuse*

My two fingers on a typewriter have never connected with my brain. My hand on a pen does. A fountain pen, of course. Ball-point pens are only good for filling out forms on a plane.
Graham Greene

Loafing is the most productive part of a writer's life.
James Norman Hall

There is no way that a writer can be tamed and rendered civilized or even cured. The only solution known to science is to provide the patient with an isolation room, where he can endure the acute stages in private and where the food can be poked in to him with a stick.
Robert Heinlein, *The Cat Who Walks through Walls*

If I had to give young writers advice, I'd say don't listen to writers talking about writing.
Lillian Hellman

Literary awards usually come late in life when the recipient is well established. It's like throwing a life belt to a shipwrecked man after he has reached safety.
Ernest Hemingway

We are all apprentices in a craft where no one ever becomes a master.
Ernest Hemingway

The simplest way to torture an author is to get his name wrong and forget what books he has written.
Gilbert Highet, *Explorations*

Nature, not content with denying him the ability to think, has endowed him with the ability to write.
A.E. Housman

Any writer worth the name is always getting into one thing or getting out of another thing.
Fannie Hurst

A writer and nothing else: a man alone in a room with the English language, trying to get human feelings right.
John K. Hutchens

A writer never has a vacation. For a writer life consists of either writing or thinking about writing.
Eugene Ionesco

[The writer] must essentially draw from life as he sees it, lives it, overhears it, or steals it; and the truer the writer, perhaps the bigger the blackguard. He lives by biting the hand that feeds him.
    Charles Jackson, recalled on his death

The artist is present in every page of every book from which he sought so assiduously to eliminate himself.
    Henry James

It is through the ghost [writer] that the great gift of knowledge which the inarticulate have for the world can be made available.
    Elizabeth Janeway

The writer cannot afford to question his own essential nature.
    Randall Jarrell, *A Sad Heart at the Supermarket*

No man but a blockhead ever wrote, except for money.
    Samuel Johnson, in James Boswell, *Life of Johnson*

For forty-odd years in this noble profession
I've harbored a guilt and my conscience is smitten.
So here is my slightly embarrassed confession--
I don't like to write, but I love to have written.
    Michael Kanin

Writers aren't like mushrooms--you can't grow them.
    Simas Kaselionis, *Chicago*

When a writer talks about his work, he's talking about a love affair.
    Alfred Kazin

I get up in the morning, torture a typewriter until it screams, then stop.
    Clarence B. Kelland

Literature plays an important role in our country, helping the Party to educate the people correctly, to instill in them advanced, progressive ideas by which our Party is guided. And it is not without reason that writers in our country are called engineers of the human soul.
    Nikita Khrushchev

When I sit down at the typewriter, I am out to change the world.
    John Oliver Killens

I like to write when I feel spiteful; it's like having a good sneeze.
    D.H. Lawrence

And it does no harm to repeat, as often as you can, "Without me the literary industry would not exist: the publishers, the agents, the sub-agents, the sub-sub-agents, the accountants, the libel lawyers, the departments of literature, the professors, the theses, the books of criticism, the reviewers, the book pages--all this vast and proliferating edifice is because of this small, patronized, put-down, and underpaid person."
 Doris Lessing

When audiences come to see us authors lecture, it is largely in the hope that we'll be funnier to look at than to read.
 Sinclair Lewis

The writer who cannot sometimes throw away a thought about which another man would have written dissertations, without worrying whether or not the reader will find it, will never become a great writer.
 Georg C. Lichtenberg, *Aphorisms*

So you're the little woman who wrote the book that made this great war!
 Abraham Lincoln, on meeting Harriet Beecher Stowe

The writers who have nothing to say are the ones you can buy; the others have too high a price.
 Walter Lippmann

Let no man write a line that he would not have his daughter read.
 James Russell Lowell

A great writer is the friend and benefactor of his readers.
 Lord Thomas Babington Macaulay

My purpose is to entertain myself first and other people secondly.
 John D. MacDonald

A writer is somebody for whom writing is more difficult than it is for other people.
 Thomas Mann, *Essays of Three Decades*

Looking back, I imagine I was always writing. Twaddle it was too. But better far write twaddle or anything, anything, than nothing at all.
 Katherine Mansfield

i never think at all when i write
nobody can do two things at the same time
and do them both well.
 Don Marquis, *Archy's Life of Mehitabel*

The writer must earn money in order to be able to live and to write, but he must by no

means live and write for the purpose of making money.
Karl Marx

Only a mediocre writer is always at his best.
W. Somerset Maugham

There is no need for the writer to eat a whole sheep to be able to tell what mutton tastes like. It is enough if he eats a cutlet.
W. Somerset Maugham

I'm a lousy writer; a helluva lot of people have got lousy taste.
Grace Metalious, author of *Peyton Place*

Russia, France, Germany, and China. They revere their writers. America is still a frontier country that almost shudders at the idea of creative expression.
James Michener

Years ago, to say you were a writer was not the highest recommendation to your landlord. Today, he at least hesitates before he refuses to rent you an apartment--for all he knows you may be rich.
Arthur Miller

When you're a writer you no longer see things with the freshness of the normal person. There are always two figures that work inside you.
Brian Moore, *Saturday Review*

The role of the writer is not to say what we can all say but what we are unable to say.
Anaïs Nin

If you are a writer you locate yourself behind a wall of silence and no matter what you are doing, driving a car or doing housework . . . you can still be writing, because you have that space.
Joyce Carol Oates

Writers really live in the mind and in hotels of the soul.
Edna O'Brien

I notice particularly the cadence of their voices, the sort of phrases they'll use, and that's what I'm all the time trying to hear in my head, how people word things--because everybody speaks an entirely different language.
Frank O'Connor, in *Writers at Work*

Always roused by the writing, always denied . . . my work died.
Tillie Olsen

When one says that a writer is fashionable one practically always means that he is admired by people under thirty.
George Orwell

A man may write himself out of reputation when nobody else can do it.
Thomas Paine, *The Rights of Man*

An essayist is a lucky person who has found a way to discourse without being interrupted.
Charles Poore

Many a writer seems to think he is never profound except when he can't understand his own meaning.
George D. Prentice

Most writers enjoy two periods of happiness--when a glorious idea comes to mind and, secondly, when a last page has been written and you haven't had time to know how much better it ought to be.
J.B. Priestley, *International Herald Tribune*

What no wife of a writer can ever understand is that a writer is working when he's staring out of the window.
Burton Rascoe

There is nothing like literature: I lose a cow, I write about her death, and my writing pays me enough to buy another cow.
Jules Renard

If you give me six sentences written by the most innocent of men, I will find something in them with which to hang him.
Duc de Richelieu (Armand-Jean du Plessis)

In Russia you can't get in the writers' guild until you turn in a manuscript--and two other writers.
Don Rickles

It's not so much that I write well--I just don't write badly very often, and that passes for good on television.
Andy Rooney

A writer who lives long enough becomes an academic subject and almost qualified to teach it himself.
Harold Rosenberg, *Discovering the Present*

The only reason for being a professional writer is that you can't help it.
Leo Rosten

A confessional passage has probably never been written that didn't stink a little bit of the writer's pride in having given up his pride.
J.D. Salinger, *Seymour: An Introduction*

A writer lives, at best, in a state of astonishment. Beneath any feeling he has of the good or the evil of the world lies a deeper one of the wonder at it all. To transmit that feeling, he writes.
William Sansom, *Blue Skies, Brown Studies*

L'écrivain doit refuser de se laisser transformer en institution. (A writer must refuse to allow himself to be transformed into an institution.)
Jean-Paul Sartre, refusing the Nobel Prize, 1964

Snoopy's advice to other writers: "Be very careful how you balance your typewriter on the top of a dog house so it doesn't slide off."
Charles M. Schulz, in Bill Downing, *Right Brain . . . Write On!*

Every writer is a frustrated actor who recites his lines in the hidden auditorium of his skull.
Rod Serling, *Vogue*

You must not suppose, because I am a man of letters, that I never tried to earn an honest living.
George Bernard Shaw, *The Irrational Knot*, preface

I write fast, because I have not the brains to write slow.
Georges Simenon

Every author, however modest, keeps a most outrageous vanity chained like a madman in the padded cell of his breast.
Logan Pearsall Smith, *Afterthoughts*

What I like in a good author is not what he says, but what he whispers.
Logan Pearsall Smith, *All Trivia*

I'd rather write a paper any day of the week than work at Wendy's in the summer.
Melinda Kay Smith

A great writer is, so to speak, a second government in his country. And for that reason no regime has ever loved great writers, only minor ones.
Alexander Solzhenitsyn, *The First Circle*

Volume depends precisely on the writer's having been able to sit in a room every day, year after year, alone.
Susan Sontag, *New York Times*

The writer is either a practicing recluse or a delinquent, guilt-ridden one; or both. Usually both.

Susan Sontag, *New York Times*

The writer is an engineer of the human soul.

Joseph Stalin

Writers are a little below clowns and a little above trained seals.

John Steinbeck, *Quote*

The two most engaging powers of an author are to make new things familiar, familiar things new.

William Makepeace Thackeray

I hold a beast, an angel, and a madman in me, and my inquiry is as to their working, and my problem is their subjugation and victory, downthrow and upheaval, and my effort is their self-expression.

Dylan Thomas

With sixty staring me in the face, I have developed inflammation of the sentence structure and a definite hardening of the paragraphs.

James Thurber, *New York Post*

Writers of comedy have outlook whereas writers of tragedy have, according to them, insight.

James Thurber, *Lanterns and Lances*

I am told that I talk in shorthand and then smudge it.

J.R.R. Tolkien, acknowledging critics who called his writing difficult to understand

I always begin my task by reading the work of the day before, an operation which would take me half an hour, and which consisted chiefly in weighing with my ear the sound of the words and phrases . . . . By reading what he has last written, just before he recommences his task, the writer will catch the tone and spirit of what he is then saying, and will avoid the fault of seeming to be unlike himself.

Anthony Trollope

Writers take words seriously--perhaps the last professional class that does--and they struggle to steer their own through the crosswinds of meddling editors and careless typesetters and obtuse and malevolent reviewers into the lap of the ideal reader.

John Updike

Failure is very difficult for a writer to bear, but very few can manage the shock of early success.

Maurice Valency

If you are killed because you are a writer, that's the maximum expression of respect, you know.
Mario Vargas Llosa

Each writer is born with a repertory company in his head. Shakespeare has perhaps twenty players, and Tennessee Williams has about five, and Samuel Beckett one--and maybe a clone of that one. I have ten or so, and that's a lot. As you get older, you become more skillful at casting them.
Gore Vidal

He was an author whose works were so little known as to be almost confidential.
Stanley Walker

Sometimes people give titles to me, and sometimes I see them on a billboard.
Robert Penn Warren

I never can understand how two men can write a book together; to me that's like three people getting together to have a baby.
Evelyn Waugh

Most writers are in a state of gloom a good deal of the time; they need perpetual reassurance.
John Hall Wheelock

Delay is natural for a writer.
E.B. White

I write in order to understand as much as to be understood.
Elie Wiesel

When I stop [working] the rest of the day is post-humous. I'm only really alive when I'm writing.
Tennessee Williams, *Pittsburgh Press*

A writer's mind seems to be situated partly in the solar plexus and partly in the head.
Ethel Wilson

Writers often don't sit down to write what comes naturally. They sit down to *commit an act of literature*.
Elizabeth Hahn Winslow

Telling a writer to relax is like telling a man to relax while being prodded for a possible hernia.
William K. Zinsser

WRITER'S BLOCK

It's a portable vacuum pack. On Melmac we use it to cure writer's block.
Alf (television character)

I've got the time for writer's block and when I don't have the time, I make it.
Erma Bombeck

We are not allowed to have writer's block in the newspaper business. Writer's block is for people who don't have deadlines.
Art Buchwald, in Bill Downey, *Right Brain . . . Write On!*

I'm sorry--I myself have never had writer's block. I learned early on that being a writer is like being a plumber. You work every day at the same time; write when you don't feel like it. Imagine a plumber who couldn't turn off a raging faucet because he had plumber's block.
Alistair Cooke, in Bill Downey, *Right Brain . . . Write On!*

I have discovered quite recently that the characteristic Freudian resistance to confessions of any sort, which are very well represented in all the writing blocks one goes through--the dizzy fits, the nauseas, and so on, and so forth, which almost every writer has recorded--are a standard pattern for all kinds of creative things.
Lawrence Durrell

You don't know what it is to stay a whole day with your head in your hands trying to squeeze your unfortunate brain so as to find a word.
Gustave Flaubert

Blocking is the panic of not knowing where to go next, and outlining is the way to avoid it . . . . I write from an outline. I don't sit down at the typewriter and expect words to come out. It starts as a general outline for the book, and then I break it down into chapter outlines, and each chapter I break down into scenes. I know where I'm going.
Judith Krantz

Writing experience seems to diminish writer's block, but not much. When you're well into the writing, you won't even remember this moment when the pen has to be forced onto the paper, the fingers forced onto the keys. The only comfort to be taken in this first confrontation with the empty page is in the knowledge that it happens to practically everybody.
James W. Lea

[Blocked writers tend to] see the rose through world-colored glasses.
Mort Sahl

There are never mornings when I can't write. I think there are never mornings that anybody "can't write." I think that anybody could write if he would have standards as low as mine.
William Stafford, *Writing the Australian Crawl*

Never say block. Say, "The baby's not born."
Susan Strasberg, in Bill Downey, *Right Brain . . . Write On!*

WRITING

Having imagination, it takes you an hour to write a paragraph that, if you were unimaginative, would take you only a minute. Or you might not write the paragraph at all.
Franklin Pierce Adams, *Half a Loaf*

The paper burns, but the words fly away.
Ben Joseph Akiba

Writing has got to be an act of discovery . . . . I write to find out what I'm thinking about.
Edward Albee

Accomplishment is directly proportional to starting.
David Anderson

I think the whole glory of writing lies in the fact that it forces us out of ourselves and into the lives of others.
Sherwood Anderson

Paper is patient.
Stanislav Andreski

Where there is too much, something is missing.
Anonymous

Talent is like a faucet; while it is open, one must write. Inspiration?--a hoax fabricated by poets for their self-importance.
Jean Anouilh

Reading maketh a full man, conference a ready man, and writing an exact man.
Sir Francis Bacon, *Of Studies*

Write down the thought of the moment. Those that come unsought for are commonly the most valuable.
Sir Francis Bacon

Convince yourself that you are working in clay not marble, on paper not eternal bronze: let that first sentence be as stupid as it wishes. No one will rush out and print it as it stands. Just put it down; then another. Your whole first paragraph or first page may have to be guillotined in any case after your piece is finished: it is a kind of forebirth.
    Jacques Barzun

Creative writing is or pretends to be a course in originality, although crabbed English teachers assert that creative writing is just a composition course in which the spelling is not corrected.
    Morris Bishop, *Atlantic*

A good goose-quill is more dangerous than a lion's claw.
    Sir Henry George Bohn, *A Handbook of Proverbs*

Writing is nothing more than a guided dream.
    Jorge Luis Borges, *Doctor Brodie's Report*

Writing, I think, is not apart from living. Writing is a kind of double living. The writer experiences everything twice. Once in reality and once in that mirror which waits always before or behind.
    Catherine Drinker Bowen

You will have to write and put away or burn a lot of material before you are comfortable in this medium. You might as well start now and get the necessary work done. For I believe that eventually quantity will make for quality.
    Ray Bradbury

Unless the written word is reserved for those occasions where it and it alone is determined to be best suited to the situation, its competitiveness in the communication market place is questionable. In this era of mixed media, writing must find its special niche.
    Mary C. Bromage

Those who write as they speak, even though they speak well, write badly.
    Comte de Buffon, *Discours sur le style*

Beneath the rule of men entirely great,
The pen is mightier than the sword.
    Edward George Bulwer-Lytton, *Richelieu*

It was a dark and stormy night.
    Edward George Bulwer-Lytton

I can testify that none of the meaning I've found in writing ever just came to me. I had

to go in and get it. As for being patient, my advice to my own children has always been just the reverse: "Be impatient."
 Norman L. Cahners

That's not writing, that's typing.
 Truman Capote, on Jack Kerouac

Writing has laws of perspective, of light and shade, just as painting does, or music. If you are born knowing them, fine. If not, learn them. Then rearrange the rules to suit yourself.
 Truman Capote, in *Writers at Work*

The pen is the tongue of the mind.
 Miguel de Cervantes, *Don Quixote*

The need to write comes from the need to make sense of one's life and discover one's usefulness.
 John Cheever, accepting the Edward MacDowell Medal

Sometimes . . . it takes me an entire day to write a recipe, to communicate it correctly. It's really like writing a little short story.
 Julia Child

The best time for planning a book is while you are doing the dishes.
 Agatha Christie

I've always believed in writing without a collaborator, because where two people are writing the same book, each believes he gets all the worries and only half the royalties.
 Agatha Christie

I couldn't write the things they publish now, with no beginning and no end, and a little incest in the middle.
 Irvin S. Cobb

One does not write a love story while making love.
 Colette, *Lettre au petit Corsaire*

Write sixteen pages, you are a pamphleteer, and may find yourself in prison . . . . Write sixteen hundred, and you will be presented to the king.
 Paul-Louis Courier

I write at high speed because boredom is bad for my health. It upsets my stomach more than anything else. I also avoid green vegetables. They're grossly overrated.
 Noël Coward

One's words must glide across the page like a swan moving across the waters. One must be conscious of the movement without a thought of what is causing it to move.
Robert Crichton, *The Secret of Santa Vittoria*

Easy reading is curst hard writing.
Robert Day

The pen is the interpreter of the heart.
Joseph Solomon Delmedigo, *Notes of Wisdom*

I love being a writer. What I can't stand is the paperwork.
Peter DeVries

Planning to write is not writing. Outlining . . . researching . . . talking to people about what you're doing, none of that is writing. Writing is writing.
E.L. Doctorow

Writing is an exploration. You start from nothing and learn as you go.
E.L. Doctorow

There is no subject so old that something new cannot be said about it.
Fyodor Dostoevsky, *The Diary of a Writer*

An excellent precept for writers: have a clear idea of all the phrases and expressions you need, and you will find them.
Ximénès Doudan, *Pensées et fragments*

As a newspaper reporter I had learned long ago that every strike of the typewriter is not a gemstone.
Bill Downey, *Right Brain . . . Write On!*

Better writers don't just write about a car, they describe a two-door sedan with faded paint. They have characters with freckles and small feet, slender fingers, warts. Readers love details, which remind them of people they know, allowing them to identify with your story.
Bill Downey, *Right Brain . . . Write On!*

Writing is manual labor of the mind: a job, like laying pipe.
John Gregory Dunne

Writing is a way to end up thinking something you couldn't have started out thinking.
Peter Elbow, *Writing without Teachers*

Writing is not just setting things down on paper; it is setting things inside someone else's head.
Peter Elbow

Good writing is a kind of skating which carries off the performer where he would not go.

Ralph Waldo Emerson, *Journals*

People do not deserve to have good writing, they are so pleased with bad.

Ralph Waldo Emerson, *Journals*

The desire to write grows with writing.

Desiderius Erasmus, *Adagia*

Neither man nor God is going to tell me what to write.

James T. Farrell

Writing to me is a voyage, an odyssey, a discovery, because I'm never certain of precisely what I will find.

Gabriel Fielding

I act as a sponge. I soak it up and squeeze it out in ink every two weeks.

Janet Flanner (Genêt), on her "Letter from Paris," published for fifty years in the *New Yorker*

Writing is a dog's life, but the only life worth living.

Gustave Flaubert

"The pen is mightier than the sword." Not unless you push it.

B.C. Forbes, *Epigrams*

How can I tell what I think till I see what I say?

E.M. Forster

Sometimes I think [my writing] sounds like I walked out of the room and left the typewriter running.

Gene Fowler, *Newsweek*

Write with the learned, pronounce with the vulgar.

Benjamin Franklin, *Poor Richard's Almanack*

I've just found out what makes a piece of writing good . . . : it is making the sentences talk to each other as two or more speakers do in a drama. The dullness of writing is due to its being, much of it, too much like the too long monologues and soliloquies in drama.

Robert Frost

Too often I wait for the sentence to finish taking shape in my mind before setting it down. It is better to seize it by the end that first offers itself, head or foot, though not

knowing the rest, then pull: the rest will follow along.
André Gide

I will try to cram these paragraphs full of facts and give them a weight and shape no greater than that of a cloud of blue butterflies.
Brendan Gill, *Here at the New Yorker*

Writing develops courage. Writers leave the shelter of anonymity and offer to public scrutiny their interior language, feelings, and thoughts.
Donald H. Graves

Thoughts fly and words go on foot. Therein lies all the drama of a writer.
Julien Green, *Diary*

Writing is for the most part a lonely and unsatisfying occupation. One is tied to a table, a chair, a stack of paper.
Graham Greene

Writing is the hardest thing I have ever done.
Judith Guest

It's the equivalent of putting on the brakes suddenly while driving uphill.
John Gunther

In general, writing courses are taken with reluctance, and taught with difficulty.
Kevin J. Hardy

The only sensible ends of literature are, first, the pleasurable toil of writing; second, the gratification of one's family and friends; and lastly, the solid cash.
Nathaniel Hawthorne

Nothing you write, if you hope to be good, will ever come out as you first hoped.
Lillian Hellman

Good writing is writing wherein you can't remove one word without changing the meaning.
Ernest Hemingway

I learned never to empty the well of my writing, but always to stop when there was still something there in the deep part of the well, and let it refill at night from the springs that fed it.
Ernest Hemingway

Real seriousness in regard to writing is one of two absolute necessities. The other, unfortunately, is talent.
Ernest Hemingway

Writing is a part-time job.
   Ernest Hemingway

Manuscript: something submitted in haste and returned at leisure.
   Oliver Herford

Writing is the only trade I know of in which sniveling confessions of extreme incompetence are taken as credentials probative of powers to astound the multitude.
   George V. Higgins

What is written without effort is in general read without pleasure.
   Samuel Johnson

Your manuscript is both good and original; but the part that is good is not original, and the part that is original is not good.
   Samuel Johnson

An incurable itch for scribbling takes possession of many and grows inveterate in their insane hearts.
   Juvenal

All writing is a form of prayer.
   John Keats

There's only a short walk from the hallelujah to the hoot.
   William Kennedy, on writing

I keep six honest serving-men
(They taught me all I knew);
Their names are What and Why and When
And How and Where and Who.
   Rudyard Kipling, *Just So Stories*

Students may not be writing as well as they used to; what's more, they never did.
   Albert Kitzhaber

I have a sign on the door that says: DO NOT COME IN. DO NOT KNOCK. DO NOT SAY HELLO. DO NOT SAY "I'M LEAVING." DO NOT SAY ANYTHING UNLESS THE HOUSE IS ON FIRE . . . . Also, telephone's off!
   Judith Krantz

In conversation you can use timing, a look, inflection, pauses. But on the page all you have is commas, dashes, the amount of syllables in a word. When I write I read everything out loud to get the right rhythm.
   Fran Lebowitz

Writing is like walking in a deserted street. Out of the dust in the street you make a mud pie.

    John Le Carre

To write is to inform against others.

    Violette LeDuc, *Mad in Pursuit*

Writing is learned by application--apply seat of pants to seat of chair and write.

    Sinclair Lewis

What release to write so that one forgets oneself, forgets one's companion, forgets where one is or what one is going to do next--to be drenched in sleep or in the sea. Pencils and pads and curling blue sheets alive with letters heap up on the desk.

    Anne Morrow Lindbergh

When once the itch of literature comes over a man, nothing can cure it but the scratching of a pen.

    Samuel Lover, *Handy Andy*

You see how each added word, like a stone tossed into a still pool, sends out ripple after ripple, each merging with and altering the others.

    Karin Mack and Eric Skjei, *Overcoming Writing Blocks*

Writing is the most demanding of callings, more harrowing than a warrior's, more lonely than a whaling captain's--that, in essence, is the modern writer's message.

    Melvin Maddocks, *Christian Science Monitor*

If you want to get rich from writing, write the sort of thing that's read by persons who move their lips when they're reading to themselves.

    Don Marquis

I think I did pretty well, considering I started out with nothing but a bunch of blank paper.

    Steve Martin

Writing is like treading water while you are draining the pool.

    Stephen McPherson

We may not all be good cooks, but we can all read the instructions on the packet.

    Sir Peter Medawar

In six pages I can't even say "hello."

    James Michener

After all, most writing is done away from the typewriter, away from the desk. I'd say it occurs in the quiet, silent moments, while you're walking or shaving or playing a

game, or whatever, or even talking to someone you're not vitally interested in. . . .
Your mind is working on this problem in the back of your head.
  Henry Miller

Writing, like life itself, is a voyage of discovery.
  Henry Miller

Writing is the hardest way of earning a living, with the possible exception of wrestling
alligators.
  Olin Miller

The point of good writing is knowing when to stop.
  Lucy Montgomery, *Anne's House of Dreams*

Writing is not just a way of spitting back what you know. It's a way of discovering
what you know.
  Donald Murray

If it's badly said, it will not be read, and will wind up dead.
  Ogden Nash

We write to be able to transcend our life, to reach beyond it . . . . When I don't write
I feel my world shrinking. I feel I lose my fire, my color.
  Anaïs Nin

Writing is a hard discipline, a demanding taskmaster. It brings rewards, some
financial and some in pure satisfaction. It also results in a great many
disappointments. This is the price that has to be paid. The only question is whether
one really wants to write enough to be willing to pay the price.
  Robert T. Oliver

If we had to say what writing is, we would define it essentially as an act of courage.
  Cynthia Ozick

Anything that is written to please the author is worthless.
  Blaise Pascal

If, at the close of business each evening, I myself can understand what I've written, I
feel the day hasn't been totally wasted.
  S.J. Perelman

The story, the essay, and even something so apparently inconsequential as a book
review . . . is already there, much in the way that Socrates said mathematical
knowledge was already there, before a word is ever put to paper, and the act of writing

is the act of finding the magical key that will unlock the floodgates and let the flow begin.

Norman Podhoretz, *Making It*

It doesn't matter which leg of your table you make first, so long as the table has four legs and will stand up solidly when you have finished it.

Ezra Pound, on using outlines, *ABC of Reading*

A people that grows accustomed to sloppy writing is a people in process of losing grip on its empire and on itself.

Ezra Pound, *ABC of Reading*

The secret of popular writing is never to put more on a given page than the common reader can lap off it with no strain *whatsoever* on his habitually slack attention.

Ezra Pound

Much of writing might be described as mental pregnancy with successive difficult deliveries.

J.B. Priestley, *International Herald Tribune*

Whenever you feel an impulse to perpetrate a piece of exceptionally fine writing, obey it . . . and delete it before sending your manuscript to the press.

Sir Arthur Quiller-Couch

Talent is a question of quantity. Talent does not write one page: it writes three hundred.

Jules Renard, *Journal*

Writing is the only profession where no one considers you ridiculous if you earn no money.

Jules Renard, *Journal*

What is writing, if it is not the countenance of our daily experience: sensuous, contemplative, imaginary, what we see and hear, dream of, how it strikes us, how it comes into us, travels through us, and emerges in some language hopefully useful to others.

M. C. Richards, *Centering in Pottery, Poetry, and the Person*

Don't try for something profound or eloquent. Let what will come, come. Something will come; something always comes to us because our brains are rarely still. Just be patient and stay with it a minute or two.

Gabriele Lusser Rico

How hard it is to make your thoughts look anything but imbecile fools when you paint them with ink on paper.

Olive Schreiner, *The Story of an African Farm*

My dream is to make my eighth grade English teacher happy.
    Allen Shaughnessy

I sweat over every word, but I'm glad it doesn't show.
    Irwin Shaw

Writing is like a contact sport, like football. Why do kids play football? They can get hurt on any play, can't they? Yet they can't wait until Saturday comes around so they can play on the high-school team, or the college team, and get smashed around. Writing is like that. You can get hurt, but you enjoy it.
    Irwin Shaw

You write with ease to show your breeding,
But easy writing's curst hard reading.
    Richard B. Sheridan, *Clio's Protest*

Clean, fresh writing is like polished sandalwood where the wood grain shows its natural beauty. On the other hand, the writings of the hosts of imitators are like lacquer ware, which shine on the outside but do not wear well.
    Shu Shuehmou

Writing is not a profession but a vocation of unhappiness.
    Georges Simenon, *Paris Review*

Thought comes with writing, and writing may never come if it is postponed until we are satisfied we have something to say.
    Frank Smith

Don't try and win the Pulitzer Prize with the first sentence.
    Jack Smith, in Bill Downey, *Right Brain . . . Write On!*

There's nothing to writing. All you do is sit down at the typewriter and open a vein.
    Red Smith

It is like fishing. But I do not wait very long, for there is always a nibble--and this is where receptivity comes in. To get started, I will accept anything that occurs to me. Something always occurs, of course, to any of us. We can't keep from thinking.
    William Stafford, "A Way of Writing"

If we knew everything ahead of time, all would be dictation, not creation.
    Gertrude Stein

Writing is the only thing that, when I do it, I don't feel I should be doing something else.
    Gloria Steinem, *Publishers Weekly*

I personally consider as tentative everything I think I have learned about the teaching of writing.
Don Stoen

Let's face it, writing is hell.
William Styron

In general, writing should be like sailing clouds and flowing water. It has no definite [required] form. It goes where it has to go and stops where it cannot but stop. One has thus a natural style, with all its wayward charms.
Su Tungpo, letter to Shieh Minshih

I am now trying an experiment very frequent among authors, which is to write upon nothing; when the subject is utterly exhausted, to let the pen still move on: by some called the ghost of wit, delighting to walk after the death of its body.
Jonathan Swift, "A Tale of a Tub"

As soon as a piece of work is out of hand and before going to sleep, I like to begin another; it may be to write only half-a-dozen lines; but that is something towards Number the Next.
William Makepeace Thackeray

How vain it is to sit down to write when you have not stood up to live.
Henry David Thoreau

A perfectly healthy sentence is extremely rare.
Henry David Thoreau

Three hours a day will produce as much as a man ought to write.
Anthony Trollope, *An Autobiography*

The machine [typewriter] has several virtues . . . . One may lean back in his chair and work it. It piles an awful stack of words on one page. It don't muss things or scatter ink blots around.
Mark Twain

Write out of love, write out of instinct, write out of reason. But always for money.
Louis Untermeyer

To hold a pen is to be at war.
Voltaire

I am working seven days a week. Some days I hit. Other days I only waste time. Most days are like that, just throwing stuff away.
Kurt Vonnegut, Jr.

Writing is so difficult that I often feel that writers, having had their hell on earth, will escape all punishment hereafter.
Jessamyn West

Advice to young writers who want to get ahead: Don't write about Man, write about a man.
E.B. White

I never knew in the morning how the day was going to develop. I was like a hunter, hoping to catch sight of a rabbit.
E.B. White

Writing to me is not an exercise in addressing readers, it is more as though I were talking to myself while shaving.
E.B. White

Writing is a coy game you play with your unconscious.
Thornton Wilder

I think all writing is a disease. You can't stop it.
William Carlos Williams, *Newsweek*

When you frame a sentence don't do it as if you were loading a shotgun but as if you were loading a rifle. Don't fire in such a way and with such a load that you will hit a lot of things in the neighborhood besides, but shoot with a single bullet and hit that one thing alone.
Joseph Ruggles Wilson, quoted in John Dos Passos, *Mr. Wilson's War*

I just sit at a typewriter and curse a bit.
P.G. Wodehouse

Don't say you were a bit confused and sort of tired and a little depressed and somewhat annoyed. Be tired. Be confused. Be depressed. Be annoyed. Don't hedge your prose with little timidities. Good writing is lean and confident. Good writing is bold; it's not kind of bold.
William K. Zinsser

I almost always urge people to write in the first person . . . . Writing is an act of ego and you might as well admit it.
William K. Zinsser, *On Writing Well*

Just because people work for an institution doesn't mean they have to sound like one.
William K. Zinsser, *On Writing Well*

WRITING ANXIETY

I find writing very nervous work. I'm always in a dither when starting a novel--that's the worst time. It's like going to the dentist . . . . I linger over breakfast reading the papers, telling myself hypocritically that I've got to keep up with what's going on, but really staving off the dreadful time when I have to go to the typewriter.

Kingsley Amis, in *Writers at Work*

At the beginning of my career I prepared myself for each session of writing by whimpering all afternoon, watching television all evening, and, after throwing up at midnight, fastening myself to the desk with shackles, to remain there until dawn.

Thomas Berger

I know I am not alone in my recurring twinges of panic that I won't be able to write something when I need to.

Peter Elbow, *Writing without Teachers*

Writing is easy. All you do is sit staring at a blank sheet of paper until the drops of blood form on your head.

Gene Fowler

I wrote the scenes . . . by using the same apprehensive imagination that occurs in the morning before an afternoon's appointment with my dentist.

John Marquand

Picture an old card table, so old and worn that the top surface is paper thin. Now imagine having to place a number of bricks on that table. Beginning writers often fail because they attempt to handle all the pressures at once. They pile all the bricks in one vertical column and the surface breaks. Mature writers respect these pressures and know they cannot face them all at the same time: they know they must use the entire surface of the table. They place the bricks in smaller piles--and the table holds.

Thomas Newkirk

Source Index

Subject Index

Boldface page numbers refer to subject headings.

About the Compilers

LILLESS McPHERSON SHILLING, Associate Professor at the College of Health Professions at the Medical University of South Carolina, specializes in educational and health communications. With Linda Fuller, she is coauthor of *Communicating Comfortably: Your Guide to Overcoming Speaking and Writing Anxieties* (1990) and coeditor of *Communicating about Communicable Diseases* (1995).

LINDA K. FULLER, an associate professor in the Communications Department at Worcester State College, is the author/(co-)editor of 18 books including *The Cosby Show: Audiences, Impact, and Implications* (Greenwood, 1992) and *Community Television in the United States: A Sourcebook on Public, Educational, and Governmental Access* (Greenwood, 1994), as well as more than 200 professional publications and conference reports. In 1996 she served as a Fulbright Senior Fellow, teaching and doing research in Singapore.

ISBN 0-313-30430-0

90000>

9 780313 304309

EAN

HARDCOVER BAR CODE